P9-ARW-500

EVERYBODY'S GUIDE TO TAX SHELTERS

*How to Avoid Taxes
Like a Millionaire*

STUART A. OBER

The Dial Press
New York

Published by
The Dial Press
1 Dag Hammarskjold Plaza
New York, New York 10017

Grateful acknowledgment is made to the following for permission to reprint
from the sources cited:
Institute for Energy Development: *Tax Shelter Desk Book* by Lewis G.
Mosburg, Jr.; Salomon Brothers: "A Scorecard for Investments"; Fidelity
Mutual Life Insurance Company: "Estate Settlement Costs"; Commerce
Clearing House, Inc.: "Federal Tax Guide 1979"; Institute for Business
Planning: *Real Estate Tax Shelter Desk Book* by Mark Levine; Executive
Reports Corporation, Prentice-Hall, Inc.: *The Shelter Desk Manual*
(1979); The Research Institute of America, Inc.: "Section 8 Housing:
Renting to the 'Poor, Huddled Masses' for Tax Advantages"; Consumers
Union: *The Consumers Union Report on Life Insurance*, fourth edition;
Commerce Clearing House, Inc.: *1980 Federal Tax Guide Reporter*.

Library of Congress Cataloging in Publication Data

Ober, Stuart A.
Everybody's guide to tax shelters.

Includes index.
1. Tax shelters—Law and legislation—United States—
Popular works. 2. Tax planning—United States—Popular
works. I. Title.
KF6297.5.Z9O23   1982   343.7305′23   81-19455
ISBN 0-385-27655-9   347.303523   AACR2

To
My Mother
and
Joanne

Acknowledgments

I owe a deep debt of gratitude to those who helped me prepare this book. Margaret Danbrot was immensely helpful with her editing and style, Jack Falcon with his advice, Margaret Granfours with her organization, Audrey Proctor and Oliver Burkeson with their typing, and Joanne Michaels with her agenting and support.

Warren Esanu of Esanu, Katsky, and Korins permitted me to impose on our friendship by agreeing to read the entire book, and making suggestions on its content. I thank him warmly for his efforts and opinions.

S.A.O.

This book is designed to provide accurate and authoritative information in regard to the subject matter covered. It is sold with the understanding that the publisher is not engaged in rendering legal, accounting, or other professional service. If legal advice or other expert assistance is required, the services of a competent professional person should be sought.

—*Declaration of Principles*, jointly adopted
by a Committee of the
American Bar Association
and a Committee of Publishers
and Associations

Contents

CONTENTS

Introduction

Here is a book on tax shelters that's not just for the rich, but for the overtaxed, underpaid, middle-income wage earner as well. It will help you use federal tax laws to shelter your income with dozens of perfectly legal loopholes you're probably overlooking. And the more you use and understand the tax laws, the fairer they become!

This book also provides a basis for informed judgments about your investment decisions. It will allow you to plan for (and to eliminate) economic and tax problems *before* you invest. It spells out the pros and cons of each suggested transaction and offers examples, worksheets, and checklists.

This book has one simple objective: to help everyone maximize the effectiveness of their hard-earned dollars through the use of tax strategies and investments that shelter principal and income. The techniques have been tested and proved successful in cutting taxes, and all of them use the tax laws themselves to pave the way.

You will find ways to make the most of tax-sheltered opportunities in stocks and bonds; how to get tax-free income from your vacation home; how to set up a trust fund for your children's education; whether it's worthwhile getting married to get a tax break; and even how insurance can protect your estate from estate taxes.

This book will lead you on the way to discovering things: expenses you never imagined were tax-deductible— like the black negligee you gave your best client as a gift (and she loved it!); when land has to be a great deal because they're not making any more of it, and when it isn't; why drilling for oil is a major leak in the tax system and how you can get in on it; and how to use flower bonds, die, and come up smelling like a rose.

Filled with countless tips on how to make the tax system work for you, this is an essential reference for the citizen who's fed up with paying too much to the government every year. The clear, "how-to" approach makes this *the* tax shelter book for up-to-date, practical, accessible advice to *every* taxpayer, regardless of age or income bracket.

The time is long overdue for the average person, the middle-income taxpayer, to be informed of the hidden— yet legal—tax shelters that are at his or her disposal.

The book should be an eye-opener on tax savings. It explains how major tax savings can be created so that you can review your own situation and discover what to do to reduce your taxes. It won't make you a tax expert. But after reading it you'll be better able to size up your tax situation and know when to seek qualified help. Knowing the tax laws and using them to your advantage may be the best revenge!

New Tax Laws Update

The Economic Recovery Tax Act of 1981 creates a wealth of opportunities for investment strategies and financial planning for those who know how to use the laws. These laws were designed to provide economic growth for the nation by stimulating productivity, lowering the personal and corporate tax burdens, restraining the growth of the federal government, and upgrading the country's factories and equipment. These tax cuts are intended to restore incentives to work, produce, invest, and save.

To remain up to date and to take advantage of the new tax law, this book includes the new changes at the end of each chapter for easy referral.

For example, in the chapter on the Individual Retirement Act (IRA), the text explains the rules concerning IRA's for 1981. The new rules for IRA contributions in 1982 are explained at the end of the chapter. Thus, a reader will be able to use this book not only for his or her 1981 tax planning, but as a reference for the years to come.

EVERYBODY'S

GUIDE TO

TAX SHELTERS

> Don't get the idea that I'm one of these goddamn radicals. Don't get the idea that I'm knocking the American system.
>
> —AL CAPONE

1

The Sheltered Versus the Unsheltered Life

In one of his *New York Times* columns Russell Baker complains bitterly about being "swindled by the American educational system, which taught me reading, writing, and arithmetic, but not taxes."

He recalls a conference with a high-school guidance counselor who asked him what he wanted to be when he grew up. In his "tax stupidity" he told her: " 'I want to be a salaried worker.' "

" 'Excellent,' she lied."

What she should have said, Baker gripes, is " 'Hold on a minute, young man. Are you aware that salaried income is taxed more heavily than almost any other kind of income in America?'

" 'She didn't, and I have been paying ever since,' " moans Baker.

That salaried income is taxed more heavily than any other kind isn't quite true. (You pay a maximum of 50% on salaried income; "passive" income of dividends, interest, and short-term capital gains is taxed at a whopping 70%.) But what the heck. The column hits home because it illustrates how the average young adult is thrust out into the cold, real world wholly untutored in a matter that touches every one of us where it hurts most: in the pocketbook. Unfortunately, most people retain their naiveté to the end of their days.

That's too bad. A little know-how can lighten your tax burden considerably. Practicing just a few simple strategies can save hundreds of dollars. Applying a few somewhat more sophisticated tactics can save thousands.

This book will help you understand the basic ins and outs of the tax game; enable you to assess your personal financial situation; and explain tax-reducing techniques—tax shelters, in other words—that are right for you.

The higher your tax bill is now, the more money the information in this book can save you. That's not to say that tax shelters are only for the very rich, as you've probably read or heard someplace. If you earn income that is taxed, chances are you can benefit from some kind of tax shelter.

You don't have to be rich to be in an upper tax bracket. The maximum tax on salaried or "earned" (personal service) income is 50% (and that doesn't include state and local taxes). If you're single with a taxable earned income of $34,200, you're in the 50% bracket. If you're married with a taxable earned income of $47,200, you're also in the 50% tax bracket. You may not live rich or feel rich, but IRS considers you rich enough to tax at top dollar rates. (The tax bracket is actually 49%—not 50%—but for the purposes of illustration and simplicity, 50% is used throughout this book.)

In the 50% tax bracket, remember of every $2 you earn above a certain amount, $1 goes to Uncle Sam. The same applies when you get a raise or a bonus. Whatever you buy costs you twice as much and you get to keep only half of any savings account interest.

Inflation, as you'll have sadly noted unless you live on

Mars, is the final kicker. That dollar out of every two that you're allowed to hang on to buys less and less.

Many people are in the 50% tax bracket without realizing it. Take Yancy, a commercial artist I know. He assumed incorrectly that because he didn't pay $35,000 in taxes on his average yearly earnings of $70,000, he hadn't made it into the elite 50% bracket.

What Yancy forgot is that tax rates are based on a graduated scale: If Yancy, as an unmarried person, earns $2,200 a year or less, he pays no taxes. He pays 14% on the next $500 he earned; 15% on the next $500; 16% on the next; and so on up until he reaches the $34,200 high-water mark, at which point he forks over 50% of every additional dollar he earns to the government.

Margaret, a single young woman with a job in public relations, made $24,200 last year and paid out $5,990—almost 25% of her income—in taxes. She had been under the misconception that she was in the 25% bracket. Wrong. Margaret is in the 40% tax bracket. If she gets a piddling $1,000 raise this year, she'll get to keep $600 of it while IRS gobbles up the rest.

If she could figure out a way to take $1,000 in *deductions*, she would shave $400 off her tax bill. And if she knew how to handle her finances so as to be eligible for a $1,000 *tax credit*, she could take that $1,000 right off the top of her tax bill and invest it, put it in the bank, use it to redecorate her apartment, blow it all on clothes, whatever.

Deductions, tax credits, these are tax shelters in the broadest sense of the term. In the first chapters of this book I'll be using "tax shelter" in that broad sense, that is, to mean any (legal) strategy that can be applied to reduce your present tax burden, help you hang on to your money longer, and give you more favorable tax treatment in the future.

A few Wall Street purists might argue that some of the techniques I describe early in the book are tax-break tactics, not true tax-sheltering devices. Let the dogmatists carp.

Breaks, shelters, whatever you call them, if your financial situation allows you to take advantage of them you'll be able to keep more of your hard-earned dollars, and that's what counts, right?

Later on in the book I'll give you a look at tax shelters in the true Wall Street sense: tax-favored investment opportunities sanctioned by Congress to encourage development in certain industries vital to our country's economic growth and stability. These investment opportunities include (but are not limited to) oil and gas, real estate, cattle breeding and feeding, and equipment leasing.

Why has Congress established tax codes giving preferential treatment to these investments? Because even though such investments can be enormously profitable, they are high-risk ventures. Without special tax incentives to attract the capital necessary to carry them out—and to cushion the impact should a deal fall flat—a reasonably sane person not afflicted with gamblemania would never go near them.

It boils down to this: By investing in tax shelters you receive immediate tax deductions that lower your taxable income. This deduction—called a write-off—also allows you to proportionately reduce your true economic loss if the investment fails to be profitable.

This book will explain step by step the kind of tax sheltering arrangements that work (and how and why they work) to allow you to reduce taxes on your present income or defer them to some future date.

It will spell out the tax laws on gifts and trusts, knowledge that can save you thousands of tax dollars.

It will show you how to use the alchemy of the tax laws to convert investment and other profits—from stocks, bonds, sale of your house or other personal property—into long-term capital gains, reducing the amount you pay IRS from a staggering 70% to a more manageable 28%!

And all of these strategies are in complete compliance with both the letter and the spirit of U.S. tax laws.

New Law: Individual Income Tax Reduction: The Economic Recovery Tax Act of 1981 reduces the top rate on all classes of income beginning January 1, 1982 from 70% to 50%. The maximum long-term capital gains rates will be lowered from 28% in 1981 to 20% in 1982 and thereafter. More on this in Chapter 2.

The Sheltered Life Is Not Immoral or Illegal!
(It May Be Fattening)

The courts have always recognized your right as a taxpayer to use the tax laws to your own advantage. Taking legal advantage of the tax laws is not playing Sneaky Pete with the government or unfairly holding back dollars that are rightfully Uncle Sam's. Utilizing legal means to reduce your tax burden doesn't even make you a less good and morally upright citizen.

As the venerable Judge Learned Hand has said: "Anyone may so arrange his affairs [so] that his taxes shall be as low as possible; he is not bound to pay that pattern which will best pay the treasury." He also said: "Over and over again courts have said that there is nothing sinister in so arranging one's affairs as to keep taxes as low as possible. Everybody does so, rich and poor, for nobody owes any public duty to pay any more than the tax law demands; taxes are enforced exactions, not voluntary contributions. To demand more in the name of morals is mere cant."

2

Rules of
the Sheltered Life

If you want to save a lot of money by taking advantage of tax breaks and shelters, you really must have at least minimal knowledge of the tax system and how it works. My publisher says not to assume too much prior knowledge on the part of you, the reader—though for all I know, some of you may be lawyers, CPAs, and other tax professionals. But I'm going to go along with the publisher's advice anyway and explain some of the basics of the tax system as though you'd been living on an ice floe in Antarctica since age two and just arrived here yesterday.

So we start at the beginning.

Our tax system deals with two major components: income and expenses. The more income you have and the less you spend it on, whether for necessities, luxuries, or taxes, the more money you'll have. The more you make, and the less you spend, the richer you will become.

Now let's look at income from the point of view of how it is taxed.

1. Tax-exempt income: You get to keep all of it, the government is entitled to none. Obviously, this is the best kind to have. This is income on which you pay 0% tax!

Is there such a thing as tax-exempt income? You bet. All the interest income from investments on municipal bonds is exempt from federal income tax, and is generally exempt from state taxes too, if you live in the state from which the bonds are issued.

Another example of tax-exempt income: IRS provides for a depletion allowance that permits you to receive tax-free some of the income or profits from a successful oil or gas drilling program. The allowance is (1) to compensate for your having invested money in the risky and expensive business of searching and drilling for oil, and (2) to partly make up to you the fact that your wells, which are a source of income to you, will eventually run dry. (In Chapter 17, oil and gas tax shelters will be discussed in detail.)

Still another example of what amounts to tax-exempt income: The government offers an investment tax credit to most corporations who go into equipment-leasing tax shelters. These operate by buying, and then renting out, hardware such as computers, pollution control equipment, heavy machinery, and even ships and aircraft to companies needing the equipment, but unwilling or unable to buy their own.

Uncle Sam wants business to thrive, not founder for lack of efficient, modern equipment (or for any other reason, for that matter). Thus corporate investors who sink money into the purchase of equipment for leasing purposes are rewarded with a tax credit. The credit, often a big one, is subtracted from its tax bill. The investment credit may be equal to the amount of taxes owed on other income—in effect, making some or all of it tax-free.

2. The next best kind of income is profits that can be taxed at long-term capital gains rates, the maximum being a measly 28%. What's a capital gain? It is profit resulting from the sale of assets such as stocks, bonds, real estate (including your home), and other tangibles which are not sold in the ordinary course of business.

9

To get long-term capital gains treatment you must hang on to the asset for at least 12 months. Then, when you sell, 60% of your profit is exempt from taxation. The other 40% is taxed at your regular tax rate multiplied by 0.4.

For example, if you're in the 50% tax bracket, your capital gains are taxed at 50% × 0.4 or 20%.

If you're in the 70% tax bracket, as you may be if much of your income is interest on stocks, bonds, etc., you will have to pay taxes on long-term capital gains at the rate of 70% × 0.4 or 28%.

(Profit from the sale of assets held less than a year is called a short-term capital gain. Such gains are taxed as regular income, at rates equal to your regular tax rate up to a maximum of 70%. Obviously, if you're thinking of selling an asset, you're better off waiting until you've owned it for at least 12 months, rather than selling earlier and paying taxes on the profit at short-term capital gains rates. There are a few exceptions to the rule and they'll be discussed later.)

3. Ordinary "earned" income, which comes to you as a salary, wages, or commissions, is less attractive from a tax point of view. As I've mentioned, 50% is the maximum tax rate on earned income—also called personal service income.

4. "Passive," or unearned, income is interest and dividend income. You've made several profitable investments and you just sit back and watch the interest accumulate. Sounds pretty great, except that if enough of your income is passive you find yourself catapulted into the 70% tax bracket.

5. There's only one thing worse, and that's no income at all. Even in the 70% bracket, at least you get to keep $30 out of every $100. As Thomas R. Duwar put it: "The only thing that hurts more than paying an income tax is not having to pay an income tax." (This may be debatable.)

That's about it for income. Now let's take a look at expenses:

1. No expense is best, obviously. But that's a state of affairs that ends forever when your parents first start making you pay your own way. You're better off not spending your money than spending it.

2. Noncash expenses, sometimes called "paper expenses," are the second most desirable. But how, you may be pardoned for wondering, can you have an expense without shelling out money?

The answer, in a word, is depreciation, the best example of a noncash or paper expense.

To understand depreciation, you have to be aware that many assets, such as real estate (an office building, for example, but not the land under it; land is never depreciable), have what IRS calls an "estimated useful life." Uncle Sam's thinking is based on the concept that things wear out, break down, and generally deteriorate until finally all they're worth is what you would get if you scrapped them: "salvage value." (Incidentally, different classes and subclasses of property have different assigned estimated useful lives.)

For tax purposes, then, the dollar value of an asset decreases by a certain percent (due to real or theoretical wear and tear) each year of its estimated useful life. The government allows you to deduct that percentage of depreciation from your taxable income. The depreciation deduction is IRS's way of compensating you for your loss.

There's no cash outlay and your asset may in fact not have depreciated very much except on paper. In real life, it may even have increased in value. For example, the market value of a building may be many thousands of dollars more now than when you bought it, say, five years ago. You can take yearly depreciation deductions anyway.

Note: If it turns out that your depreciation deductions exceed the actual deterioration of an asset, then when you sell that asset, the government recoups the excess depreciation by taxing it as ordinary income. Your profits from the sale, if any, are taxed at long-term capital gains rates if the property was held for at least 12 months.

3. Cash expenses that are tax-deductible are the next most attractive. If you're self-employed or own your own business you already know that a mass of business-related expenses, from postage stamps to the rent you pay for office space, are tax-deductible.

Even as an employee you may have a fair number of tax-deductible business expenses. For example, you can deduct the cost of special uniforms you wear on the job, special tools or equipment you need to perform your work, professional journals and trade association fees, as well as required job-related travel expenses, including meals and hotels (remember, none of these items is tax-deductible if your employer has reimbursed you for out-of-pocket expenses).

On a somewhat more sophisticated plane, as an investor in an oil and gas tax shelter, you can deduct from your regular earned income your share of the cost of intangible drilling expenses.

Don't underestimate the value of deductible expenses in lowering your tax bill. And for heaven's sake keep track of them. The higher your tax bracket, the more important they become.

To see why this is so, let's suppose you're in the 40% bracket. You go down to the local liquor store to buy two bottles of bourbon costing $10 each. One is for your personal use and the other is to keep in a closet at the office to help clinch an after-hours deal.

The first bottle costs you $10 because personal expenses are not deductible. But the second bottle, which is a business expense and thus deductible, in effect costs you just $6. That's because in the 40% tax bracket, a $10 deduction is worth a tax saving of $4.

4. Deductible expenses that can only be added to what's called "basis" don't give you quite the same big tax breaks as straight-out business deductions, but they're still

worth taking advantage of. In order to explain why, let's backtrack and start with the concept of "basis."

If you buy a $90,000 house and live in it casually, making only a minor repair here and there when necessary, then no matter how much you put down in cash to buy the house and how much is mortgaged, the basis of your home is $90,000.

If you decide to sell it a year and a half later and are able to get $98,000 for it, you have made a profit of $8,000, which is taxed at capital gains rates. In this example, basis really is cost.

Now let's suppose you live in that $90,000 house for the same year and a half, but you add a redwood sundeck which costs you $2,000. You can't deduct the $2,000 from your income or depreciate it. That $2,000 is not tax-deductible because it's an improvement expense on your *personal* residence. It's your house, you live there, the deck is for your own private pleasure. However, you can add that $2,000 to the cost basis of your home, bringing it up to $92,000. In other words, $92,000 is the new basis. If you sell the house for $98,000 you have to pay capital gains tax on only $6,000 ($98,000 − $92,000), a nifty saving.

5. Expenses that are in no way tax-deductible are the worst, at least in terms of dollars and cents. (My recent vacation to Mexico wasn't tax-deductible, but it was one of the best cash outlays I ever made.)

What everyone should be aware of is that the higher one's tax bracket, the more expensive nondeductible outlays of cash become. If you're in the 50% tax backet, dollar-a-loaf bread costs you $2 on income over and above $34,200 (if you're single) or $47,200 (if you're married), because you had to earn $2 to come up with $1 after taxes.

There's not much you can do about nondeductible expenses that are in no way business-related, such as food, clothing, and shelter, except to look for bargains. But from a tax point of view they should be avoided whenever possible.

New Law: Long-Term Capital Gains Reduced: The maximum long-term capital gains rate will be lowered from a measly 28% in 1981 to an even more measly 20% in 1982 and afterward. This is a result of the maximum tax rate dropping from 70% in 1981 to 50% in 1982. Thus, after 1982 there will be no difference in the tax rate between "earned" or "unearned" income.

Here's why the maximum tax rate is only 20% on long-term capital gains: On long-term capital gains, 60% of your income is exempt from taxes, while the other 40% is taxed at your tax rate, whatever it happens to be. If 40% of the long-term capital gains is taxed and 50% is the highest possible tax rate in 1982, then 40% times 50% equals 20%.

Let's look at an example: If you made $1,000 in long-term capital gains, 60% (or $600) is entirely free from taxes. On the remaining 40%, or $400, if you are in the maximum 50% bracket, 50% of the $400 goes to Uncle Sam, or $200. This is 20% of the $1,000, assuming you were in the 50% tax bracket. If you were in the 30% tax bracket, the tax rate would be 40% times 30%, so that only 12% of $1,000, or $120, would go to taxes.

New Law: Interest, Penalties, and Estimated Tax:

Interest: The new tax law provides for *annual* adjustments of the interest rate on deficiencies or overpayments, with the rate to be set at 100% of the September 1981 prime rate. The next change will occur on February 1, 1982. In future years the change will take effect on January 1.

Negligence penalty: Besides the existing 5% penalty for negligence, there will be an additional penalty equal to 50% of the interest on a deficiency attributable to neglect or intentional disregard of rules or regulations. This new penalty applies to taxes due after 1981.

Valuation overstatement penalty: On returns filed after 1981, a new graduated penalty will be imposed where overstating a value results in a deficiency. The penalty percentage is (1) 10% if the overstatement is 150% or more, (2)

20% if over 200%, but not more than 250%, and (3) 30% if over 250%.

The penalty does not apply unless the underpayment is at least $1,000, nor does it apply if the property has been held by the taxpayer for over five years as of the close of the tax year of the overstatement.

This penalty applies to individuals, personal service corporations, and closely held corporations (over 50% of the stock owned by five or less people).

All or part of the penalty may be waived by the IRS (but don't count on it), if the taxpayer can show a reasonable basis for the valuation claimed, and that the claim was made in good faith.

False withholding certificates: Starting in 1982 the civil penalty for claiming withholding allowances based on false information is increased to $500 from $50.

Overstated tax deposit: A penalty equal to 25% of any overstated deposit claim will be levied for returns filed after August 14, 1981. This term applies to claims involving failure to deposit or claims of deposits in excess of the amount actually deposited. This is in addition to all other penalties. Reasonable cause will avoid this penalty.

Corporate estimated taxes: For the tax year beginning 1981, corporations whose taxable income is more than $1 million in any of the three preceding years must pay estimated tax of at least 60% of the current year's tax regardless of their tax liability for the preceding year. For tax years beginning in 1982, the percentage that must be paid increases to 65%, in 1983 to 75%, and in 1984 and afterward to 80%.

3

Tax Breaks for
Lower, Middle, and
Astronomical Tax Brackets

At the beginning of this book I mentioned that some of the tax-saving strategies we'd be taking an up-close look at in the first few chapters are what Wall Street purists would call tax *breaks*, not shelters. Well, here are some simple tax breaks available to almost everyone—plus how best to take advantage of them.

Even if you consider yourself an old pro at doing your own taxes, and regardless of whether you see yourself as a lower-, middle-, or upper-income taxpayer, I suggest you carefully read through the following sections. You may know it all now; then again, you may pick up something new.

Let's start with a few of the tax breaks that are built right into the system—or rather, printed plain as day on every federal tax return.

Personal Exemptions: Form 1040 clearly shows that you, as a taxpayer, are allowed a personal exemption of $1,000. That means you can subtract $1,000 from your gross earnings for the year and you do not need to pay taxes on that $1,000.

You can do the same for your spouse if you're married. And you can slice off an additional $1,000 for each of your children under 19, or as long as they remain students, as long as you provided more than half their support during the tax year.

Same goes for mothers, fathers, mothers- and fathers-in-law, grandparents, grandchildren, stepchildren (but not your stepchildren's children), aunts, uncles. If they earn less than $1,000 per year and you provide half or more of their support, you can claim them as dependents and pare your gross taxable income by $1,000 each.

If you and/or your spouse are 65 or older, you're allowed an additional $1,000 exemption. And if you are blind at the close of a tax year, you may deduct another $1,000.

Zero Tax Bracket: The ultimate tax shelter, though it's certainly not a deal I would want to be in, is to fall in the "zero" tax bracket. It isn't that people unfortunate enough to fall into this category earn no money, but they earn so little that the government allows them to keep it all.

You qualify for zero tax bracket treatment (1) if you're married, filing separately, and earning a maximum of $1,700 per year, or (2) if you're married, filing jointly, and earning a total of $3,400 or less, or (3) if you're single or the head of a household and earn $2,300 or less.

Filing Jointly: No doubt you already know that if you're married, regardless of your tax bracket, you may choose to file a joint return with your husband or wife, or elect to file separately.

When you file jointly, the incomes of husband and wife are combined and for tax purposes attributed on a 50-50 basis, half to each spouse.

Generally, filing a joint return is best, though there may be times when filing separately makes more sense. (We'll get to these exceptions later.)

What's so great about filing jointly? It often results in a lower tax bill. Because of our graduated tax system, and because by filing jointly the total family income is combined and then divided in half and attributed equally to husband and wife, earnings are "averaged," in a sense. (This is not to be confused with "income averaging," which we'll go into later.)

In households where the incomes of husband and wife are widely divergent, joint filing may lead to significant tax savings indeed! Take my neighbors Mary and Joe. Mary made $19,600 last year as a photographer's representative. Joe stayed home with their one-year-old and earned no income, though he claims to be hard at work on the Great American Novel between diaper changings and trips to the park. (Knowing Joe, my guess is that he'd rather be a full-time parent, novel or no novel.)

Anyway, if Mary had filed separately as a married person, her taxes for the year would have been $5,170. But she chose to file jointly with Joe and their tax bill was $3,372—a neat savings of almost $1,800. Joe's $0 earnings combined with Mary's almost $20,000, then divided by two, dragged their average way down, resulting in the big tax benefit.

Filing Separately: Now for some of those special circumstances where filing separately puts you ahead. One case is if both spouses work and one of them reports unusually large medical expenses.

John and Linda, who are friends of some friends of mine, are a good example. They're both in their early twenties, both pull down salaries in the mid-teens, but Linda sprained her back last year in a gymnastics class. Her injury, though not serious, was painful, and sent her from G.P. to orthopedist to chiropractor and back again. Then a dental checkup revealed she needed extensive treatment for pyorrhea. It was a year of big medical and dental expenses for Linda, but not for John.

According to the tax laws, medical expenses (dental expenses included) are deductible only to the extent that they exceed 3% of one's adjusted gross income.

If John and Linda filed jointly, Linda's medical expenses,

though high, would not have exceeded 3% of their total adjusted gross income. But her medical bills did amount to more than 3% of her *own* adjusted gross income. To take advantage of the medical deduction—which in their case was greater than the advantage of filing jointly—they filed separately last year.

Joint filing is allowed and is ordinarily advantageous when one spouse has died during the tax year. But here's another exception to the rule: If the estate of the deceased happens to be insolvent, meaning that its assets are inadequate to satisfy the demands of creditors who are no doubt hovering like vultures waiting for their share of whatever is left, the surviving spouse is better off filing separately. Otherwise, he or she would be subject to liabilities that would not otherwise occur.

Filing a joint return may also result in a greater tax disadvantage to an estate if the surviving spouse is earning more than the deceased did. Then, if a joint tax return were filed, the estate would be liable for the tax of the decedent as well as the tax of the surviving spouse.

Standard Deductions: In addition to the $1,000 exemption for yourself and each dependent, you're allowed an automatic deduction of a certain specified amount (depending on your filing status). This standard deduction, now called the zero bracket amount, is built right into the tax-rate schedules. In other words, you don't have to do any additional figuring to claim it. You simply turn to the tax-rate tables at the back of your 1040 instruction booklet to find the amount you owe. The government has already calculated your zero bracket deduction into that amount.

However, it's helpful to know that the zero bracket deduction for a single taxpayer is $2,300. For married people filing joint returns it's $3,400. And for spouses filing separately, the zero bracket amount is $1,700.

Taking the zero bracket deduction has been called the lazy man's way of doing taxes. No need to sit down with a pile of canceled checks to determine what you spent on visits to the doctor or dentist, prescription drugs, interest payments on charge accounts and loans, charitable contributions, state and local taxes, etc. Just take the zero bracket deduction and be done with it!

The truth is that for many people, tallying their deductible expenses *is* ultimately a waste of time. To get a tax break by itemizing deductions, the total amount of itemized deductions must be greater than your aforementioned zero bracket amount. You may have written checks right and left all year long on potentially "itemizable" deductions only to find at tax time, when you haul out your records, that your total deductible expenses fall short of your zero bracket amount. If that happens, stick with the zero bracket amount. Obviously.

Itemizing Deductions: Even though you may end up taking the zero bracket amount anyway, I think it's worth figuring your taxes both ways—by itemizing deductions and comparing the total with your zero bracket amount. I especially encourage you to try itemizing if you've had unusually high medical bills or have several loans or a mortgage outstanding on which you're paying interest. Itemizing can lead to a substantial savings.

For example, consider what happened when the Wilson family (Mom, Dad, two kids) decided to try itemizing:

Last year, their adjusted gross income was $20,000. The tax tables (with built-in zero bracket deduction) indicated their taxes for the year to be $3,460.

However, their total itemized deduction came to $4,500 —$1,100 more than their zero bracket amount of $3,400. By subtracting the $1,100 (the difference between their zero bracket amount and their total itemized deductions), their total taxable income was reduced to $18,900. The tax tables indicate that the tax due on $18,900 is $3,185. By itemizing deductions, they were able to save $275 ($3,460 −$3,185). The Wilsons should definitely itemize.

Adjusted gross income		$20,000
Less: Total itemized deductions	$4,500	
Less: Zero-bracket amount	$3,400	
Excess itemized deductions		1,100
Taxable income		$18,900

If the Wilsons' deductions did not exceed the zero-bracket amount of $3,400, there would be no point in itemizing deductions.

Here's a technique that many smart taxpayers have learned to take advantage of: It involves doing a few advance calculations to determine whether itemizing deductions for the current tax year will save any money. If it looks as though itemizing isn't going to work to your advantage this year, then, if possible, stall payments for itemizable expenses until after January 1 of the following year. At least there is a chance that you *may* be able to make a profitable deduction of those expenses next year.

For example, if you can pay a large medical bill in December 1980 or in January 1981, a year during which you anticipate more heavy medical bills and other deductible expenses, then put off till '81 what you could pay in '80.

The same technique applies to charitable contributions and other deductible expenses over which you have some degree of control.

Incidentally, you may be able to claim more itemizable deductions than you realize. For an idea of the wide range of possible deductions (some of them seemingly far-fetched, yet allowable by IRS) take a look at this list.

Deductions for Everyone!

1. The black lace negligee you gave as a business gift to your best client. (You can deduct up to $25 in total gifts per client per year)

2. Your old clothing and furniture that you gave to the Salvation Army or church group
3. Scenic views (if you contribute open-air or scenic easement to the local, state, or federal government you can get a deduction!)
4. Wheelchairs and crutches
5. Abortions (if performed in a general hospital and if the operation is not outlawed by the state)
6. Acupuncture
7. Air-conditioning units (if prescribed by a doctor to relieve breathing difficulty or allergies)
8. Contributions to Alcoholics Anonymous
9. Alimony—periodic payments
10. Answering service as a business expense
11. Apartment maintained solely for business
12. Artificial teeth and limbs
13. Athletic club dues, if used primarily for business
14. Bad debts
15. Tickets for (if business related) performances
16. Birth-control pills (if obtained under a prescription by a physician)
17. Vasectomy
18. Blackout losses (fully deductible for business, in excess of $100 if nonbusiness)
19. Seeing-eye dog and the expenses of keeping it fed and happy
20. Bodyguard (if you received a kidnapping threat)
21. Car telephone (if medically qualifiable)
22. Contributions to a cemetery company
23. Payment to Christian Science practitioners
24. Christmas cards as business expense
25. Contact lens insurance
26. Treatment of drug addiction
27. Head-hunting fee (executive search)
28. Foreign business conventions (not more than two a year)

29. State and local taxes on gasoline
30. Home stereo system (if medically qualifiable)
31. Payments to kidnappers (less $100 theft loss deduction)
32. Subscriptions to magazines (if magazines are used in income-producing activities)
33. Psychiatrists
34. Wig (if recommended by physician to avoid mental upset)
35. Whirlpool bath (if for medical purposes)
36. Plastic surgery (if medically prescribed)
37. A swimming pool (if recommended by a physician and you can prove that it alleviated a physical ailment)
38. Organic food (if prescribed by a doctor)
39. Sonic boom damage
40. Smog damage
41. This book

Income Averaging: This is a tax-sheltering device available to virtually every taxpayer who finds himself with unusually high income during one year. For the person whose income has risen by at least $3,000 since the previous year, this option can lead to sizable savings.

The regulations on income averaging allow it to be used with almost all kinds of income, including salaries, commissions, bonuses, professional fees, interest income, dividends, wagering income, capital gains, ordinary income from sole proprietorships or partnerships, and income in the form of gifts or inheritances.

Only two types of income are not eligible for averaging: Trust accumulation distribution and premature distribution of pension funds, both of which will be taken up in chapters to come.

To understand how income averaging works, let's imagine that you win $40,000 in a state lottery. If that's not your dream come true, maybe you'd rather pretend that the stock you bought 15 days ago has suddenly gone shooting up and you just sold it for a $40,000 profit. Whatever.

If you had to pay taxes on the additional $40,000 all at once your tax bill would be astronomical and you'd have little of your windfall left to enjoy. Income averaging reduces the amount of taxes you must pay.

Here's a step-by-step guide to income averaging. If you don't get it at first reading, go through it again. It'll become clear.

1. Get out your old tax returns and add up your taxable income for the past four years. Divide by 4 to get the average. Then multiply that average by 120%. The result is called your average base period income.

2. Subtract the average base period income from this year's taxable income. Multiply the result by 20% and add to your average base period income. Compute the tax on that amount.

3. Subtract the tax arrived at in step 2 from the tax due on your average base period income alone. Multiply the result by 5 and add this to the tax on your average base period income. The figure you end up with is the amount due on this year's taxable income.

(If you want to take the easy way out, pick up a Schedule G, which offers a simplified approach to the machinations of income averaging, making the computations easier to comprehend and maneuver.)

My friend Neil is a example of how income averaging saves tax dollars.

A little background on Neil: He's married and his earnings as a sales representative hovered at about $20,000 for a few years. (His average base period income was 120% of this, or $24,000.) Last year he changed jobs and did so well his new boss rewarded him with a $40,000 bonus. True story!

Now $24,000 + $36,000 = $60,000 (what Neil earned last year). But the tax on $24,000 plus the tax on $36,000 is a lot less than the tax on $60,000—and that's how Neil saved money:

This year's taxable income		$60,000
Average income, last 4 years	$20,000	
Plus 20% tax	4,000	
	$24,000	
Average base period income		24,000
Average base period income subtracted from this year's taxable income = "averageable income"		36,000
Tax on base period income ($24,000) plus 20% of averageable income (20% × $36,000) = tax on $31,200		6,682
Less tax on base period income		4,337
Tax on 20% of averageable income		2,345
Tax on 20% of averageable income × 5		11,745
Plus tax on base period income ($24,000)		4,337
Tax due on this year's income ($60,000)		$16,062

If Neil hadn't taken the trouble to average his income, his taxes on the $60,000 would have been $19,678. Income averaging saved him $3,616!

Income averaging isn't always an unmixed blessing. You should be aware of what you might lose should you decide to average your income.

If really big sums of money are involved, you may average yourself right out and go over the 50% maximum tax rate on personal service income, a maximum that no longer applies when you opt for income averaging. And you may lose the advantage of excluding certain earned income from sources outside the U.S. These foreign earnings must be included in the taxable income for the computation year as well as in the base period years, if you income-average.

To be on the safe side, make sure to figure your taxes

both ways—the regular way and by income averaging—before you make a final decision in favor of the latter.

Stocks and Bonds: You don't have to be rich to own stocks or bonds, or some of each. In a 1975 New York Stock Exchange survey of shareowners it was estimated that more than 33% of stock owners had incomes of less than $15,000 a year and though wages and prices have gone up considerably since then, there's no reason to believe that the situation has changed much. Then, as now, millions of people of average means own corporate bonds and/or shares in American businesses.

Though I wouldn't recommend investing in stocks or bonds to anyone who is hard-pressed to put food on the table, if you have a few extra dollars to play around with, can afford to lose, and understand some basic principles, you may be able to lighten your tax load considerably by investing in stocks and bonds.

Let's ignore dividends and interest for the moment and simply think of stocks and bonds as assets that can be bought and sold—sometimes for a profit, sometimes at a loss. Stocks and bonds, like any assets held for more than a year and sold for a profit, are subject to long-term capital gains treatment, which means that the profit is taxed at a maximum rate of 28%.

If you sell at a profit stocks or bonds held for twelve months or less, you end up with a short-term gain, which is added to your ordinary income and taxed along with it at your going tax rate.

Now here's where it gets interesting: Capital gains can be offset by capital losses. If you somehow end the year with greater capital losses than gains—not such a difficult feat when you're playing the market—you can deduct up to $3,000 worth of those losses from your ordinary income!

Short-term capital losses, resulting from the sale of assets you have held for twelve months or less, can be deducted from your ordinary income, on a dollar-for-dollar basis, up to the $3,000 limit. In other words, if you sustain $2,000 worth of short-term capital losses, you can deduct the full $2,000 from your gross income for the year.

Long-term capital losses are a slightly different matter. You need to sustain $2 of long-term capital losses to deduct $1 from your ordinary income. Again the $3,000 limit applies. If you had $4,000 worth of long-term capital losses you can deduct $2,000 from ordinary income.

What happens if you sustain capital losses in excess of $3,000 in a single tax year? IRS allows you to carry those excess losses over into the following year (or years), at a limit of $3,000 per year, until the entire amount of your capital losses has been deducted!

loss carry forward

Suppose you sustain $5,000 in short-term capital losses in 1980. You can deduct $3,000 (the upper limit) from your ordinary gross income for 1980. The remaining $2,000 can be deducted from your 1981 income. Or you can save the deduction for some time in the future whenever you need it.

In the case of long-term capital losses, for which you need to lose $2 to obtain a $1 deduction, if you sustained an $8,000 long-term capital loss in 1980 you could write off a maximum of $6,000 to get a $3,000 tax deduction from your ordinary income. You'd be left with $2,000 worth of long-term losses—or $1,000 worth of deductions—to use in subsequent years.

Naturally, you'll want to plan carefully so that you'll get the most mileage out of excess capital losses. If your overall tax picture looks pretty good in 1981, "save" your losses so they can be deducted from ordinary income in '82. Or '83. Or whenever. There's no time limit.

Of course you have to invest money to sustain losses and get the deductions in the first place and that kind of strategy may not be your cup of tea. But knowing how to maneuver in the area of capital gains and losses is an important factor in many tax-saving tactics. Understanding the basics of these maneuvers takes away some (not all!) of the scary aspects of investing in stocks, bonds—or anything else, for that matter.

One other important thing you, as a taxpayer, should know about stocks: The first $100 of dividend income is tax-exempt. This means that if you have the wherewithal to invest in a few shares of blue-chip stocks—enough to give you an annual return in dividends of about $100—it's definitely worth your while to do so.

A Tax Break from Renting?
Sometimes Yes, Believe It or Not

Most people automatically assume that buying a house or co-op is a better deal, taxwise, than renting. They figure they can deduct property taxes and interest paid on the mortgage. And they're right. But those deductions don't always result in a tax break.

Remember, you're entitled to a standard deduction, which, if you're single, is $2,300, and if you're married and file jointly, is $3,400. As you know, you can either take the standard deduction or itemize your deductions. You can't do both.

Thus, if you are married, file jointly, and have only $2,000 worth of property tax and mortgage interest deductions, but no additional deductions, you'd actually lose $1,400 worth of deductions if you itemized ($3,400, your standard deduction, minus $2,000, your itemized tax and mortgage interest deduction).

In looking at renting versus buying from the angle of tax deductions only, I've excluded from consideration the very important investment potential of real estate and the fact that property tends to appreciate in time. Your $1,400 tax break may look rather insignificant compared to the long-term profit potential of owning your own home.

In the example above, I've also assumed that property tax and mortgage interest were the *only* itemized deductions. The fact is, if you had a number of other deductions, you'd probably come out ahead after all if you owned rather than rented.

Just an added point in passing: If you take the standard deduction instead of itemizing, you don't get tax benefits for making charitable contributions. (But then again, true charity has nothing to do with tax savings—right, Scrooge?)

New Law: Indexing of Personal Exemptions and Zero Tax Bracket: To prevent "bracket-creep" (the effect of inflation lifting everyone into higher tax brackets), beginning in 1985, the income tax brackets, the personal exemptions, and the zero tax bracket amount will have annual adjustments measured by the Consumer Price Index.

New Law: Marriage Deduction: Married couples who file jointly are now allowed a deduction in computing adjusted gross income, thus eliminating what was once a "marriage penalty," due to different tax rates for single, head of household, and married taxpayers. Beginning in 1982, based on the lower-earning spouse's "qualified earned income," the first $30,000 receives a deduction of 5% of the amount earned (up to a maximum of $1,500). In 1983 and thereafter the deduction on the lower-earning spouse's income will be 10% (up to a maximum of $3,000). For spouses earning equal amounts, the deductions from income may be computed using either spouse's income.

This deduction is available only to spouses who file jointly and who do not claim the benefits applicable to income earned abroad.

New Law: Stocks and Bonds: Beginning in 1982 and thereafter, the long-term capital gains rates will be reduced from 28% to 20%. See Chapter 2 under "New Law: Long-Term Capital Gains Reduced."

New Law: Child Care and Dependent Expense Credit:
The new law liberalizes the credit that working parents
can claim for child care and dependent expenses. For 1981
the maximum credit is $400 (20% of the first $2,000 of
expenses) for one child, and $800 (20% of the first $4,000
in expenses) for two or more children.

Beginning in 1982, the credit will be increased and
changed depending on a sliding scale of a family's income.
For one child, the credit for couples with adjusted gross
incomes of $10,000 or less will be a maximum of $720 (or
30% of the first $2,400 in expenses). For two or more chil-
dren, the credit will be $1,440 (or 30% of the first $4,800).
The credit is decreased by 1% for each additional $2,000
of income (or fraction thereof) above $10,000 up to
$28,000. Taxpayers with adjusted gross incomes over
$28,000 will be entitled to a 20% credit, limited to the two
or more child maximum of $1,440.

New Law: Employer-Provided Child Care: Child care
assistance provided by an employer (when under a written
nondiscriminatory plan) is not included in an employee's
gross income. This applies to remuneration after 1981.

New Law: Adoption Expense Deduction: If you legally
adopt a child with special needs (as determined by the
state of adoption), up to $1,500 of deductions are available
after December 31, 1980, for "qualified adoption expenses,"
such as adoption fees, lawyers fees, or court costs. A "child
with special needs" is one who is handicapped or a member of a minority group.

**New Law: Exclusion for Income Earned Abroad, or
America, Love It and Leave It:** From the way the new
tax law reads you'd think the government wants you to
leave. Starting in 1982, qualified U.S. citizens and resident
aliens working abroad are entitled to a $75,000 exclusion
election from gross income to be increased $5,000 annually
up to $95,000 after 1985.

If this were not enough, a housing cost exclusion will be

allowed for "housing expenses" (including utilities and insurance but not taxes and interest, which are separately deductible), over a base housing amount (which is currently $6,059, 16% of $37,871, the present salary of a grade GS-14 government employee).

The test for physical presence is liberalized to 330 days in any 12 consecutive-month period from the 510 days in any period of 18 consecutive months now required. Deductions and credit attributable to excluded income will not be allowed. Thus foreign taxes paid on excluded income cannot be credited against U.S. taxes.

> The tax collector must love poor people—he's creating so many
> of them.
>
> —BILL VAUGHAN

4

Tax Breaks for Stockholders
—Securities Without
Becoming Broker

You don't have to be rich to own stocks. A 1975 New York
Stock Exchange survey of shareowners estimated that more
than 33% of them had incomes of less than $15,000. An
annual income of $15,000 meant more then than it does
now, but the point remains: millions of people of average
means own shares in American businesses.

There's a good chance that you're one of them. If so,
some of the tax breaks we'll be considering in the following
pages will have a distinctly slimming effect on the figure
you owe to Uncle Sam in taxes for this year and years to
come.

The $100 Dividend Exclusion: In Chapter 3 I pointed
out that as an individual taxpayer, you can deduct up to
$100 in stock dividends from your taxable income for the
year. Now let's look a little closer at this ruling.

If you're married and you and your spouse both have
dividend income, you may each deduct up to $100 of that
income from your gross income for the year. But you can't

treat your combined dividend income as a lump sum. In other words, if dividends from stocks owned by the husband amount to $170, and dividends from stocks owned by the wife amount to $30, you can deduct only $130 of dividend income from your combined gross income for the year— the maximum $100 for the husband's dividend income of $170, plus the $30 in dividend income from the wife's stock.

One way to maximize your dividend income deduction, if you're married, is to have stock owned jointly in both your names. If this is done, the husband and wife with $170 and $30 respectively in dividend income can deduct the full amount—$200—from their gross income for the year.

Taking Advantage of Stocks with Tax-Free Dividends: If you really want to minimize your tax bill on dividend income, see a broker about shifting some of your investments into stocks that pay tax-free dividends.

Most stocks paying tax-free dividends are utility company issues. Their dividends are nontaxable to the investor because the cash earnings of these companies are more than offset by their tax losses, which are caused by accelerated depreciation, investment tax credits, sales of investments for losses, and other entirely legal tax strategies on the part of company management that allow earnings to pass on to the investor tax-free.

Unfortunately for you, the investor, some new tax laws— especially those disallowing the use of accelerated depreciation for tax purposes, a concept we'll take up in detail later —are making it harder and harder to find companies paying tax-free dividends. Thus there's no guarantee that the utility company paying tax-free dividends this year will be doing the same next year.

Here are a couple of precautionary don'ts and a do pertaining to investing in stocks that pay tax-free dividends:

Don't assume that the utility companies pay tax-free dividends.

Don't assume that the utility company that paid tax-

33

free dividends last year will be able to continue the practice this year.

Do check with a broker before investing in a utility company that has been paying tax-free dividends. Its situation may have changed.

Another thing to be wary of when investing in stocks that pay tax-free dividends is that these dividends reduce your tax basis of the cost of the stock, as they are treated for tax purposes as return of principal. You may find when you sell the stock—even if you sell it for the same price you paid for it—that you are subject to capital gains taxation on the amount you received as tax-free dividends.

For example, suppose you buy XYZ stock at $30 per share, receive $4 in tax-free dividends on each share, and sell the stock later for your original cost, $30 per share (the original cost to you of the stock, remember). IRS, maintaining that your adjusted cost basis on the price of the stock is $26, may swoop down and tax you on $4 at capital gains rates, the $4 difference per share between the $30 price at which you sell the stock and the $26 adjusted cost to you.

If your original cost of XYZ is $30 per share:

Original cost and original basis (per share)	$30
Tax-free dividends received (per share)	− 4
Adjusted basis (per share)	$26

If you later sell the stock of XYZ for $30 per share:

Proceeds from stock sold (per share)	$30
Adjusted basis (per share)	− 26
Capital gains (per share)	$ 4

However, if you sell the stock after holding it for over a year, you will be able to get capital gains treatment. Thus, you will have converted ordinary income into capital gains!

Getting the Most Out of Capital Gains and Losses. The Revenue Act of 1978 went a long way in helping investors maximize their return from capital gains. As of November 1978, 60% of your long-term capital gain on the sale of stock or real estate or any other property came back to you tax-free. Only 40% of your capital gain is taxed, rather than 50% as under the old rules.

Formerly, if you had a long-term capital gain of $20,000, $10,000 would come back to you tax-free, and the other $10,000 would be taxed at your tax bracket. If your tax bracket was 50%, you would have to pay the government $5,000 in taxes. Under the new laws you only have to pay $4,000.

According to the Pre-Revenue Act of 1978, 50% of long-term capital gains is taxed:

Long-term capital gains	$20,000
Tax-free (50%)	− 10,000
Subject to tax	$10,000
(For 50% tax bracket)	× 50%
Tax	$ 5,000

But according to the Revenue Act of 1978, only 40% is taxed:

Long-term capital gains	$20,000
Tax-free (60%)	− 12,000
Subject to tax	$ 8,000
(For 50% tax bracket)	× 50%
Tax	$ 4,000

Thus the saving given by the Revenue Act of 1978 is $5,000 − $4,000 = $1,000.

Let's look at some basic concepts and rules that are necessary to maximize the tax benefits you can receive from capital gains and losses.

1. Your long-term gains are used to offset your long-term losses. The difference is your long-term gain or loss.

2. Your short-term capital gains are offset by your short-term capital losses. The difference is your short-term gain or loss.

3. If you had both long-term and short-term capital gains, you must keep them separate. Add your short-term gains to your ordinary income. Take 40% of your long-term gains and add that to your ordinary income.

4. If you have more net short-term capital gains than net long-term capital losses, treat the remaining net gain as short-term.

5. If your net long-term gains exceed your net short-term losses, the remaining net gain is treated as long-term.

6. If you have more net short-term losses, you can deduct them dollar for dollar against your ordinary income up to $3,000 (in one year only).

7. If you have net long-term losses, you can offset them up to $3,000 (in one year only) of ordinary income, although it takes $2 of long-term capital loss to offset $1 of ordinary income. In no case, however, can your long-term and your short-term losses combined offset more than a total of $3,000 in one year.

8. Any remaining short-term or long-term losses can be carried forward indefinitely.

In your tax planning, keep in mind the following:

1. Try to balance your gains off against your losses.

2. Try to avoid taking more net long-term losses than you have gains. If you do this you are wasting your losses, as it takes $2 of net long-term losses to offset $1 of ordinary income.

3. It may be useful to take up to $3,000 in net short-term losses that you can deduct dollar for dollar against ordinary income.

4. As a rule, keep your losses short-term and your gains long-term.

Keep in mind that market conditions should take precedence over tax considerations in deciding when to take capital gains or losses. However, remembering the above rules and applying them will definitely maximize your net returns.

How to Get a Tax Break by Selling Your Stock Rather Than Taking the Dividends: As we've seen, you are not required to pay taxes on dividend income of up to $100. Once past that $100 maximum, dividends are taxed as ordinary income rather than at the more attractive capital gains rates.

For tax purposes it may be more advantageous to simply sell the stock and, if you've held it for more than a year, get long-term capital gains treatment on your profit, than to keep the stock, receive the dividend, and be taxed at ordinary rates on the dividend income. This is an especially good strategy to keep in mind if you were planning to sell the stock some time in the future anyway, since the price of a stock generally increases after a dividend has been declared.

Be sure to sell the stock before the "ex-dividend" date (the date that the stock is sold without the dividend), or you, and not the new owner of the stock, will receive the dividend! A stock sells ex-dividend four full business days prior to the record date (the date which determines who gets the dividend).

Timing is everything in making this strategy work.

"Selling Short Against the Box"—Last-Minute Tax Strategy When New Year's Just Around the Corner: "Selling short against the box," a favored strategy among sophisticated investors, is probably so called because in days gone by investors kept their securities in little locked black boxes. At any rate, that's how the origin of the term was explained to me. The strategy allows you to defer taxable recognition of gains or losses from stock sales from one year to the following year. Here's how:

When you sell short, you're selling shares you do not

own in the hope that you can buy them and close the transaction at a lower price than you paid, thus earning a profit. When you sell short against the box you sell shares that you already own, locking in your profit or loss, but you don't close the transaction (by buying them back) until the next year. Hence, you have obtained the profit that you desired, and have postponed its tax effect. You now have use of some "tax money" for an entire year.

Here's how John, a client of mine, sold short against the box. By the middle of December 1979 John had made a 15-point gain on 100 shares of X stock; but all indications were that the stock had greater downside risk (meaning its price was likely to slide) than upside potential. Naturally, John wanted to keep the gain he had made, but didn't want to pay taxes on it until next year. If he sold it outright, he'd have to pay taxes on a $1,500 profit for tax year 1979.

Instead, John instructed me to "short the stock against the box." "Shorting the stock" means that you borrow shares from your broker and sell them in the hope that they decrease in price. If the stock goes down you'll be able to buy it back cheaper and give the shares back to your broker, making a profit on the difference.

John was shorting the stock he already owned (had in his "box"), so as to lock in his profit (or loss, if taking a loss is advantageous to the overall tax situation) regardless of whether the stock went up or down. If the stock went down 10 points, his long position would lose $1,000 but his short position would gain $1,000. He could close out his position on the first trading day of the new year or thereafter by delivering the long position against the shorted stock. The transaction occurred for tax purposes in the new year, 1980. John now had until April 1981 to play with the government's money.

Warning: You can't turn a short-term gain into a long-term gain by going short against the box. Your holding period ends the day you short the stock, even though you have postponed the tax consequences. Trying to justify this to IRS will have the same dismal consequences as coming up against a stone wall.

How to Time Stock Losses for Best Tax Advantages: As discussed in Chapter 3 there may be times when you can save money on taxes by taking a loss on a stock or another asset.

Ordinarily the sale date of the stock determines the year in which you can take the loss. In other words, if you sell stock J at a loss on December 28, 1981, you will reap the desired consequences on your 1981 tax return.

However, in taking a loss on a short sale, the sale date—and thus possibly the year in which the tax consequences occur—is determined by when the stock is actually delivered, which is *five business days after the order to sell* (the execution date). Short sales executed on December 28, 1981, will actually be delivered in the first week of January 1982, and the tax consequences of such a sale will apply to your 1982 tax return.

How to Clean Up on a Wash Sale: A technique that allows you to retain a stock and take up to a $3,000 loss on it at the same time is called a wash sale.

(In case your memory needs refreshing, short-term capital losses resulting from the sale of stock or other assets you have held for less than a year can be deducted dollar for dollar from your gross income for the year, up to a maximum of $3,000. But you need to sustain $6,000 of long-term capital losses in order to deduct the maximum $3,000 from your gross income. Thus how long you've held a stock affects the maximum loss you can deduct on a wash sale.)

Here's a situation in which you might clean up:

Let's assume that if you sold stock K today you would sustain a short-term loss of $3,000, and you desperately need that loss to offset taxes on some unusually high profits you've made during the year. Yet all indications are that stock K is worth keeping in your portfolio.

What do you do? You buy new shares of stock K in the amount of $3,000 and then tell your broker to sell the original shares. Neat, huh?

There's a catch. There always is with techniques as simple as this one. According to IRS, your wash sale deduction will be disallowed unless you buy the new shares either 31 days before or 31 days after you sell the old shares.

Your broker will tell you to count the number of days. Find the last date in the year that you can qualify for the loss and count backward 31 days: This gives you the last possible date on which you must have bought new shares to replace the old ones you plan to sell.

Better still, don't wait until December to plan a wash sale. Start thinking and acting in October or November.

State Transfer Taxes—How to Figure Them to Your Advantage: If you have long-term capital gains on stock sales you should deduct your brokerage commissions and state transfer taxes from your profits when reporting the gain to IRS, right?

Wrong. Many—probably even most—investors subtract brokerage commissions and state transfer taxes, if any, from long-term capital gains on stock sales, and it costs them dearly. Let's say you've made long-term capital gains of $2,000 on a batch of stock you sold this year. Your brokerage fees on the deal are $150, and state transfer taxes are $100. If you deduct the total, $250, from $2,000 profit, you'll report an adjusted long-term gain of $1,750 to IRS. So far, so good. Except you're cheating yourself.

Here's a better way to figure state transfer taxes. Deduct the brokerage commission from your long-term capital gain. This gives you $1,850 that can be taxed at the attractive maximum long-term capital gains rate of 28% (70% times 40%).

As for the state transfer tax, that can be deducted from your ordinary income. The transfer tax, if deducted from your ordinary income (taxed at a 50% maximum) may be worth almost twice as much to you in tax benefits as it would be if you subtracted it from your long-term gain (taxed at a 28% maximum). How's that?

Let's say Philip had $1,000 worth of income taxed at 50%, $1,000 worth of long-term capital gains taxed at 28%, and $100 worth of state transfer taxes which are deductible. Let's compare what happens when Philip deducts the $100 from long-term capital gains, and what happens when he correctly deducts the $100 from his ordinary income. The wrong way:

Ordinary income	$1,000	Long-term capital gains	$1,000
Tax bracket	× .50	State transfer taxes	− 100
		Taxable balance	$ 900
		Tax bracket	× .28
Tax due	$ 500	Tax due	$ 252
Philip keeps	$ 500	Philip keeps	$ 748
($1,000 − $500)		($1,000 − $252)	

Philip keeps a total of $1,248 ($500 plus $748). The right way:

Ordinary income	$1,000	Long-term capital gains	$1,000
State transfer taxes	100	Tax bracket	× .28
Taxable balance	$ 900		
Tax bracket	× .50		
Tax due	$ 450	Tax due	$ 280
Philip keeps	$ 550	Philip keeps	$ 720
($1,000 − $450)		($1,000 − $280)	

Philip keeps a total of $1,270 ($550 + $720). Philip ends up with $22 more (for each $100 of state transfer taxes) by taking his state transfer taxes off his ordinary income. The higher your tax bracket the more favorable results this will produce for you. That $22 Philip saved could have paid for this book, plus a couple of drinks to celebrate!

"Earmarking" Stocks for Greater Tax Benefits: Stock certificates don't have ears, but you can still have your broker earmark them according to certificate number and date purchased. (The broker probably won't do this as a matter of course; you'll have to make a specific request.)

Why would you want to earmark your stock? Because unless you do, IRS operates under the assumption that the first 100 shares of a company's stock that you sell are the first 100 shares you bought. It's the old "first-in, first-out" assumption.

Trouble is, when you've purchased the same company's stock at various times and at different prices, it's not always to your advantage to sell the original 100 shares first. Depending on your tax situation and the price of the stocks, you may benefit by unloading the second or third block of 100 shares.

Selling the block purchased at the highest price results in your paying a smaller capital gains tax than you'd pay on the sale of a block of lower-priced stock.

To see how this works, suppose you bought 100 shares of M stock at $10 per share on June 1, 1977. Your broker records its date of purchase and certificate number—say, #1000. A year later you purchase 100 more shares of M stock, this time at $15 per share. This time the earmarked certificate number is #2000.

On July 1, 1979, when M stock is up to $25 per share, you decide it's time to sell 100 shares. You instruct your broker to sell certificate #2000, for a capital gain of 100 shares × ($25 − $15) = $1,000. Without earmarking, IRS would assume you sold your original 100 shares of M stock, for a capital gain of 100 shares × ($25 − $10) = $1,500. That's going to mean more taxes.

If you want to take a loss to offset other taxes, the strategy can be reversed. If you bought 100 shares of N stock at $20 on June 1, 1977, and another 100 shares at $30 on July 1, 1977, and sold 100 shares of N stock at

$25 on August 1, 1979, you can take a loss by identifying the shares sold as those you purchased on July 1, 1977—but *only* if your stocks have been recorded and identified by date of purchase and certificate number.

Otherwise, IRS will apply the "first in, first out" ruling, and instead of taking a loss, you'll be taxed on a gain.

Earmarking can be used flexibly to plan gains and losses for a given year. Don't miss out on it!

If your broker is holding your stock, you should (at the time of the sale) have him designate in writing the specific shares that are being sold. Chances are you'll come out ahead!

New Law: Dividend and Interest Income: During the 1981 tax year taxpayers can exclude dividend and interest up to $200 on a separate return and $400 on a joint return. The Act repealed this dividend and interest exclusion for the 1982 tax year and thereafter, and reinstated the dividend exclusion of $100 on a separate return and $200 on a joint return. The $200 is available on joint returns regardless of which spouse received the dividend.

New Law: Dividend Reinvestment: The new law allows a public utility to establish dividend reinvestment plans under which shareholders can choose to receive dividends in common stock (which would be exempted from taxes up to $750 per year or $1,500 per year for a joint return), rather than in cash. This rule is effective January 1, 1982, and will last through 1985.

A person receiving a stock dividend would defer tax liability until the stock is sold and is taxed on a capital gains basis. If the stockholder had a choice of receiving the dividend in stock rather than in cash, the stock dividend would then be taxed as ordinary income. Stock received as dividend will have a zero basis.

The stock must be newly issued common stock to qualify. Not every utility will qualify, and those that do will not necessarily elect to provide stock. A shareholder will have to make an election for this exclusion to apply. Shareholders owning at least 5% of the value of the stock or of the voting power in a corporation, estates, trusts, and nonresident aliens are not eligible for this exclusion.

New Law: Capital Gains and Losses: Beginning in 1982 and thereafter, the long-term capital gains rates will be reduced to 28% from 20%. See Chapter 2 under "New Law: Long-Term Capital Gains Reduced."

New Law: Commodity Futures Straddles: A major abuse in the tax system had been the use of commodity straddles to defer income and to convert ordinary income and short-term capital gains into long-term capital gains. In a commodity straddle an investor holds equal long and short positions in futures contracts in the same commodity with different delivery dates. The two positions, called "legs," are expected to move in opposite directions but with little change in an investor's overall position, as a gain in one leg would offset the loss in the other leg, thereby minimizing the risks.

The new law changed the following:

Marked-to-market: Under the new act regulated futures contracts entered into after June 23, 1981 are "marked-to-market" at year end (meaning that they are treated as if sold on the last day of the tax year and any gain or loss is determined by its value on that last day), and taxed on the realized or unrealized net gain at that time. Commodity straddle losses will be allowed only to the extent that losses exceed unrealized gains on offsetting positions.

Marked-to-market gains and losses are combined with any gains and losses from futures contracts recognized during the year and are taxed as follows: (1) 60% of the combined gain and loss is long-term, and (2) 40% is treated as short-term capital gain or loss. This works out to a maximum tax rate of 32% on gains on regulated futures contracts for 1982 and thereafter.

Net losses, after giving effect to the marked-to-market

rule for regulated futures contracts, can be carried back three years by noncorporate taxpayers against the smaller of (1) net regulated futures gains, or (2) the capital gain for the year. Net losses cannot be carried back to years ending on or before June 23, 1981. Any loss unused after carryback is carried forward. For corporations the three-year carryback provisions under present law are not affected.

Loss deferral: For straddles involving property other than regulated futures contracts that are marked-to-market, losses are deferred to the extent there are unrealized gains in offsetting positions. Disallowed losses are deferred to future years, but only if the property subject to the loss is actively traded personal property other than stock. Excluded also are long-term stock options and real estate.

Wash sale and short sale: Wash sale and short sale principles of the present law are to be extended to straddles.

Capitalization of interest and carrying charges: Interest and carrying charges to purchase or carry a commodity held for investment will not be deducted currently, but are added to the basis of a commodity held as a straddle.

Hedging exception: Hedgers, those who own the actual commodity itself and who take a counterbalancing position in a regulated futures contract to protect against loss, will be exempt from the marked-to-market, loss deferral, and capitalization rules.

Treasury bills: Two basic changes are provided in the taxation of government bonds:

1. Treasury bills and other short-term government obligations issued at a discount and payable at a fixed maturity date less than one year from the issue date will be treated as capital assets in determining gain or loss. The old law defined them as not being capital assets, and thus they generated only ordinary income.

2. Any gain realized on the sale or exchange of a government obligation is treated as ordinary up to "the ratable share of the acquisition discount" (the portion equal to the

ratio of the number of days the bond is held to the number of days between the date of acquisition and the date of maturity). For example, if a bill is bought six months before maturity and is held for three months, one half of the gain is treated as interest and is taxed as ordinary income, and the balance is taxed as short-term capital gain.

Dealer identification of securities: Broker-dealers must identify securities held for investment on the day the securities are acquired. Before this change a dealer could wait 30 days to make this identification.

Treatment of cancellations, lapses, and similar transactions: Cancellations, lapses, and similar terminations that have been given ordinary income or loss treatment are now treated as capital gains or losses.

Transition rules: For all regulated futures contracts held on or before June 23, 1981, the taxpayer may elect to have the new rules apply. He or she may elect to have the marked-to-market rules apply to all regulated futures contracts held during the taxable year that includes June 23, 1981, the tax calculated under this election using the 1982 tax rates. If this election is made, the taxpayer may elect to pay the tax related to the futures contracts held in two to five annual installments with interest.

New Law: Incentive Stock Options Changes: Executives who receive stock options from their companies will find the new tax code very attractive, as might those employees who usually do not receive stock options since stock options may now become part of their compensation package. The new law allows incentive stock options to be taxed similarly to the treatment given pre-1976 qualified stock options. An employee is not taxed at the time of the grant nor on the exercise of the option, but is taxed at capital gains rates only when the stock is sold (provided that the stock is held at least two years after the date of the grant *and* one year from the date of exercising the option).

A stock option gives the holder the right to purchase a

specified number of shares at a set price over a designated period of time. If the stock price rises over the set price of the option, the holder of the option makes a sure profit. If the stock price is under the set price of the option, the option holder is not out of pocket a penny.

Existing stock options: The new rules apply immediately to any options granted after 1975 and exercised or outstanding after 1980. Although the new law applies primarily to new options, it makes existing options attractive provided they meet the requirement of the new options. An employer must make an election to have the incentive stock option rules apply, for options granted from January 1, 1976 and before 1981. The value of the stock subject to these elective options may not exceed $200,000 in the aggregate or $50,000 for any calendar year. Changes in the post-1975 option plans must be within one year from the date of enactment to conform to the new rules.

Newly granted options: For newly granted options the following conditions must be satisfied for an "incentive stock option" to qualify:

1. The stockholders must approve a plan within 12 months before or after the plan's actual adoption specifying the number of shares of option stock to be issued and the employees to receive the options.

2. The option is granted within ten years of the date the plan is adopted or approved by the shareholders, whichever comes first.

3. The options must be exercised within ten years of the date of the grant.

4. The option price must equal or exceed the fair-market value of the option stock at the time the option is granted.

5. The employee, immediately before the granting of the option, may not own more than 10% of the total voting power of all classes of stock, unless the option price is at least 110% of the fair-market value of the stock and the option isn't exercisable for more than five years after it is

granted.

6.   The option is not transferable except at death. It is exercisable during the employee's lifetime only by the employee.

7.   The option is not exercisable while there is any outstanding incentive option granted to the employee from an earlier time. The value at the date of the grant of options to any employee in any calendar year may not exceed $100,000 plus a limited carryover of prior unused amounts.

8.   The employee must stay with the company granting the option until at least three months before the option is exercised.

5

Tax Breaks with Bonds

When you buy a stock you're buying equity—a share, or piece of the action of a corporation or other issuing agency.

But when you buy a bond the money you pay for it represents a loan to the issuing agency, which may be a corporation, a utility company, the federal government, or a municipality. The bond is a kind of promissory note issued to you, the lender, by the borrowing agency, which promises to pay you interest on the principal of your loan, usually at a stated rate, over a number of years until the bond matures. At that point you get your principal back and, if you haven't already taken it in installment payments over the years, you also get interest on the principal.

The tax breaks offered by bonds are quite interesting—and different from those available to stockholders.

Municipal Bonds—A Way to Tax-Free Income: There are different kinds of bonds, but for now let's focus on municipals, which are offered by states, counties, cities, or their agencies to raise money for special local projects: road building, construction of tunnels or bridges, improvement of mass transit systems, and the like.

The most interesting thing about municipals, at least for our purposes, is that they provide interest income that is exempt from federal income taxes! Usually, but not always,

49

*This table will allow you to figure out the equivalent taxable yield
you would have to obtain to equal the tax free yield of a municipal bond.
Locate your tax bracket and then read across.*

1980 Joint Return Taxable Income*	Tax Bracket	Tax Free Yield				
		4.00%	4.50%	5.00%	5.50%	6.00%
			Equivalent Taxable Yield			
$ 16,000 - $ 20,200	24%	5.26%	5.92%	6.58%	7.24%	7.89%
$ 20,200 - $ 24,600	28	5.56	6.25	6.94	7.64	8.33
$ 24,600 - $ 29,900	32	5.88	6.62	7.35	8.09	8.82
$ 29,900 - $ 35,200	37	6.35	7.14	7.94	8.73	9.52
$ 35,200 - $ 45,800	43	7.02	7.89	8.77	9.65	10.53
$ 45,800 - $ 60,000	49	7.84	8.82	9.80	10.78	11.76
$ 60,000 - $ 85,600	54	8.70	9.78	10.87	11.96	13.04
$ 85,600 - $109,400	59	9.76	10.98	12.20	13.41	14.63
$109,400 - $162,400	64	11.11	12.50	13.89	15.28	16.67
$162,400 - $215,400	68	12.50	14.06	15.63	17.19	18.75
$215,400 -	70	13.33	15.00	16.67	18.33	20.00

* After deductions and exemptions.

municipal bond interest is also exempt from state taxation
if the bondholder lives in the state where the bonds were
issued.

Who benefits most from investing in municipal bonds?
Let's put it this way: If I had a favorite great-aunt with
$500,000 from life insurance proceeds, I'd invest a large
portion of it for her in a portfolio of top-quality muncipals.
At 6½% tax-free interest income per year—a fairly standard
rate for good-quality municipal bonds—she'd get a return
on her investment of $32,500 a year, tax-free. That plus
her Social Security payments would allow her a pretty good
measure of freedom from economic worry in the autumn
of her life. Municipals wouldn't make her rich. But her
principal would be secure and the income would be
adequate for her needs. (I don't really have a favorite great-
aunt with $500,000 to invest, but if I did, I assume she'd be
the kind who'd be content with the simpler things of life.)
Another sort of investor who might be attracted to muni-

			Tax Free Yield				
6.50%	7.00%	7.50%	8.00%	8.50%	9.00%	9.50%	10.00%
				Equivalent Taxable Yield			
8.55%	9.21%	9.87%	10.53%	11.18%	11.84%	12.50%	13.16%
9.03	9.72	10.42	11.11	11.81	12.50	13.19	13.89
9.56	10.29	11.03	11.76	12.50	13.24	13.97	14.71
10.32	11.11	11.90	12.70	13.49	14.29	15.08	15.87
11.40	12.28	13.16	14.04	14.91	15.79	16.67	17.54
12.75	13.73	14.71	15.69	16.67	17.65	18.63	19.61
14.13	15.22	16.30	17.36	18.48	19.57	20.65	21.74
15.85	17.07	18.29	19.51	20.73	21.95	23.17	24.39
18.06	19.44	20.83	22.22	23.61	25.00	26.39	27.78
20.31	21.88	23.44	25.00	26.56	28.13	29.69	31.25
21.67	23.33	25.00	26.67	28.33	30.00	31.67	33.33

cipals is the high-tax-bracketed professional or business-man/woman. The tax-exempt high-yield income offered by these bonds motivates many people of slightly to substantially above average means to invest part of their earnings in municipals.

It's not a bad strategy. Compare the tax-exempt bond yield with taxable-interest income investment alternatives and you'll see what I mean.

What with the recent close calls in Cleveland and New York City (both tottered disastrously on the brink of defaulting on their municipal bond obligations), many investors naturally wonder whether municipals represent a truly safe, stable investment.

Most in the financial community continue to believe in the relative safety of municipals. Among securities they're rated second in stability and safety only to obligations (bonds) issued by the federal government. The strongest appeal of municipals, aside from their tax-exempt status, has been protection against loss of principal. During the Depression, when municipal bonds were put to their strongest test, only 0.5% of all bonds issued suffered any loss of principal, and less than 2% defaulted, that is, failed to pay interest or principal on time. The vast majority of the tiny minority of bondholders who sustained losses were eventually repaid all interest and principal due them.

Obviously all municipal bond issues are not equally safe and I would not suggest investing in municipals until you:

1. Review your financial situation with a broker, and

2. Should municipals appear to be a good investment choice for you, check up on the bonds you are interested in, in Moody's Investor Service or Standard and Poor's. Both are independent rating agencies that assess every aspect of risk associated with the bond issues available.

While you're browsing through Moody's or Standard and Poor's, you'll notice that municipals are subdivided into four basic categories: (1) general obligations (GOs), which are backed by the full taxing power of the issuer, (2) limited tax bonds, secured by a pledge of specific tax proceeds, (3) revenue bonds, secured by income from a specific project, such as toll roads or water or utility systems, and (4) hybrid "double-barreled" bonds, payable from more than one source of funds.

How to Buy Bonds That Are Exempt from Federal, State, and City Taxes: If you want to invest in bonds that offer interest income that virtually *no* taxing agency can touch, consider municipals issued in Puerto Rico, the Virgin Islands, and Guam.

Interest on bonds issued in Washington, D.C., is exempt from federal income tax; in many states it is also exempt from state taxation.

If you buy a bond issued by your own state or city, chances are that the interest income is exempt from federal, state, and local taxation, but there are exceptions. Illinois, for example, taxes interest on its own bonds.

If you are interested only in bonds that are exempt from federal, state, and city taxes, check with your broker *before* you buy.

The Municipal "Bond-Swap" Strategy for Greater Tax Advantages: If you want to establish a capital loss to offset high taxes in other areas, you might consider a municipal bond swap, where you sell some of the bonds you own and use the proceeds to buy other municipals of comparable value to establish a loss or to update a tax-exempt portfolio. To engineer a capital loss you sell your bonds at a lower rate than you paid for them and "swap" them (really, you buy them with the money you receive for your old bonds) for comparable bonds that entitle you to the same amount of principal at maturity as the bonds you sold. No tangible loss of capital is involved; but there will appear on your books a capital loss for tax purposes.

Here comes the interesting part: The loss you incur by bond swapping is then applied to offset capital gains. If your capital losses exceed your capital gains for the year, you can deduct any excess losses, up to a maximum of $3,000 for the year, from ordinary earned income.

Important: When considering this strategy keep in mind that to offset each dollar of ordinary income, you need $2 in long-term capital losses. However, short-term capital losses are deductible dollar for dollar against ordinary income.

Another potential benefit of municipal bond swapping is that you may be able to pick up bonds with a higher yield than the ones you previously held. This will increase your tax-free income.

If the bond-swapping tax strategy appeals to you, don't wait till the end of the year to get going. Capital losses can be established at any time during the year, and the more time you give yourself or your broker to shop around in the bond markets, the better your chances to obtain good bonds that suit your purposes.

Why Borrowing for Munis Is a No-No: So you want

53

bonds but you don't have the ready cash. Then you should sell some stock or other asset to get the money.

Reason: You can't borrow to buy municipal bonds. If you do, IRS will surely disallow any deductions you claim for interest on the loan. In fact, the government has gone so far as to rule that borrowed money doesn't actually have to be used to buy tax-exempt municipals in order to disallow a claim for interest deductions. There need be only a "sufficiently direct relationship" between the municipal bond and the borrowing.

Claiming a deduction for interest on money borrowed to purchase tax-exempt municipal bonds is one version of what is called double dipping. Don't do it.

How To Buy a Tax-Free Bond Even Though You Thought You Couldn't Afford To: Tax-free municipals can be bought in denominations as small as $1,000 if purchased individually, or less if you invest in a mutual fund of municipal bonds. A fund may be the perfect solution if you have no expertise in bonds and no desire to get any, and you don't have a lot of money. The fund pools money of small (and large) investors and purchases a diversified portfolio of tax-exempt municipal bonds. The bond interest that the fund receives is passed on, federal income tax–free, to you. In some states, such as New York, there are bond funds that buy bonds only from within the state, making them triply exempt from state, city, or federal taxes! These funds also allow the "little guy" to participate!

A Few Words About the Drawbacks of Municipal Bonds for the Small Investor: First, they're expensive. Municipal bonds generally sell in denominations of at least $1,000.

Second, municipal bonds are not as liquid as other bonds and many other types of assets. For this reason, it's not a good idea to have a large portion of your money tied up in municipals. If you need money fast and need to unload the bonds quickly, you may have to sell at a substantial loss.

And third, municipal bond yields tend to be lower than

those of high-rated corporate bonds. If you are in a high tax bracket, the tax-exempt interest factor of municipals may count for more than the higher taxable rates of the corporate bonds. But if you are in a middle tax bracket, the tax saving on the municipals may not be worth getting.

As a general rule, the higher your tax bracket, the more you need tax relief; the lower your bracket, the more important your opportunities for growth and a high return on your investment.

How to Convert a Municipal Bond Yield into Its Taxable Equivalent: The following formula will help you decide whether it makes more sense to invest in a tax-free municipal bond or a higher-yield corporate bond.

$$\text{Equivalent taxable yield} = \frac{\text{coupon yield of municipal bond}}{100\% - \text{tax bracket}}$$

Here's how Donald, a client of mine, used the formula to decide between investing in a 10% corporate bond and a 7% municipal bond. Donald is in the 40% bracket.

$$\text{Equivalent taxable yield} = \frac{7\%}{100\% - 40\%} = \frac{7}{60} = 11.667\%$$

According to the formula, the corporate bond would have to yield 11.667% to equal the return of the 7% tax-free municipal. My client chose the municipal bond.

If you're making an average income, say if you're single and earning $10,000 in the 24% tax bracket, your return on a 6% tax-exempt bond is only worth as much as a 7.9% taxable bond:

$$\text{Equivalent taxable yield} = \frac{6\%}{100\% - 24\%} = \frac{6}{76} = 7.9\%$$

You would be better off buying a high-rated 10% corporate bond.

Treasury Bonds—Sure, Safe Exemptions from State and Local Taxes: U.S. Treasury bonds are the safest securities available, backed as they are by the creditworthiness of the U.S. government. If the federal government runs out of money with which to pay its obligations, it can always raise taxes. Most cities can raise taxes, but the feds have an option not open to any municipality: they can print more money.

As a rule of thumb, the higher the risk to the investor, the greater potential return on the investment. Because treasury bonds are the closest thing there is to a no-risk investment, they tend to yield a lower rate of interest than that of other bonds and securities. (Treasury bond yields have been more attractive lately.)

It may come as a surprise to learn that the yield on treasury bonds issued by the federal government is not exempt from federal income taxes! But that's the way things are.

If the return is so low and is not even exempt from federal income taxes, why bother with treasury bonds at all? Well, for one thing the exemption from state and local taxes does not go unappreciated in places like New York City, where city taxes eat up a sizable chunk of one's yearly income.

If you hold treasury bonds longer than one year they are taxed at favorable long-term capital gains rates.

The value of one group of treasury bonds, known as flower bonds (for more about them see Chapter 13), immediately jumps to par (face value) upon death of the investor and can be very useful in paying off estate taxes.

Savings Bonds—The Bargain Basement Tax Shelter at $25. Do people still buy savings bonds? Sure they do. And they buy them for the same reasons that other people invest in municipal bonds that cost over 50 times as much: for interest income and for tax shelter benefits.

Savings bonds, if held for eleven years, offer 8% compounded at the end of the eleven-year maturity period. While this ain't nothing to write home about (practically everything else held for long term yields more, including savings account certificates, investments in money market funds, corporate bonds, you name it), it's still *something*. And it would be a mistake to discount entirely the tax shelter aspects of savings bonds. The interest is exempt from state and city taxation. Exemption from local taxes may not be of any great benefit to those in a low tax bracket or in areas where local taxes are low, but it offers substantial tax relief to high-bracketed investors who reside where local taxes approach astronomical proportions, as they do in New York City. (It is paradoxical that the $25 bargain basement tax shelter may be more useful to the wealthy than to the lower middle class who, presumably, make up the bulk of the buyers.)

The purchaser of a savings bond buys a $50 face amount bond for $25. If held to maturity, the face amount is guaranteed to be paid at the maturity date.

Series EE savings bonds, to give them their formal name, offer another tax benefit: Interest accumulation is exempt from federal taxation until the bonds reach maturity or until you cash them in, whichever comes first. At that point federal taxes are due on the amount of accumulated interest, which will be taxed according to your then-current tax bracket. This can make Series EE bonds a wise investment as you approach retirement age: by the time the bonds mature, you will probably be in a lower tax bracket than you were when you bought them. You can also elect to report the interest year by year.

The Series HH government savings bonds come in denominations of $500, $1,000, $5,000, and $10,000. When you buy a Series HH bond you immediately pay the face amount and then receive an interest check starting six months after the issue date of 7½% of face value compounded semiannually until the bond reaches maturity in ten years.

One tax advantage of Series HH is that Series E (these were similar to the EE but cost $18.75 and had a somewhat lower yield and shorter maturity) and Series EE bonds can be turned into HH's without paying tax on the E's or the

EE's. The tax deferment on the E's and the EE's continues. You only pay federal income tax on the HH bond interest as it is currently paid, and the tax on the increase in value on your E and EE bonds won't be payable until you cash your HH bond in.

This bond-switch strategy has a broader application than you might suspect. Picture a hypothetical Mrs. Jones whose husband dies, leaving her $40,000 in Series E bonds. Two years later the bonds reach maturity. If Mrs. Jones cashes in her Series E bonds then the income she receives will place her in a bracket that makes her ineligible for welfare payments. However, a tax-free exchange from Series E to Series HH saves the day and the welfare payments keep coming in. Regardless of your personal feelings about the dole, it must be admitted that bond switching is a happy solution for Mrs. Jones and others like her. You see, there *are* tax shelters for the poor!

How to Shelter Income and Your Kids with Series EE Bonds: Savings bonds make great gifts for kids, at least those who don't earn any money, since the child's zero tax bracket effectively cancels out any federal taxes (besides state and local) that might otherwise be due. For this strategy to work the bonds must be issued in the child's name. Before your children start to earn a living, it might make sense to cash in the bonds so as to pay little or no income tax. Because your child's zero tax bracket will offset federal taxes, Series EE bonds provide good vehicles to save for your children's college education.

A final note about Series EE bonds and kids: Although the face value of a Series EE bond is $50, you pay only $25 per bond (the difference of course between what you pay and what you get at maturity is interest income). Your children may be temporarily fooled into thinking you've sacrificed more for them than you really have. (If they still believe that when they reach college age, don't send them to college!)

How to Keep Savings Bond Gifts Out of Your Estate: If

your name appears on a bond as co-owner and you die, the bond may be included in your estate. To make sure that doesn't happen, see to it that the bonds are issued in only one name: that of the donee.

New Law: All Savers Certificates: The new tax law provides for up to a $1,000 ($2,000 for a joint return) exclusion of interest on so-called "All Savers Certificates" offered by banks and thrift institutions from October 1, 1981 to December 31, 1982. The certificates have a one-year maturity and yield up to 70% of the Treasury bill rate.

This is a once-in-a-lifetime exclusion, so if under this provision you claim a $600 interest exemption on your '82 return, you can only claim up to $400 on your '83 tax return.

These certificates should be purchased by those in the over-30% tax bracket, as a greater return can be earned through other sources. Assuming you invest $10,000 in a Treasury bill yielding 15%, you will earn $1,500 before taxes. If you are in the 50% tax bracket, you keep $750, in the 30% bracket you keep $1,050, and in the 20% bracket you keep $1,200. However, if you purchase $10,000 in the all savers certificates, on which you receive 70% of the Treasury-bill rate (70% of 15% in this example), or 10.5% times $10,000, you receive $1,050 tax exempt. Thus, these certificates make sense for over-30% tax bracket individuals.

You should also check whether your state exempts these certificates from state taxes. Also make sure you will not need the funds before the year is up, as there is a penalty for the loss of the tax exemption for any certificate redeemed early. You can likewise lose the exemption if you borrow money to buy these certificates. Pledging a certificate as collateral is also considered to be a redemption.

This exclusion is available to individuals, and within certain limits to an estate, where the estate receives a qualified certificate as a result of the decedent's death. A partnership is not eligible for the exclusion, although individual partners may exclude their distributive share of interest paid on these certificates held by the partnership, up to each partner's individual limit on the exclusion.

Trusts, corporations, real estate investment trusts, Subchapter S corporations, and regulated investment companies do not qualify for this exemption.

His name was George F. Babbitt. He was forty-six years old now in
April 1920, and he made nothing in particular, neither butter nor
shoes nor poetry, but he was nimble in the calling of selling
houses for more than people could afford to pay.

—Sinclair Lewis

6

Gimme Shelter;
or, How to Get Maximum
Tax Benefits from Your Home

So you own your own home. Or you're thinking of buying
one. Not a bad idea. With a home of your own you've got
a roof over your head and a pretty good tax shelter for your
money, too.

Of course you know that interest payments on your
mortgage as well as real estate taxes are deductible. Likewise,
if you've bought into a cooperative apartment, the percentage of the monthly maintenance fee applied to cover interest and taxes is deductible.

The tax shelter potential of your home doesn't end with
mortgage interest and real estate tax deductions. They're
important; but there are many, many more tax benefits
available to homeowners.

How to Cut Your Fuel Bill and Save on Taxes Too

Thanks to the new Energy Law you can now get tax credits
for making energy-conserving improvements on your home
—improvements you'd probably want to make anyway,

what with the escalating cost of fuel. To qualify for the credits, improvements must have been made on or after April 20, 1977.

The law covers two areas: home improvements, such as the installation of storm windows and insulation; and investments in alternative private energy sources, such as solar heating and wind-powered generators.

Home Improvements: You can subtract 15% of the first $2,000 spent—a maximum of $300—from your tax bill for energy-saving improvements to your home: the installations mentioned as well as thermostats and weather stripping. To those of you whose thoughts immediately and naturally leapt to the idea of redecorating for tax credits, I'm sorry to say that drapery, carpets, and wood paneling do not qualify, even if they have an insulating effect.

The credit is available only for improvements on your principal residence, which must have been built or substantially completed on or before April 20, 1977. Vacation homes and newer homes don't qualify. It may be claimed by owners of condominiums, cooperative apartments—and renters, too!

Solar-Heating Devices and Wind Installations: The tax credits here are even more generous. You can get a credit of 30% on the first $2,000 that you spend, and 20% on the next $8,000—up to a maximum credit of $2,200—for installing equipment that transforms sunlight or wind into energy for your home. (Don Quixote, where are you now?)

Solar and wind equipment qualify when installed in *new* as well as in existing residences; otherwise, the rules are similar to those for home improvements.

Repair, Don't Improve

One of the oddities of the tax laws is that you can deduct certain expenses for repairing your income-producing property, but not for improving it!

On second thought, maybe IRS knows its business after all. Repairs, such as repainting the exterior of your property, keep your property in good operating condition. Improvements—putting in a new floor, for example—extend the useful life of your property and add to its value, which means they must be capitalized, their cost being added to the "basis" of your house.

Some distinctions between a repair job and an improvement:

1. A *repair* does not add to the value of the property.
2. A *repair* does not prolong the life of the property.
3. A *repair* keeps the property in good condition.
4. An *improvement* increases the value of the property.
5. An *improvement* prolongs the "useful life" of the property.
6. An *improvement* makes the property adaptable to new and different uses.

Cost is not a guideline. Most people associate lower costs with repairs and higher costs with improvements, but they are wrong. Even if the final repair bill is high, that doesn't change it to an improvement. You can still get a deduction.

If repairs and improvements are being done simultaneously—for example, if a major plumbing repair is being made in the kitchen while the kitchen itself is being enlarged (definitely an improvement), be sure to keep separate records specifying the work done and the costs for the two projects. Otherwise you run the risk of having to capitalize the combined costs.

Another expense for the home owner who buys his home on a mortgage is "points," the one-time charge paid to the mortgage lender for giving the mortgage, in addition to the regular interest payments.

Payment for points is deductible to the buyer provided that:

1. The charge is for the use of the money and is paid in connection with the purchase or improvement of a principal residence.

2. Charging points is the established lending practice in the area and the buyer has not paid more than the customary number of points charged there.

Caution: Be sure that the points are paid by you rather than letting the lender withhold the money for points. The tax court has held that if the lender withholds the money for points the deduction must be made over the period of the loan instead of immediately.

How to Get Deductions for
Business Entertaining in Your Home

Do you ever take clients (old, new, or prospective), employees, contractors, agents, or other business connections to lunch or dinner? If so, you know that the cost of entertaining for business purposes can be deducted from your taxable income—assuming that your company doesn't reimburse you for the expense.

Well, the same rules that allow you to take deductions for entertaining people you do business with at restaurants and clubs apply equally to entertaining in your home.

The Tax Code says that for entertaining to be legit, the following requirements must be met:

1. The get-together must have a business purpose. (Presumably you're allowed some time out for social chitchat and other pleasantries.)

2. Food and/or drinks must be served in an atmosphere conducive to business discussion (that is, reasonable peace and quiet; the kids tucked away for the night or discreetly off in their own rooms; Beethoven, possibly, on the stereo, but no disco).

3. There must be no distracting influences. This means, more or less, that the evening should include no nonbusiness guests. The couple next door, no matter how sparkling,

would constitute a distracting influence if they aren't somehow involved in the business being discussed or conducted.

Deductions taken for the cost of entertaining business connections at home, though entirely proper if the above rules are adhered to, may be closely scrutinized by an IRS agent should you have the misfortune to be audited. So make sure to have receipts for any expenditures over $25 and to keep a detailed record of your expenses, recording them in a diary at or soon after the time the expenses are incurred.

If more than 50% of your business activity takes place in your home, you are also allowed to deduct business-related expenses for household upkeep. Otherwise you can only deduct out-of-pocket costs of food and drink for you and your business guests.

Office at Home as a Tax Deduction

If you have a sideline business that you run from your home, such as moonlighting as a consultant or managing rental properties or writing magazine articles, you're eligible to deduct office-at-home expenses.

To qualify, your office at home must be (1) used exclusively for business purposes (a desk plus file cabinet in the front hall or tucked away in a corner of the den or family room doesn't count); (2) used on a regular basis; (3) the principal place in which your sideline business activities are conducted, or the place where you meet clients during the normal course of your business.

"Home" for this purpose needn't be your actual dwelling. Nearby structures, such as a barn used as an artist's studio, also qualify.

You may deduct expenses for an office at home only as

they relate to the part of your home that is used in the business.

For example, June, a free-lance writer I know, lives in a four-room apartment in Manhattan. She uses one room as an office and is therefore entitled to deduct 25% of her rent as a business expense. She also deducts 25% of her electric bill. If she owned the apartment and paid local taxes, she could deduct 25% of them too.

Other deductible home office expenses include cost of stationery, postage, telephone, office furniture and equipment, and business-related repairs to the office area.

All office-at-home expenses should be backed up with records, canceled checks, receipts, and diary entries.

If you're not self-employed or engaged in a sideline business, but simply bring extra work home from the office on a now-and-then basis, forget about using the office-at-home deduction—new tax laws have mostly disallowed it. If you try for this deduction you'll have to convince IRS that you bring the work home for the convenience of your employer and not yourself. Good luck!

Selling Your Home

Whether it's a house, condominium, co-op apartment, mobile home, or vacation home, your home can provide you with favorable tax treatment unavailable to you otherwise. And if you know the rules, it can get you a few tax-free extras.

Your deductions for mortgage interest and local taxes are not part of the tax-sheltering techniques we're going to consider now. It's only when you sell your home that true tax-sheltering tactics come into play.

Let's begin with some basics. When you sell your house you'll have to pay taxes on any profit you make; the bigger the profit, the more taxes. Now you don't want to lower the selling price of your house just to avoid paying taxes on the profit—that just goes against human nature. Yet you want to make sure that you don't pay any more in taxes than you legally must, right?

To keep your taxes to a minimum, you must make a careful computation of the cost, or in tax terms the "basis," of your house. Often the basis of a house is considerably greater than the amount you paid for it.

1. Include your cash down payment plus your mortgage.

2. Include expenses connected with the purchase of your house that were not immediately deductible: legal fees, title search, title insurance, broker's commissions, survey expenses, appraisal costs, and so on. It is important to keep a careful record of these expenses. Added to your down payment and mortgage, they will increase your basis so that the taxable profit will be less when the time comes to sell.

3. Include the cost of improvements of a permanent nature. A few pages back we discussed the difference between repairs and improvements. The cost of repairs cannot be added to your basis; but the cost of an improvement—which adds value to the house and/or prolongs its life—counts as a capital expenditure and can increase your basis, perhaps by several thousand dollars. Here's a list of some of the more common improvements:

> Basement waterproofing
> Installation of central air conditioning
> Electric wiring (new or replacement)
> Laying a new floor
> Installing a new heating system (or converting from oil to gas)
> Landscaping
> Enlarging the house by adding new rooms or a new wing
> Adding or tearing down walls or partitions to get more efficient use of existing space

Adding a porch, sun deck, or swimming pool
Replacing the old plumbing system and/or sump
    pump
Installing a new roof or reshingling the old one
Adding storm windows
Termite-proofing
Plastering and/or reinforcing existing walls

Figuring the Amount of Gain on the Sale of Your House:
Calculate your adjusted basis, which consists of the original
cost plus purchase expenses plus the cost of improvements.
Subtract casualty losses or depreciation if applicable.

Now calculate the selling price by subtracting from it any
expenses you pay in connection with the sale. Here are some
of the more common expenses incurred by the seller. (It's
possible that few or none of them will apply to you; you
should be aware of them anyway.)

Abstract of title
Advertising
Appraisal fee
Broker's commission
Contract of sale drafting fee
Deed-drafting fee
Deed-recording fee (if paid by seller, not by buyer)
Escrow fee
Legal fee
Points paid
State transfer tax
Surveying
Title certificate
Title insurance
Title opinion
Title registration change

If you sell your house and use the proceeds to pay off
an existing mortgage you may incur a prepayment penalty,

for paying the mortgage before it is due. You can add the prepayment penalty, as interest, to the cost of selling your house.

Money you spend to make an old home more attractive to prospective buyers can be added to the cost of selling, if the following conditions are met: (1) The work must be done within 90 days before the contract of sale, and (2) the work must be paid for within 30 days after the sale.

Now subtract your adjusted basis, plus all expenses connected with the sale, from the selling price.

Here's a real-life illustration: A client of mine, Janet, bought a house in 1972 for $30,000, including legal fees and broker's commission, which she had to pay when she took title. In 1977, to the tune of $5,000, she added a den. Her total adjusted basis was $35,000.

In 1980 she sold her house for $60,000. Selling it cost her $5,000 in broker's commissions, legal fees, and transfer taxes, leaving $55,000 as the amount realized from the sale.

Her capital gain on the sale was $20,000: $55,000, her adjusted selling price, less $35,000, her adjusted basis.

Janet loves to throw out in casual conversation that she sold her house for twice what she paid for it, which of course implies 100% profit. However, she and her accountant uncle were careful to adjust the basis of her house upward as much as possible and to count in every penny spent in connection with selling the house, so that her capital gain, the amount on which she would have to pay taxes, was kept to a minimum.

How to Negotiate a No-Tax Sale of Your Home: If after selling your house you buy another one that costs at least as much as what you received from the sale of the first, you pay no tax on the transaction.

Tom, an old college classmate of mine, did it this way. In 1975, he bought a house in a rundown inner-city neighborhood that was on its way up again—fast. He paid $50,-000 for the house, quickly spent $10,000 on improvements, and sold it in 1979 for $100,000. The sale was accompanied by $5,000 worth of selling expenses. His capital gain was $35,000.

Selling price		$100,000
Less selling expenses		− 5,000
		$ 95,000
Less cost of old house	−$50,000	
Less cost of improvements	−$10,000	
	−$60,000	
		−$ 60,000
Capital Gain		$ 35,000

If Tom had not immediately gone out and purchased another house (which he did), he would have been taxed on a capital gain of $35,000. Tom knew that if he was not to pay any capital gains tax, his new house would have to cost as much as he received for the old one. Tom knew that the expenses of fixing his old house to make it more attractive are considered when he determines how much of his gain is tax-free. Tom knew that the fixing up had to be paid for within 30 days after the sale and must be done within 90 days before the contract of the sale. To figure that amount, he subtracted his selling expenses ($5,000) plus the amount he spent on fixing up the old house ($10,000) from the selling price:

Selling price		$100,000
Less selling expenses	−$ 5,000	
Less cost of improvements	−$10,000	
	−$15,000	−$ 15,000
Adjusted Sales Price		$ 85,000

As a result of these calculations, Tom, who's pretty good at watching out for number one and will probably be "trading up" for the rest of his life, wouldn't even look at houses costing less than $85,000. In fact, he ended up buying one for $115,000.

The basis on his new house, incidentally, is not $115,000, but $115,000 less his $35,000 untaxed gain on the old house, or $80,000.

What would have happened if Tom had fallen in love with a house costing less than $85,000? Let's pretend that Tom bought a new house costing $79,000. In that case, he would have to pay capital gains taxes on $6,000—the difference between the adjusted sale price of the old house ($85,000) and the cost of the new one ($79,000).

He would also have to adjust the basis of this $79,000 home by $29,000 (the gain of $35,000 on his old home minus the $6,000 on which he would now have to pay capital gains taxes). Thus the basis on his new home would be $50,000.

The moral: When you sell an old house, plan to buy a new one costing at least as much as you got for the old one. Otherwise you will be taxed at capital gains rates on your profit.

In theory, you can buy house after house for the rest of your life and never pay a penny of capital gains tax on your profits.

This strategy comes with a couple of strings attached. For one, to obtain the tax break the house you sell must have been your principal residence. Same goes for the house you buy; your intention must be to live there. This disallows the capital gains tax break on selling and buying vacation homes.

However, there's nothing in the tax code to prevent you from selling a house and replacing it with a condominium (or vice versa), or from going to co-op apartment to boathouse to geodesic dome for that matter. So long as both your old and your new dwelling meet the principal-place-of-residence definition, and your new one costs as much as you received for the old one, you may be eligible for the tax break.

I say "may be eligible" because other stipulations have to do with timing. You must buy your new house and take up residence there within a 36-month period extending from 18 months before to 18 months after the sale of the old house.

An exception to the rule is made for a member of the armed forces who is on active duty after his or her house was sold, in which case he or she is allowed additional time to buy and move into a new house.

The Revenue Act of 1978 also allows you an exception if your job forces you to relocate. If this is the case, you are entitled to multiple tax-free "rollovers" (changes in residence) exempt from the regular replacement period rules, so long as you conform to the regulations governing deductions for moving connected with job relocation. (These regulations will be discussed later in this chapter.)

If you buy a new house and then sell or dispose of it *before* you sell your own residence, the new house will not qualify as replacement property. If the new, never-been-lived-in-by-you house is sold at a profit, you'll have to pay a capital gains tax.

Timing is also a factor if you're building a new house rather than buying an existing one. To get the capital gains tax break construction on the new house must begin no sooner than 18 months before or later than 18 months after you sell your old house, and you must be living in the new house within 24 months of the sale. In calculating whether you'll have to pay capital gains taxes on profit from the sale of your old house, you may include only the cost of construction that has been completed by the end of 18 months after the sale.

A helpful hedging device to make sure that building is completed within the time limit is to add a penalty clause to your builder contract.

Remember: To qualify for the capital gains tax break under the postsale two-year rule, you must have entered into the contract to purchase the new home before construction will start. If you contract to purchase a house that is already under construction, it must have been completed and you must be in residence by the end of 18 months after the sale of your old house; otherwise, no capital gains tax break.

How to Figure Capital Gains and Losses if You Live Where You Work: If your principal residence and your principal business occupy roughly the same space—say, if you live in a house on your farm or in an apartment over your store—your capital gains or losses (and the taxes you may or may not have to pay on the sale of your residence) must be treated separately from those connected with your business, as though your dwelling and your business property were two distinct places.

How to Use the Installment Plan to Pay Off Capital Gains on Your House: If part or all of the gain realized from the sale of your house is subject to taxes, there's another strategy to lighten your tax load: Pay on the installment plan.

With this method you can avoid paying all of your capital gains taxes at once and dole them out to the government in partial payments over a specified time.

Paying on the installment plan is not something you can elect to do on the spur of the moment after the sale of your house. The sale of the house must be set up in a certain way.

The key is to arrange with the buyer to receive no more than 30% of the selling price of your house in the year of the sale. You pay capital gains taxes only on the percentage of profit you receive during the year, rather than paying the bill in a lump sum.

Becky, a divorced mother of two, used this strategy. She bought a house for $20,000 and sold it five years later for $100,000. (Where real estate is concerned, Becky obviously is a woman of keen judgment.)

The long-term capital gain on the sale of the house was $80,000. Taking all that money in a lump sum, though tempting, would saddle Becky with the obligation to pay capital gains taxes on her profit in an equally lump sum, which raised a lump in Becky's throat.

So Becky arranged to take $30,000 (30% of the purchase price) as a down payment in the year she sold her house, and to take back a purchase mortgage for the remaining $70,000, payable to her at 9% interest over seven years.

That way she not only deferred tax payments on her gain, but since the buyer is paying her interest on the unpaid balance, she is actually making money on sums that otherwise would have gone to Uncle Sam. Nice work if you can get it.

If the idea of using the installment plan method to defer payment of capital gains taxes on profits made from the sale of a house appeals to you, I strongly urge you to consult with a lawyer or accountant in drawing up the contract.

The most important point is: If you take more than 30% of the selling price in the first year, the entire capital gains tax falls due that year. This is written into the Tax Code and applies even though you may not receive full payment on the house for several years.

There are pitfalls to watch out for when negotiating this kind of installment mortgage. For example, if the buyer had paid Becky $20,000 in December 1980, at the signing of the contract, and another $20,000 in January 1981, during the title close, Becky would have had to pay the entire capital gains tax bill, due in 1981. Reason: IRS has proclaimed that all payments made before and during the year of the sale must not exceed 30% of the purchase price of the house if capital gains taxes are not to be due all at once. The IRS would have counted the whole $40,000 as if paid in 1981.

How to Get More Cash Now Plus Installment Mortgage Tax Treatment: There's a way to get more immediate cash from the sale of your house and do it without forfeiting the capital gains installment tax break. The method may require a certain amount of chutzpah and/or a friend or acquaintance who happens to be an officer at a bank or savings and loan association. (It's always a good idea to cultivate the people where you do your banking.)

Here's how the Warrens, who sold their house to the Sills, used this strategy:

The Sills bought the Warrens' house for $120,000. Their cash down payment was $36,000, the 30% maximum first-year payment on an installment mortgage arrangement. The Warrens, who are rather well connected, borrowed the difference—$84,000—from a bank, pledging the Sills' mortgage as collateral! They have the use of the $84,000 and also continue to collect mortgage payments, with interest, from the Sills, using the interest on the Sills' mortgage to pay off the interest on their own loan from the bank.

The wrong way to do it would be for the Warrens to discount the Sills' note before maturity. This would create an immediate tax on all of the deferred gain because it would have the effect of the Warrens' disposing of their house, as they no longer owned the notes. Using the correct method, the Warrens retain ownership of the notes.

A Once-in-a-Lifetime Tax Break:
Turning 55 Years Old

Hard to believe, but true: The government gives you a fat tax break just for turning 55.

Anyone 55 years of age or older who has used his or her house as a principal residence for at least three of the preceding five years, and who elects the exclusion, is eligible for tax-free profits of up to $100,000 on the sale of the house.

Not only that, IRS imposes no stipulation that a replacement house be purchased.

If profits from the sale amount to more than $100,000, tax-deferring strategies can be used to postpone payment of capital gains taxes on the excess amount.

Sandy and Ed, for example, both in their early sixties, sold their home for a $120,000 gain. They opted for the $100,000 tax exclusion and *immediately bought another house*, deferring the capital gains taxes on the remaining $20,000. In other words, they successfully avoided paying one cent of tax on a gain of $120,000.

The $100,000 exclusion can be used only once. If the gain from the sale of your house is less than $100,000, you do not get credit for the balance and cannot use any part of it in the future.

Nevertheless, this is a tax break that makes growing older look better and better.

Strategies for Vacation Home Owners; or,
How to Take a Holiday from Taxes

Most of the tax breaks we've considered apply only to principal residences; vacation homes have been excluded. If you've the good fortune to own a vacation home, you may be eligible for certain other tax benefits, especially if you're willing to restrict your *own* use of the house and rent it out to others for part or most of each year.

Admittedly this is a trade-off, and you have to decide which is more important to you: unlimited access to (and enjoyment of) your vacation home, or tax benefits that allow you to keep most or all of your income from renting the house, plus potential tax shelter for some of your other income. Whichever way you lean, it's good to know your options.

Let's see what kind of deductions are available to you as owner of a vacation home. You can take the same mortgage interest and local tax deductions as any other homeowner. If you rent out your vacation home, you can also claim deductions for maintenance and depreciation connected with the "business" (or income-producing) use of the house. The percentage of maintenance costs and depreciation you can deduct is related to the amount of time your vacation house is occupied—or available for occupancy—by tenants.

For example, you can take maximum maintenance and depreciation deductions if you don't use the vacation home (1) for more than 14 days in a year, or (2) 10% of the number of days in the year that you rent the property, whichever is greater. If you rent your vacation home out for 250 days, you can use it not more than 25 days, as (2) is greater. If you rent for less than 141 days, you can use it up to 14 days.

The deductions you take for maintenance and depreciation can be subtracted from your gross income for the year. The obvious benefit to you is that, as a result, you pay taxes on less income!

If you decide to rent your vacation home for two weeks or less of each year, IRS says you don't have to report rental income on your tax return. It's found money and you can pocket it all. As a trade-off for this tax-free income, you won't be able to claim any rent-related deductions. However, you still can deduct all your interest and property taxes.

Not a bad vacation home that takes a holiday from taxes.

How to Get Good Tax Mileage Out of Moving

If you move for work-related reasons, chances are you can claim deductions for moving expenses, most of which apply whether your move is dictated (maybe "suggested" is a better way of putting it) by your employer, or whether you are self-employed and decide on your own to move to an area offering better business opportunities.

To qualify for moving-expense deductions you must meet the following criteria:

1. Your new office or place of business must be at least 35 miles farther away from your old home than the old job was from the old home.

2. You must be employed full-time at the new location for at least 39 weeks during the 12 months following your move.

If you and your wife or husband file a joint return, this stipulation is considered to have been met if either of you was employed in the new area for 39 weeks of the 12 months following the move.

3. If you are self-employed, you must work at the new location for at least 78 weeks out of the 24-month period following your move.

If you qualify, direct moving expenses are fully deductible. You can claim the whole cost of crating and moving furniture, other household goods, and personal effects. You can claim the cost of in-transit storage of these items if the circumstances of your move require it.

Also fully deductible as a direct moving expense is the cost of getting your car to your new home. If you drive it there yourself you can either itemize your expenses or deduct a flat 9¢ per mile plus tolls and parking fees.

You can also claim travel expenses for getting yourself, your family, and even your pets to the new house. If you all pile into the car and drive there together, you can itemize driving expenses or deduct a flat fee as mentioned above. If you take a train, plane, or bus, your fares are deductible. Whichever way you go, you can claim the cost of food and lodging.

In fact, just about the only thing you can't claim is the cost of altering rugs and draperies to fit your new house. (Sorry, I forgot for a moment that IRS also says you can't claim the expense of relocating your yacht.)

Certain other moving expenses are classed as indirect by IRS. You can claim deductions of up to $3,000 in indirect moving expenses, which include (1) premove house-hunting expenses; (2) the cost of food and lodging if your new house is not ready for occupancy when you get there, or if you arrive in the new location without having found a suitable place to live; and (3) certain expenses connected with selling your old house and buying or renting a new one. Among the deductible expenses of selling an old house and renting or buying a new one are brokers' commissions, legal fees, title costs, and the cost of settling on an unexpired lease, if any.

No more than $1,500 of the $3,000 limit on indirect moving expenses can be deducted for house-hunting and temporary living expenses.

You cannot qualify for the premove house-hunting deduction unless you already have a job in the new area when you go out looking. You also must have traveled at least once from your old residence to the new area and back again.

To be eligible for the temporary living expense deduction, the expenses must be incurred within any 30 consecutive days after obtaining (or being assigned to) your new job.

We said that if you sell your house you can avoid paying capital gains taxes on the profit if your new house costs more than your old, and if you move into it within 18 months of the sale. You can take advantage of this tax break more than once in an 18-month period if your reason for moving is job-related.

If your employer reimburses you for some or all of your moving expenses, you must report the reimbursement on Form 1040, which also provides instructions for making appropriate readjustments if you were not fully reimbursed.

What If Disaster Strikes Your Home?

Every day somebody's house is destroyed by fire or flood, tornado or hurricane, or the property must be sold under threat or imminence of condemnation. Of course, you don't expect any of these things to happen to *your* house, but read the following just in case.

If calamity strikes and you receive compensation for being deprived of your residence (from an insurance company or, sometimes, from your local or state government), an "involuntary conversion" has occurred. Through no fault of your own, your property ain't what it used to be, and it has been at least partly "converted" to compensation of some kind.

If the insurance company or condemning authority replaces your home with another, no gain will be recognized. Though you might prefer to have your old house back again, you are at least relieved of having to pay taxes on the conversion.

But if the involuntary conversion results in a taxable gain—if you receive a lump sum of money or, as sometimes happens, a nonresidential property that more than compensates for your loss, you have tax consequences.

You can avoid paying taxes immediately on your gain by using your compensation to replace your old house with another one, as discussed above, within a specified time.

If your old house was totaled by fire or natural disaster, the replacement period begins at the time the property was destroyed and ends two years after the close of the taxable year in which you first realize any part of the gain.

If your house was condemned for public use or sold under threat or imminence of condemnation, the replacement period begins on the date you receive notice of threatened condemnation and ends two years after the close of the first taxable year in which you receive your gain on involuntary compensation.

If you apply to IRS for an extension of the replacement period your request will probably be granted.

What You Should Know About Casualty Loss Deductions; or, How to Make the Most of the Worst: The term "casualty," besides referring to losses from sudden disasters such as floods, storms, fires, and bolts of lightning out of the blue, includes losses that result from vandalism, sonic boom, ice damage to trees and shrubbery, and other mundane events.

You can claim deductions for casualty losses of any kind of property—personal property, including your house and its contents, and business property.

To claim casualty losses resulting from theft or damage to personal property, you must itemize deductions on your tax return rather than take the standard zero bracket deduction.

It's important to have evidence to back up your claims; otherwise there is the possibility that IRS will not accept them. A wise thing to do is to take a series of "before" pictures of your property from all sides and various angles. Do it as a matter of course soon after moving into your house. If disaster strikes, document it with "after" pictures.

Another way to justify casualty loss claims is to have an independent appraiser make out a written report listing and evaluating your property "before," including exterior details and landscaping as well as furniture, household goods, and valuables (cameras, furs, jewelry, etc.). Such an advance appraisal can save you thousands of dollars in casualty loss tax deductions and insurance compensation "after." (Incidentally, the appraisal fee is tax-deductible.)

Keep all canceled checks, receipts, and other proofs of payment for personal property. The more evidence you have to back up your claims, the less chance of their being disallowed.

81

You can claim only the cost of property that has been lost or damaged. Claims on personal injury, loss of wages, and/or the expense of renting a place to stay if your house is temporarily rendered unfit for human habitation do not qualify for casualty loss deductions.

Losses are deductible only to the extent that they exceed $100 per loss. If lightning strikes your $200 redwood picnic table, you are eligible for a maximum tax deduction of $100. If there is a storm and the cost of cleaning up afterward is $150 you can claim a $50 deduction. If your $50 ornamental door knocker is stolen, forget it. Your loss does not exceed the $100 minimum.

IRS has a heart of stone: Sentimental value counts for nothing where casualty loss is concerned. You cannot add extra dollars to your claim on the basis that the item destroyed or stolen was a keepsake or heirloom.

When trees or shrubbery are destroyed by high winds or ice, the rules are strict and somewhat subjective. You can claim deductions only if the damage results in a decrease of value of the property as a whole. If your house is approached by a winding drive bordered by stately sycamores, the loss of one or more trees makes the property less valuable. But a single old oak tree way off at the back corner of your lot? It's impossible to predict how IRS will interpret your claim. (I know what I'd do about that old oak tree: Wait till fall; photograph it in its most glorious colors and from its most attractive angle; then hope that if the oak is ever struck by lightning the IRS agent handling my claim has a weakness for trees.)

Generally you can deduct casualty losses on the return filed for the year in which the loss was sustained, even though repair work does not begin until the following year.

Regulations are liberal for residents of specified disaster areas. They can deduct losses on the return filed for the year in which the loss was sustained and are also eligible to claim a refund if the loss occurred just after they filed returns for the previous year.

In the event of a huge casualty loss in a disaster area that exceeds your total income for the year, taxes for that year will be waived. You can even arrange to have your loss carried back to recover taxes that you paid in the previous three years; or you can carry your losses forward and deduct them over the next seven years. These allowances apply to business as well as personal casualty losses.

Of course, any reimbursement of loss that you collect from an insurance company or from special disaster relief aid must be figured into your claim for a casualty loss tax deduction. If your stereo equipment, valued at $750, is insured against theft, and your insurance company issues you a check for $500, your loss is $250. Subtract from that the $100 IRS minimum (remember, tax laws specify that losses are deductible only to the extent that they exceed $100) and you have a legitimate claim for a casualty loss tax deduction of $150.

New Law: Gain on Sale of Your Home: You now have either two years before or after the sale of your principal residence to replace it by either a purchase or constructing a new house to be able to obtain a tax-free rollover (deferral) of gain from your sale. This deferral of tax is provided if your new principal residence is acquired at a cost at least equal to the sales price of your old residence. Previously the replacement period by purchase was 18 months before up to 18 months after the sale's date (two years after for newly built homes).

This change is effective for sales or exchanges on principal residences made after July 20, 1981, or to sales or exchanges before that date if the previous 18-month rollover period did not expire by July 20, 1981.

New Law: Installment Sales: Although not part of the Economic Recovery Act of 1981, a law was enacted toward the end of 1980 changing the method of reporting installment sales if made after October 19, 1980. The buyer no longer has to receive 30% of the selling price of the house in the year of the sale in order to qualify. An installment sale basis is automatic provided at least one payment of any amount is received after the close of the tax year in which the sale occurs, no matter what the percentage that the buyer receives in the year of the sale. A taxpayer electing the installment method must show the computation of the gross profit on his or her tax return for the year of the sale.

To figure the taxable income from installment sales, just multiply the gross profit ratio for the sale (which is the gross profit divided by the total selling price) times the amount of money received. For example, if you sold some land for $3,000 for which you originally paid $2,000, your profit is $1,000, and your gross profit ratio is $1000 profit/ $3,000 sales price, or ⅓. If you receive installments of $1,000 per year for 3 years, the income reported each year is ⅓ times $1,000, or $333 per year. The installment method of reporting gain does not change the status of the gain as capital gain or ordinary income. This method may be used for both non-real estate dealers and dealers alike.

New Law: Land Sale Between Relatives: If property is sold under an installment method after June 30, 1981, and no interest arrangement is specified, or if the interest provided is less than a prescribed rate, interest will be imputed into the agreement at a rate determined by the Treasury. For contracts that don't provide for at least a 9% interest rate, the current imputed rate is 10%.

On installment sales of land made between members of the same family, the maximum rate under the new law, also effective after June 30, 1981, is a maximum of 7%. This lower rate applies to sales or exchange prices that do not exceed $500,000 (when added onto the aggregate sales price for prior qualified sales during the calendar year). Above $500,000 in sales or exchanges the higher rate would go into effect.

New Law: Once-in-a-Lifetime Tax Break at 55 Years or Older: Now you can exclude up to $125,000 ($62,500 if married filing separately) of gain from the sale of your principal residence if you are 55 years or older. This goes into effect after July 20, 1981.

There is just one thing I can promise you about the outer space program: your tax dollar will go further.

—WERNHER VON BRAUN

7

Tax Sheltering with Collectibles

Chinese ceramics, stamps, rare books, coins, and paintings by the old masters (and some newer masters, too) have outperformed the stock and bond market over the past several years, sometimes to an extent that takes one's breath away. (The chart shows what I mean.)

	Compounded Annual Rates of Return		
	1968–79	1969–79	1978–79
Gold	19.4%	16.3%	55.0%
Chinese Ceramics	19.1	18.0	31.1
Stamps	18.9	15.4	60.9
Rare Books	15.7	16.5	7.8
Silver	13.4	9.1	62.5
Coins	12.7	13.0	10.0
Old Masters' Paintings	12.5	11.6	22.1
Diamonds	11.8	12.6	4.0
Oil	11.3	11.8	6.2
Farmland	10.9	10.5	14.2
Housing	9.6	9.2	13.7
Bonds*	5.8	6.1	3.3
Stocks**	3.1	2.9	5.3
Consumer Prices	6.5	6.1	10.5

* Salomon Brothers Index
** Standard and Poor's Composite
Rates of return are for the periods ended June 1

It was all so predictable—the new rage for collectibles. With escalating inflation investors raced hither and thither for tangible assets—objects of value they could actually hold in their hands—as a means of anchoring their (the investors') worth against the aimless sinking of the dollar. Many have blessed the day when they made their first investment in art, books, stamps, or coins (gold and silver objects definitely fall into the "collectible" category, but precious metals are part of another story, one that goes beyond this volume). But the big question about collectibles has yet to be answered: Will they continue to appreciate in value, or are they subject to the law of gravity that says what goes up must come down? Only time will tell.

The Risk Factors: Fine art, including painting, sculpture, and so on, will give you an overview of the risks involved. Like many other collectibles, fine art is not "liquid." If you need to sell quickly, chances are you will suffer a loss—that is, unless you already know of a buyer who is dying to get his or her hands on that minor Monet of yours.

None of the conventional wisdom seems to apply to art. Supposedly you should stay away from fads. At least that is the advice most often given by the "experts." Yet some of the pop art of the sixties, which at the time seemed so faddish, is fetching good prices today.

Another piece of advice often given is: "Buy first-rate artists." Makes sense. But if several decades ago you bought paintings executed by the most admired English portraitists of the eighteenth and nineteenth centuries, you'd be lucky now to get half what you paid for them.

Still another piece of advice that doesn't always work to your advantage is to buy from a reputable dealer. This makes sense at least in theory, but never forget that even the most scrupulous gallery owner will be prejudiced in favor of the artists handled by his or her gallery.

Two Ways to Invest in Collectibles: If the idea of investing in collectibles attracts you, there are two ways you can proceed:

1. You can invest as an individual, being guided by your personal taste. Without questioning your taste, I remind you that some types of collectibles appreciate more slowly than others, and the genre that appeals most to you may not appreciate at the rate you hoped it would. So you may prefer to be guided by an expert financial adviser. Collecting, at this stage of the game, can cost you plenty: A rare book, for example, may carry a price tag of upward of $10,000!

(On the other hand, I know people who've turned a respectable profit on childhood collections of comic books, baseball cards, cigar-box labels, and cereal box-top giveaways.)

2. You can invest as a member of an organized investment syndicate. Many syndicates specialize in one area, such as works of art, antique furniture, Persian rugs, coins, stamps, gems, or books.

Both ways are risky, but the second is particularly treacherous. As an individual collector, you can at least buy what you like and get pleasure from your investment—the kind of pleasure you won't get from contemplating a stock certificate.

Take fine arts again. If your painting also appreciates in value, so much the better. But if you invest in an art-buying syndicate, be prepared to lose your shirt. The syndicate pools money from investors to acquire superexpensive art works. It usually holds on to these works for at least ten years to allow time for significant appreciation. For all that time your money is frozen in the deal. Not all the money you contribute to the syndicate goes toward paying for the artworks; there are storage charges, insurance, and often hefty commissions and management fees. As one of perhaps dozens of investors in a work, you may never be able to enjoy it in your own home (in fact, you might only view it once). There may be constant squabbling among investors about who gets to display the work.

There are good, honest people in charge of running some of the art syndicates, but there are also unethical types with little or no knowledge of art who are out to make an easy buck from gullible investors. They will take a high management fee off the top of the pooled investment money, and then buy third- or fourth-rate works for the syndicate. Only years later, when an attempt is made to sell these works for a profit, do the investors realize the extent to which they have been had.

If you plan to invest in collectibles through a syndicate, it is always a good idea to bring in an independent appraiser to evaluate and authenticate the work in question before it is bought.

Tax Advantages of Investing in Collectibles: Though the risk is high, the tax advantages are not inconsiderable:

1. Collectibles are treated as capital assets. You can get capital gains tax treatment when and if you sell.

2. You can defer capital gains taxes on collectibles if you exchange one item for another instead of selling. For example, if you buy a painting for $100,000, hold it for four years, then exchange it for a painting worth $200,000, you need pay no taxes on your $100,000 gain until you sell the new painting. Note: This option is for collectors and investors only. Dealers may not defer taxes this way.

3. Of interest, to me at any rate, is the fact that in many instances collectibles may be purchased for Keogh plans and IRAs (Individual Retirement Accounts). (See Chapter 9.)

The Growing Use of Collectibles for Tax Evasion Purposes: To the dismay of IRS, crafty collectors and syndicates have devised several ingenious and not-so-ingenious ways to evade taxes on collectibles.

Stamps, diamonds, and other small but valuable items can be easily carried undetected across U.S. borders; money in the form of taxable goods is thereby transferred out of the country. Collectibles are sometimes passed from owner to heirs in devious, secretive ways that make the transfer difficult if not impossible for IRS to uncover. Some collectors dodge taxes by just not declaring the capital gains on items they sell.

And then there's the old charitable contribution dodge whereby a donor makes a gift of collectibles—their value appraised at inappropriately inflated rates—to museums and other institutions. In return for the gift the donor claims a "charitable" contribution deduction that actually leaves him with a big tax profit. To curb this abuse, IRS now has its own panel of appraisers to evaluate any collectible that is donated as a charitable contribution, if its worth is stated to be in excess of $20,000.

New Law: Collectibles in Retirement Accounts: To the dismay of many collectors all amounts invested by IRAs or Keoghs in collectibles after December 31, 1981 will be treated as taxable distribution for income tax purposes. Thus, if you purchase $1,000 of collectibles in your IRA or Keogh after December 31, 1981, IRS will consider this a distribution from your retirement account and will tax you accordingly. Trustees and fiduciaries will still be able to purchase collectibles with funds that they manage.

Benjamin Franklin wrote: "In this world nothing can be said to be certain, except death and taxes." What the taxpayer resents is that they don't come in that order.

—ANONYMOUS

8

Life Insurance as a Tax Shelter

Talk about misnomers and euphemisms! Life insurance doesn't insure you against living. It insures you against dying and ought to be called death insurance!

What it does do, of course, is provide death benefits to the insured's beneficiaries when the insured goes the way of all flesh. Tax-sheltered benefits as well, it's important to add, since life-insurance policy proceeds are generally exempt from federal income taxes.

An interesting, little-known fact about life insurance is that when a person fails to pay taxes, IRS can go after that person's assets, including the cash value of any permanent life-insurance policies. So to IRS life insurance is also a form of tax insurance.

It's not death benefits but tax-sheltered "life benefits" that we'll be concerned with here. Many kinds of life insurance are flexible vehicles that can be used to stash away money now on a tax-deferred basis, allowing it to grow tax-free until the policy—and presumably you—have matured. Or until you decide to cash the policy in.

Whole Life Insurance: Sometimes called "ordinary life"

91

or "straight life," this offers two things for your premium money. Of each dollar you pay, some goes for death benefits and some goes into building up cash value.

Interest is earned on the money that accumulates as cash value, though the rate is low: about 4% during the early years of the policy, and about 5% later.

The return on whole life insurance is too skimpy to make it an attractive investment or savings plan. For the middle-income person, money market funds, corporate bonds, and so on are wiser choices. But whole life has a special appeal to many in the highest tax brackets (40% to 70%) because the increase in cash value attributable to interest earned on the premium is exempt from yearly taxation, which is hardly the case with the interest you accumulate in your savings account!

If you turn in your policy for cash—one of your options with whole life insurance—you don't have to pay tax on all of it. First you can subtract all the premiums you paid. If the total paid in premiums exceeds the cash value, you owe no income tax. If the cash value exceeds the total paid in premiums, taxes are due only on the difference.

If you're not earning dollars in the 40% to 70% tax brackets, why pay extra premiums to build up cash value? Of course, you need life insurance if you have a wife or husband and children depending on you for support. So what do you do? According to a Consumers Union study, your best bet is to get term insurance, which is life insurance pure and simple, with no extra cost for built-in savings. Term insurance is much cheaper than whole life.

The Tax Advantages of Annuities—From Retirement to Death: An annuity is the opposite of life insurance. It provides regular payments to the insured, usually beginning when he or she retires, until death. In the classic annuity you hand over one big chunk of money to the insurance company at the beginning. In other annuity programs you are required to make regular payments over a period of years. In either case, the insurance company manages your money and pays it back to you in regular amounts monthly, quarterly, or yearly.

Your contributions or "premiums" that pay for the annuity contract are usually not tax-deductible unless under a qualified plan. However, interest accumulates tax-free over the years. Only at retirement, when you begin to receive your checks, are you required to pay taxes on annuity income; and by then you will presumably be in a lower tax bracket and the damages should be minimal.

The well-heeled aunt of a friend of mine, for example, bought a $100,000 single-premium deferred life annuity with an interest rate of 10% compounded annually. At the end of 20 years, just about the time she will turn 70, her $100,000 will have grown to $672,700.

If this woman (assuming that she were in the 40% tax bracket) invested the same amount in a 10% savings account compounded annually, she would end up with only $320,700. That $352,000 difference (significant even to this wealthy woman whose only money worry has been how to invest wisely and conservatively) is due to the fact that, savings account interest is subject to taxation, which removes sizable chunks from the interest each year. In an annuity program, interest piles up tax-free.

To find out more about annuity contracts available to you as an individual and their tax implications, check with a qualified life insurance agent or life-licensed stockbroker.

How to Save on Taxes Through a Job-Sponsored Annuity Program: Some organizations, including tax-exempt foundations, public school systems, and state and city hospitals, make tax-sheltered annuities available to their employees. You can check with your employer or the person who looks after employee benefits at your company to see if an annuity program is available.

If you're eligible to pay into an annuity program as an employee, the amount you contribute to the program re-

93

Format for Measuring Term Versus Whole Life*

All figures in the table below are rounded to the nearest dollar. Numbers in parentheses are negative. Data are based on CU's 1973 cost survey. A 5 percent return rate is assumed.

Age	Term Premium	Term Dividend	Term Face Amount	Whole Life Premium	Whole Life Dividend	Yearly Savings of Term Policyholder	Accumulated Savings of Term Policyholder	Cash Value of Whole Life Policy†
37	$136	$ 12	$25,000	$561	$ 43	$ 394	$ 1,345	
39	136	19	25,000	561	61	383	2,314	
41	159	28	23,000	561	94	335	3,292	
44	159	40	23,000	561	163	279	4,804	$ 4,250
47	197	49	21,000	561	236	177	6,222	
49	197	54	21,000	561	278	141	7,182	
51	241	54	18,000	561	304	70	8,085	
54	241	64	18,000	561	331	53	9,555	9,354
57	313	74	16,000	561	359	(37)	10,958	
59	313	87	16,000	561	377	(42)	11,993	
61	382	90	13,000	546	394	(141)	12,935	
64	382	118	13,000	546	422	(140)	14,509	14,502

* Each reproduction bears the following copyright designation and *no other legend:* Copyright 1980 by Consumers Union of United States, Inc., Mount Vernon, NY 10550. Excerpted by permission from The Consumers Union Report on Life Insurance, Fourth Edition.

† Includes the terminal dividend—a dividend paid by some companies upon termination of the policy.

duces your gross income by the amount of your contribution, up to the limit of an exclusion allowance. In most cases, the exclusion allowance is 20% *after* salary deduction, or 16⅔% of your unreduced salary.

To calculate your exclusion allowance, multiply your gross salary by 16⅔%, which gives you 20% of your reduced salary, the key amount in this calculation.

To illustrate: If your salary is $10,000 per year, multiply that by 16⅔%. The result, $1,667, represents your exclusion allowance for the year—the amount you can deduct from your gross income as contribution to an employee annuity program. Just to check this, 20% of the reduced salary of $8,333 ($10,000 less $1,667 = $8,333 × 20% = $1,667) equals $1,667.

Using a Trust to Get More Coverage—and Pay Less Taxes on It: People who want or need a large amount of life insurance have the option of setting up a trust (or contributing to an existing trust); thereby they hope to obtain professional guidance and management on such matters as selecting the right policies, making premium payments, deciding how income to beneficiaries should be distributed, and the other exhaustingly detailed and boring work connected with insurance.

Another plus for the trust: Taxes are lower on trusts than on individuals, so more after-tax dollars are available for premium payments. A trust may be able to purchase more life insurance per dollar than you could on your own.

See an attorney or estate planner to investigate the potential advantages of buying insurance through a trust.

Tax-Wise Insurance Tactics for Employers: Too many employers and company executives overlook the potential uses of life insurance in business. The right kind of policy will not only help smooth the way in difficult transitional periods, as when a key man or partner dies, but will aid in overall tax planning. Here are a few examples of what I mean:

1. "Key man" policies: Let's say you're an employer and one of your top executives brings in a large portion of your company's business. What are you going to do if that key man (or woman) keels over from a heart attack or dies in a plane crash? Personal feelings aside, how is the loss of this key person going to affect your business?

Naturally, you can't predict all the consequences of losing a key person. But did you know that you can soften the financial blow to your company if your key man suddenly dies by taking out insurance on his life? In this case, you, as employer, would be both owner and beneficiary of the policy. Premiums are not deductible by the employer and the proceeds are received income tax-free.

2. Life insurance as part of an employer's benefit package: As an employer you may decide to include life insurance for an employee as part of an employee benefit program. If you pay the premiums, and if your company has no ownership rights or beneficial interest in the policy (that is, if family members of employees, and not you or your own company, are in line to receive death benefits), then the premium payments are usually deductible as additional compensation for the employee's services.

The estate of a beneficiary of an employee's life-insurance policy paid for by an employer is ordinarily allowed to exclude from taxation up to $5,000 in death benefits.

3. Insurance to fund a stock redemption agreement: Here you buy a policy in order to assure that money is available to your corporation to buy out any interest in the firm claimed by family members of the deceased.

Suppose that you and your best friend have formed a small corporation. If your best friend dies and his share of the business is transferred through his estate to his wife, you may be in for some problems. You and she may not see eye to eye on business matters. You may not even like each other. Or she may remarry and you'll be in business with her second husband. You are yoked together in a business arrangement that neither of you is happy about. You'd buy her out if you could—and she'd be happy to be bought out—but where's the money to come from?

To prevent this unhappy scenario from coming true, you and your friend can enter into a "buy-sell" agreement dictating a disposition of the stock and setting a value. To fund the agreement insurance policies will be purchased. If your friend dies you get his interest in the business, while his family is the beneficiary of the life-insurance policy; and similarly if you die.

The transfer of stock to surviving shareholders under an insurance-funded stock redemption agreement does not ordinarily result in any additional taxing of the deceased's estate. It also serves to fix the value of the stock for estate tax purposes.

Life insurance can protect small business from forced liquidation or merger due to heavy death taxes and can provide liquidity to estates. An insurance-funded redemption of stock under the provisions of Section 303 of the Internal Revenue Code allows a corporation to redeem part of a deceased stockholder's shares without the redemption price being treated as a dividend (which would be taxable as ordinary income). Instead, the redemption price is treated as a capital transaction, as payment in exchange for the stock. The redemption price probably would not result in a capital gain, as the tax basis of a decedent's stock is its fair market value at the time of death.

Life Insurance as Protection of Partnership Interest: If your business is a partnership, you may want to take the same approach as the one just cited for corporate stock redemption, to make sure that in the event of your partner's death, you are not saddled with the spouse or child of the deceased as a new and possibly unwanted partner.

In a partnership, premiums paid for insurance on the life of one partner by another are *not* deductible to either partner. Nor are the premiums deductible if you insure your own life and name your partner as beneficiary. Sorry, but that's the breaks.

Life-Insurance Premiums and Sole Proprietorships: Premiums paid by a sole proprietor for insurance on his or her own life are not deductible as a business expense—even if business funds are used to purchase the insurance. Nor can an employee of a business run as a sole proprietorship deduct the premium for his taxes when the employee purchases insurance on the life of the sole proprietor.

That doesn't mean that an employee cannot or should not insure his boss's life. After all, if your employer dies and you're out of a job, who knows how long it will be until you find another; insurance proceeds can make the hunt-and-search period a whole lot more comfortable.

The Liquidity Factor: Sometimes the proceeds of life-insurance policies provide the cash necessary to protect small businesses from forced liquidation or merger due to heavy death taxes. Consider the following scenario:

The owner of a small business dies. The business, worth let's say about $100,000, is left to the owner's daughter. Death taxes levied against the business and the deceased's estate amount to a heavy $20,000. The daughter can't get the $20,000 for taxes immediately out of the business, whose assets are not that liquid. Nor does she have $20,000 of her own.

But the owner had the foresight to take out extra life insurance on himself—enough to cover projected taxes on the estate and business. Liquid assets provided by life insurance save the day!

Without the additional insurance the daughter might have to sell the business—possibly at a heavy loss—in order to raise money for taxes.

What You Should Know About Death Proceeds from Insurance Purchased for Business Purposes: Whether the beneficiary is an individual, a trust, a corporation, a partnership, or the insured's estate, proceeds from life-insurance policies taken out for business purposes are generally exempt from income tax if the proceeds are paid out in a lump sum.

This, plus the many other benefits of insuring the life of a business associate (or taking out additional insurance on one's own life for business purposes) has affected the thinking of many who view business life-insurance policies as more than just an interesting idea; rather, as an indispensable part of sound business management.

Before you plunge into buying extra life insurance, discuss your needs—personal or business—and your financial situation with a competent insurance agent. An individual with a Chartered Life Underwriter (CLU) designation is generally a professional well-versed in this field.

Life insurance, it has been said, is the ultimate tax shelter: "It can be set up so it produces no current income; none of it is taxable to the beneficiary; and the insured never knows the pain of paying taxes on it either."

New Law: Individual Income Tax Reduction: The new law reduces the top rate on all classes of income from 70% to 50% beginning in 1982.

I'm a middle-bracket person with a middle-bracket spouse
And we live together gaily in a middle-bracket house.
We've a fair-to-middling family; we take the middle view;
So we're manna sent from heaven to Internal Revenue.

—PHYLLIS MCGINLEY

9

IRA and Keogh Retirement Plans: Key to Retirement Millions for the Middle Class

Ever stop to think about how the years flash by? Seems like just yesterday you were in college, right? But the fact that you're reading this book probably means your school days are well behind you. Time flies. The older you get, the quicker it seems to go. And all of a sudden, you're facing retirement. Then what?

If you've been financially successful, you'll be trotting around, seeing and doing all the things you never had time for in your working years.

But what if you've failed to build up a fortune? What if your income has been just "average"—enough to get by, with maybe a few bucks left over for vacations, dinners in nice restaurants, theater tickets now and then? You've got a lot of pleasant memories, but memories don't pay the electric bills, let alone give you the means to live in dignity, free of nagging money worries when you reach retirement age. And Social Security payments, as you well know, will provide for little more than the bare necessities.

If you're covered by a company pension or profit-sharing

plan and maybe manage to make some good investments, you'll probably be OK when you reach what the insurance companies used to call your "golden years" until everybody got sick of the euphemism. In fact, if you're a member of a company-sponsored pension or profit-sharing plan, you may not even want to bother reading past the next paragraph or so in this chapter, because you may not be eligible to take advantage of what may be the most important tax-saving, money-sheltering strategy of them all.

I'm talking about setting up an Individual Retirement Account (IRA) or Keogh Plan (HR-10). Congress provided for both in the Employment Retirement Income Security Act (ERISA) to help individuals who do not benefit from a company-sponsored pension plan.

Either plan can assure you hundreds of thousands of dollars for your retirement years. (How much money you'll get has a lot to do with how young you are when you set up the plan.)

Not only that, the tax advantages of a qualified retirement plan are twofold: (1) every dollar you invest in either plan is tax-deductible in the year the contribution was made; and (2) all income from either plan—whether dividend, long-term capital gain, or just plain interest—is completely sheltered from taxes until you begin to draw on the money. If you wait until you're retired, you'll most likely be in a much lower tax bracket than you are now, so your money will be taxed at a much lower rate.

It all sounds too good to be true, but it's true.

IRA and Keogh Plans are not without their critics. It's often pointed out, usually by people who don't have the sense to recognize a good deal when they see one, that there are penalties imposed for withdrawing the money prematurely. The penalties consist of (1) an obligation to pay income tax on the amount withdrawn, and (2) a 10% surcharge on the value of all of the assets in the account, even though only a small portion is withdrawn. So? You just don't touch the money except in cases of direst emergency. And if things ever get *that* bad, you'll be mighty happy to have the money to draw on in the first place.

The other common criticism of these plans comes from people who believe that if they put money away into an IRA or Keogh account, they'll be locked into that one investment. They're wrong about that.

It's possible to select a flexible plan that allows you to control how your money will be invested, that is, which stocks, bonds, mutual funds, or money market funds to buy, when to sell, and when to switch from one to another. These flexible plans can be set up through a brokerage house, savings bank, or mutual fund.

As for who's eligible for an IRA or Keogh Plan, you may be able to count yourself in if you work and are not covered by a company-sponsored pension or profit-sharing plan.

Individual Retirement Accounts (IRAs): Who Qualifies?

Exclusions: Individual Retirement Accounts are for people who work for a company, but who do not participate in any of the following:

1. A pension, profit-sharing, or stock bonus plan sponsored by the employer
2. A qualified annuity or bond purchase plan sponsored by the employer
3. A government retirement plan
4. A Keogh (HR-10) self-employment plan

Contributions: How much do you contribute to an IRA? The more the better, within the limits of up to $1,500 per year or 15% of your earned income, *whichever is less.*

If you earn $12,000 a year, you can contribute $1,500

(15% of your income would be $1,800, which is more than $1,500).

If you earn $7,000 a year, you can contribute only $1,050 per year (15% of $7,000).

The limitation is modified for those who are married to a spouse who doesn't work. Then the upper limit is $1,750.

A husband and wife who are both eligible to set up IRAs can set up two separate accounts, each contributing up to the lesser of $1,500 or 15% of income.

Note: You are not required to contribute the maximum amounts or *any* amount once your account has been set up. You can contribute 15% of your income for two years in a row, then nothing for a year, then 5% the next year and back up to 15% the next. Paying the maximum is best, because it will generate the most income; but everyone has good years and bad and there may be times when other expenses take priority.

Should a windfall come your way, however, you can't make up for past years when you contributed less than your maximum. (You can put some extra money in your savings account, but you won't get the IRA tax advantage.)

When to Contribute: The sooner you start a plan, the more interest income will accumulate over the years. Also, if you make a big payment to your account in January it will generate more income for that year than a payment made in December. A payment can be made as late as December 31 and still be deductible from your income for the year.

Receiving Retirement Benefits: You can withdraw money from your IRA at any time, though there are penalties for early withdrawal. You can apply for regular penalty-free retirement income from your plan as early as age 59½. You *must* apply for income from the plan by age 70½.

You can get your money in a lump sum, which will be taxed as regular income, although you have the privilege of five-year income averaging to spread out the tax burden if you wish. Or you can receive regular installments, payable over a period of years that does not exceed the life expectancies of you and your spouse, as figured from insurance company tables.

An IRA for Ira: Ira, a single guy, 25 years old, lives in the town where I grew up. We got to talking one day. Turned out that Ira's company, a small manufacturing firm, has no employee retirement program. I mentioned he could contribute 15% of his salary or up to a maximum of $1,500 per year, and blah, blah, blah went through the whole thing with him. He has a gross income of $10,000 and was interested in knowing how much he'd save in taxes with an IRA.

Here's how the figures went:

	Without IRA	With IRA
Total Income	$10,000	$10,000
Minus tax-deductible IRA contribution	0	1,500
Taxable income	10,000	8,500
Taxes	1,387	1,072
Tax savings with IRA	0	$ 315

Ira was impressed with the idea of saving $315 on his tax bill each year, and it was this that convinced him to set up an IRA. But he was flabbergasted when he grasped the entire significance of what he'd done. If he contributes $1,500 to his account every year for the next 40 years (until he's in his mid-sixties), and his money accumulates interest at a steady 8% rate, he'll have $419,671.50 when he's ready to retire!

Tax-Free Rollovers: If you're enrolled in a qualified employer-sponsored retirement plan and you leave your job, you can set up your own IRA and transfer the funds (rollover) accumulated in your old employer's plan to your own. You must set up your IRA and transfer funds into it within 60 days of receiving the money from the old program.

Self-Employment Retirement Programs
(Keogh Plans, or HR-10s): Who Qualifies?

The Keogh Plan takes its name from the New York congressman who sponsored the original legislation in 1962.

Eligibility: You are eligible to set up a Keogh Plan if you are any of the following:

1. Self-employed
2. The sole proprietor of a business
3. A partner with more than a 10% interest in a business

Contributions: If you are eligible for a Keogh Plan you can contribute up to $7,500 per year, or 15% of your earned income, *whichever is less.*

If you are self-employed and have no one working for you, you can contribute less than the maximum, or even nothing, in bad years when your entire income has to cover other expenses. But as with an IRA, the more you contribute each year the better it will be for you in the long run.

If you set up a Keogh Plan for yourself, you must establish similar plans for any full-time employees who have worked for you for three or more years. You must contribute the same percentage of the employee's salary as you contribute for yourself. You may exclude part-time and seasonal employees.

There are so many rules and regulations and variations thereof governing Keogh Plans as they relate to employer/ employee contributions that your best bet is to consult an attorney to determine your obligations.

If you want to set up a retirement program only for yourself, and choose not to contribute to an employee's retirement fund, you can set up an Individual Retirement Account (IRA) instead of a Keogh Plan.

Receiving Retirement Benefits: As with an IRA, you can begin to withdraw income from your Keogh account, penalty-free, beginning at age 59½. You must apply for withdrawal of funds by the end of the calendar year in which you reach age 70½.

If you become disabled, benefits can be paid out to you immediately, regardless of your age. If you die, benefits can go immediately to your spouse or other beneficiary named when you set up the plan.

Generally, all amounts that are distributed are taxed as ordinary income. You can take out the money in a lump sum. If you do, part of it will be taxed at long-term capital gains rates and the other part as ordinary income. You may be eligible for special ten-year income averaging privileges that will lessen your immediate tax burden. Check with IRS or an attorney to get the details on capital gains and income averaging.

Premature Distribution of Income: If you withdraw a portion of your Keogh funds prematurely, there is a 10% tax penalty on the entire amount in your account, and the funds withdrawn will be taxed as ordinary income. The part of your account, if any, that consists of your voluntary contributions as an employer can be withdrawn without penalty at any time.

A Keogh Plan for Carol: Carol came to me as a client seeking tax shelter advice. Her financial situation was basically good but my feeling was that she wasn't quite ready for oil or real estate tax shelters, since she hadn't made any plans for the far-off future. I told her so and suggested she set up a Keogh account. As a $40,000-a-year self-employed publishers' representative, Carol certainly qualified. Since she was an unmarried woman with a single person's tax-filing status and no dependents, a Keogh could make a significant difference on her tax return.

Here's how the figures worked out for Carol:

	Self-Employed Without a Keogh	Self-Employed With a Keogh
Total annual income	$40,000	$40,000
Minus tax-deductible annual Keogh contribution	0	6,000
Taxable income	40,000	34,000
Taxes	13,190	10,200
Tax savings	0	$ 2,990

Carol's yearly contribution of $6,000 (15% of $40,000) to a Keogh Plan would reduce her tax bill by almost $3,000! If she continues to contribute to the plan at that rate for the next 30 years, and if her money accumulates tax-free interest at a steady 8% annual rate, Carol will have a total of $734,076 to draw on when she retires at about age 60.

Excess Contribution to IRA and Keogh Plans

Some people just can't get enough of a good thing and overcontribute to their IRA or Keogh Plans, either because they have the extra money and want to try for a bigger tax deduction and a speedier accumulation of interest, or because they've simply forgotten their upper limit. Whatever the reason, IRS makes it very clear that deductions for excess contributions will be disallowed. In fact, if excess funds are not removed from an account by the time you file your federal income tax for the year, a nondeductible 6% excise tax will be imposed on the excess.

New Law: Individual Retirement Account (IRA) Changes: Beginning after December 31, 1981, the new law raises the amount allowed as a deduction on IRAs to the lesser of (1) $2,000, or (2) 100% of your compensation.

The spousal (for a nonworking spouse) IRA limit was increased from $1,750 to $2,250. Equal amounts will no longer have to be contributed to each spouse's account. A minimum of $250 will have to be directed to the nonworking spouse's IRA, although additional amounts may be contributed if the working spouse desires.

Additionally, in the event of a divorce the working spouse may make deductible contributions up to $1,125 annually to an IRA that may be credited to alimony or compensation payments.

An employee already covered by a company pension plan will now be able to contribute an additional $2,000 per year ($2,250 for a spousal IRA) to an IRA. This may occur either through a company-offered IRA or through a separate IRA, at the option of the employee.

All amounts invested in collectibles by IRAs or Keoghs after December 31, 1981 will be treated as taxable distribution for income tax purposes. See Chapter 7 under "New Law: Collectibles in Retirement Accounts."

New Law: Keogh Changes: Starting in 1982, the maximum deductible contribution to a Keogh will be $15,000, which is twice the old limit. The 15% contribution limit of your income remains as before.

The new law also says that any loan to an individual from his or her Keogh program or the use of any interest in that plan as security for a loan will be treated as taxable distribution.

Any funds prematurely withdrawn from a Keogh or an IRA will be subject to a 10% penalty.

An individual is free to determine how he or she wants to invest the money in a Keogh or an IRA, except for insurance policies (in which money accumulates tax-free and that might escape taxation when a person dies), collectibles (see Chapter 7), and investments paid for with borrowed funds.

A taxpayer can claim depreciation on all sorts of things—except oneself.

—ANONYMOUS

10

You, Inc.: Incorporation as a Tax Shelter

General Motors is a corporation. So is General Electric. So is Exxon. No surprise, but doesn't every honest taxpaying citizen get all hot under the collar and scream out for restrictive legislation when they read about the super-duper tax write-offs and other tax advantages of these giants? There oughta be a law!

There's another way to look at it: If you can't beat 'em, join 'em. Incorporate yourself—or, rather, your business—and take advantage of some of the privileged tax treatment enjoyed by the corporate behemoths.

Incorporating yourself will probably not affect the volume of your business or make your firm an overnight success. But that's beside the point, which is to avail yourself of the tax-sheltering benefits IRS bestows on the corporation.

What's a Corporation, Anyway? A corporation is a separate legal business entity, authorized by the state in which it was created. It has its own name, can enter into contracts and own property, is taxed as a taxpayer (but at much lower rates than high-bracketed individuals), can sue and be sued, and exists in its own right, distinct from those who own it.

A corporation is owned by its stockholders. The authority to run a corporation lies in the hands of the board of directors, elected by the stockholders. The board appoints the managers of the company.

If you're a self-employed businessperson or professional you don't need a whole board of directors and a staff to manage your corporation. Generally, all you are required to have is a president and a secretary. (The secretary is an officer of the corporation, not an office secretary as in typist.) You can appoint yourself president and anyone you like as secretary.

Why Incorporate?:   There is a long list of advantages to incorporating yourself or your business. And there are a number of reasons why incorporating might not be in your best interests. Those reasons will be spelled out later. For now, let's look at the pros:

1.   Corporate income tax rates are less steeply graduated than those for personal income tax. They run to 17% on the first $25,000 of income; 20% on the second $25,000; 30% on the third $25,000; 40% on the fourth $25,000; and 46% on amounts in excess of $100,000.

State and local taxes are not to be discounted, however. Some states hit corporations hard; others are very gentle.

2.   The profits of a sole proprietorship or partnership must be paid and taxed to the owners in the year earned, but there are ways for corporations to keep certain sums ("retained earnings") from one year to the next. (Usually, but not always, earnings are retained to finance specific projects.)

3.   Employees of corporations are eligible to participate in tax-free life insurance, as well as medical, disability, salary continuation, pension, and profit-sharing plans. You may deduct from your corporate income the dollar amount of all contributions to these plans.

Life insurance in the form of one-year renewable term policies with face value of up to $50,000 (Section 79 insurance) is available to groups of ten or more; IRS also allows smaller corporate groups, including a "group of one," to qualify for these policies. The corporation can deduct the cost of the premiums from its gross income—nor is the benefit treated as taxable income to the holder of the policy. It's one of those no-lose situations. As owner/employee of the corporation, you get the deduction, plus the tax-free benefit if you receive insurance funds. (Coverage of more than $50,000, however, is taxable as "imputed income" to the owner of the policy, but taxes, based on the age of the individual, are low.)

Group term life insurance can be a great blessing to corporate owner/employees who have had difficulty in obtaining life insurance through other channels.

The corporation can deduct from its gross income up to $5,000 in death benefits paid to a deceased employee's beneficiary. No tax is paid by the beneficiary.

Comprehensive medical insurance and reimbursement of medical expenses and drugs are available to corporate employees and their dependents. The corporation can deduct from its gross income the entire cost of these plans, as a corporate business expense. The benefits are not treated as income to the recipient. In fact, the corporation can make these payments directly. Another no-lose situation.

Likewise, disability and salary continuation plans are available on the same fully deductible basis. An employee of a corporation is eligible to receive workmen's compensation, something unavailable to sole proprietors.

4. The corporation gets favorable pension tax treatment by providing contributions to pension plans for its employees that are tax-deductible as a business expense.

    a) If they choose a *defined benefit plan*, whereby the benefit is determined currently by a specific formula based on salary, service, a specific amount, or a combination of all of these, the contribution is the amount necessary to provide the required benefit, with the maximum benefit of $110,625 or 100% of annual salary, whichever is lower.

In a *defined contribution plan*, where the benefit is whatever can be generated by the funds contributed plus interest and investment results, the contribution is based on a fixed percentage of salary, with a maximum contribution of 25% of salary up to $36,875 per year.

This is better than the Keogh Plan with its limit of 15% of salary up to $7,500.

b) The corporation's contributions are not currently taxed to the employee as current income. Income-tax liability is postponed until the employee receives the benefits. The only exception is if the plan provides life insurance, in which case a small tax liability is incurred.

c) The retirement fund grows tax-free. Income is accumulated tax-free, allowing the fund to grow larger and faster.

d) The benefits are usually received by the employee at lower tax rates, as he or she will probably be in a lower tax bracket when the benefits are disbursed. The benefits are subject to tax treatment as ordinary income when they are received under a monthly income distribution. If you elect to receive qualifying lump-sum distributions of your retirement income you can get favorable long-term capital gains treatment to the extent of the employee's pre-1974 active participation in the plan, and the ordinary income portion can qualify for ten-year averaging (which can also be elected for the entire distribution).

Corporate pension plan funds can be invested in stocks, bonds, art objects, antiques, gems, gold or silver bullion, stamps, or coins, as well as in mutual funds, money market funds, savings certificates of deposits, and other "conventional" investments.

5. The stockholders of a corporation—or you, as owner/employee of your own one-person corporation—are not personally liable for corporate debts beyond the amount of capital investment in the company. Your personal assets (your home, other real estate, investment income from sources outside your own corporation, etc.) are protected should any lawsuits be initiated against the corporation. As owner or partner of a nonincorporated business you are no doubt already aware that business creditors can go after your personal property if you don't pay up in good time; indeed, your personal property may be in jeopardy in any lawsuit arising from your business activities.

6. A corporation, which is a distinct entity, can establish its own line of credit. As owner/employee, your personal borrowing power is separate from that of the corporation.

7. By issuing shares (or stock) corporations have the means of securing additional capital without borrowing. Placing a fair valuation on the stock and determining the number of shares that should be sold are matters best discussed with an accountant or attorney wise in the ways of corporate tax law.

8. Deferred compensation plans are available to shareholders and employees; they lessen the immediate tax bite that would otherwise be levied.

9. As owner/employee of your own corporation, it should be easy to transfer some of your ownership, represented by your stock, to others—your children or spouse, for example. Because of the way corporate tax laws are written, you can probably transfer more of these assets without having to pay the gift tax imposed on ordinary transfers of property. If the time comes when you want to take advantage of this option, take up the matter with an

accountant or attorney, as the rules about these transfers tend to be complex.

10. If a car is necessary for business purposes, your corporation can own it, deduct the cost of insurance, maintenance, repairs, gas, etc., from gross corporate income.

11. Because it's an entity with a "life" of its own, a corporation lives on even if you or another major shareholder die. By leaving your shares of the corporation to your spouse or children, you may be bequeathing a valuable asset. (The exceptions are obvious. A self-incorporated free-lance artist cannot very well leave her business to her husband and children and expect it to be much of an asset.)

12. Your corporation can have a safe-deposit box that your heirs can open on your death without having a federal or a state tax official present. Only personal safe-deposit boxes are sealed on the death of their owner; corporation boxes are not.

Why Incorporation May Not Be for You: Now let's hear it from the opposition:

1. Profits are subject to corporate tax. When the profits are distributed to stockholders as dividends they are again taxed, as income ("double taxation"). However, in most small corporations not much earnings are left to be taxed after salary and pension contributions.

2. Corporate activities are limited by provisions in the corporate charter. Your charter may not let you be flexible enough to take advantage of business opportunities that come up.

3. Minority stockholders are almost always subject to the power and wishes of the majority. If you are the sole stockholder, or one of the majority stockholders, this is a plus factor. But if you are one of several partners in a business, and a minority partner at that, the likelihood is that your capital investment will net you only a small percentage of the total stock, and you may lose your "voice," if a decision is made to incorporate.

4. It's usually difficult for a deceased stockholder's family to get income out of a business. The business can decide not to declare dividends. Also, a widow, unless she actually works for it, cannot receive a salary from the corporation.

Measuring the Effects of Incorporating: A young woman I'll call Joanne, who owns her own dress design company with a total yearly income of about $100,000, was wondering about the advantages of incorporating. When we first spoke, she was running her business as a sole proprietorship and did not contribute to a Keogh Plan, though she was eligible. Together, we calculated how much she could save yearly on taxes if she continued business operations as a sole proprietorship with a Keogh Plan, as a corporation, and as a corporation with a pension plan. Here's how the figures came out:

	Sole Proprietorship	Sole Proprietorship with Keogh Plan	Corporation	Corporation with Pension Plan
Total business income	$100,000	$100,000	$100,000	$100,000
Minus cost of benefits (deductible)	0	7,500	0	12,500
Taxable income after deducting benefits	$100,000	$ 92,500	$100,000	$ 87,500
Minus earnings taxable to owner (salary)	100,000	92,500	50,000	50,000
Taxable to business	0	0	50,000	37,500
Business tax payable	0	0	9,250	6,750
Taxes of owner	43,260	38,760	15,460	15,460
Total taxes payable	$ 43,260	$ 38,760	$ 24,710	$ 22,210
Savings with Keogh Plan		$ 4,500		
Savings with corporation			$ 18,550	
Savings with corporation with pension				$ 21,050

By incorporating with a pension plan (the best choice) Joanne was set to save a staggering $21,050 a year in taxes!

How to Set Yourself Up as a Corporation: Most people are attracted by the prospect of incorporating because of the income-tax savings they hope to enjoy. Self-employed executives, free-lance artists, and professional people are the most likely candidates for self-incorporation. As a rule it probably doesn't pay to incorporate unless you are making in excess of $30,000 per year.

The hardest step in incorporating is making the decision. Joanne's case was clear-cut; there were no factors militating against incorporating. Your own situation may be different, and I suggest you talk the matter over with an attorney and an accountant before you decide.

Assuming you've discussed all the angles with your advisers and your decision is to take the plunge into incorporation, the next step is to choose the attorney to set up the corporation. Attorney fees for this run from about $200 to $700, depending on such things as the state, the complexity of the arrangements to be made, and the current income from your business.

You can save the attorney fee and do the incorporating yourself. There are several how-to books that explain the procedure in detail, and if you really put your mind to it you may be able to negotiate do-it-yourself incorporation without coming to grief over it later on. I don't advise do-it-yourself incorporation, however. Better to hand the job over to a professional and have it done properly. (Besides, if you can't afford $200 to $700 for an attorney, incorporation may not be for you; your business income probably isn't sufficient to make it worthwhile.) Additional fees will be charged for setting up various plans, such as medical and pension.

Be prepared to discuss with your attorney (1) your business purpose and its future objectives and (2) the state in which you incorporate. You may find it advantageous to incorporate in a state other than the one in which you live and in which you will do business. You and your attorney should check the tax structures of various states. Find out which states are least restrictive in their requirements for corporate charters. You'll want to have a charter as broad as possible, allowing you to branch out into other business activities if you choose. Some states hold stockholders partly liable for services the corporation has contracted for and/or for wages of employees. Some states restrict or bar the right to issue no-par stocks (stocks which can significantly reduce corporate taxes and franchise fees). Some states take forever to issue a charter. Some states have "blue-sky" laws that impose severe restrictions on issuing stock to the public.

The states that are least restrictive in general are Delaware, Maryland, New York, New Jersey, Pennsylvania, Nevada, and Tennessee.

There are more points to discuss with your attorney:

1. A name for your corporation (this can be secured by writing or calling the office of the Secretary of State, Department of Corporations, in the capital of your corporate home state. Have second and third choices in mind in case your first preference is already taken, and remember that you can be penalized for doing business under a name that tends to mislead the public)

2. The location of the business

3. The principal shareholders, their functions, and remunerations (a good attorney will help define the responsibilities of all parties from the start, avoiding a lot of future confusion and bad feelings)

4. The amount each shareholder will invest, and on what terms

5. The manner in which salaries will be distributed, and who will have control

When these crucial points have been discussed, clarified,

and decided upon, your attorney will help you file under the laws of your corporate home state, and assist you in drafting your articles of incorporation, corporate charter, and corporate bylaws. Even if your charter is simple and your company small, you can anticipate a wait of several weeks before approval is granted. In the meantime, if you've an artistic bent, you can design your corporate seal.

You may not need an attorney for the last few steps: obtaining a license (if necessary to practice your profession in your corporate home state), issuing stock certificates, and assigning property to the corporation. You will also have to draw up employment and compensation agreements, and apply for your employer identification, state employee, and sales-tax numbers from the IRS district director. Finally, set up a bank account, list your phone, print your stationery and business cards, and hang out your shingle!

Corporate Caretaking: It's vitally important to run your corporation according to state and federal standards. Slipshod corporate caretaking is to be avoided at all costs; otherwise IRS may disallow your corporate tax status. I've heard a sad tale about a casual, happy-go-lucky type who neglected to follow standard guidelines for doing business as a corporation, and as a result found himself personally liable for debts because IRS mercilessly stripped away his corporate privileges.

The rules for corporate caretaking are not all that difficult to adhere to, but adhere you must. Here are some:

1. You should call regular meetings of the board of directors and stockholders. (Meetings needn't be frequent.) Someone must record the minutes of each meeting.

2. Accounting reports, statements, insurance policies, and receipts must all be issued in the corporate name. Corporate checks must be used for all disbursements, and the corporation—not individual shareholders—must be billed directly for purchases of goods and services.

3. The corporation must own the equipment, supplies,

and accounts receivable. These items cannot be owned by you individually.

4. The corporation must file annual corporate income-tax returns, withhold from wages and pay Social Security taxes for all employees, deduct income taxes from employee salaries, and pay unemployment compensation taxes.

An attorney or accountant will fill you in on the finer points of corporate caretaking as it is defined in your corporate home state. Or you may want to write directly to the office of the Secretary of State, Department of Corporations, in the capital of your corporate home state, for a list of the required procedures.

No Hoarding of Retained Earnings Allowed!: One of the privileges of a corporation, remember, is to retain a "reasonable" portion of income for corporate use (for expansion or upgrading of the facilities, for investment, whatever) rather than distribute all income to stockholders. "Hoarding" sums in excess of what IRS considers to be "reasonable" ("reasonable" being determined by the estimated needs of your particular industry or business) is punishable by a heavy tax surcharge.

The surcharge was instituted to make corporate officers think twice about retaining earnings that would otherwise be paid out to stockholders as dividends. After all, taxes on dividends are a source of revenue for the treasury.

How do you know what amounts are reasonable to carry over from one year to the next? Take it up with your accountant; if in doubt, err on the conservative side.

Section 1244 Stock for Fail-Proofing Your Corporation: When you go into business there is always the risk of failing. If you lose everything you can get a capital loss deduction, but this is limited to low-taxed capital gains, with perhaps some small amount of ordinary income. Here's a way of starting a business that can give you a full deduction against ordinary income from any loss on your business: using Section 1244 stock.

Section 1244 stock is common stock of a small business corporation, which is defined as a corporation with the total amount of money and property it receives for its stock, as a capital contribution, and as paid-in surplus not exceeding $1 million. In case of loss, the maximum loss allowable on sale or worthlessness of such stock as a deduction against ordinary income is up to $50,000 per year on a single filing, and up to $100,000 per year on a joint return. Any loss above this is treated as a capital loss.

This deduction is available to any individual or partnership that is the original purchaser of the stock, but not to estates, corporations, or trusts, or to anyone who bought or received the stock by gift or by will from the original owner.

How to Get a Fat Tax Break on Investment Income for Your Corporation: Here's one of the less-known tax breaks available to corporations: When a corporation invests in the common or preferred stock of another corporation, 85% of the dividend income goes untaxed! To put it the other way around, your corporation pays taxes on only 15% of dividend income, Note: Dividends for preferred stock issued by utility companies before October 1, 1942, are the exception. They are only a little more than 60% tax-free.)

What it really boils down to is that the tax rate for your corporation on any stock dividend income it receives is 6.9% maximum. How's that again? Well, 46% is the maximum income-tax rate for a corporation. Multiply 46% times 15%, the percentage of dividend income on which taxes are due, and you get 6.9%.

Interest income from sources other than common or preferred stock may be taxed as follows:

First $25,000	17%
Second $25,000	20%
Third $25,000	30%
Fourth $25,000	40%
In excess of $100,000	46%

To see how investment income from dividends on common or preferred stock tallies with income from, say, bonds, let's do some comparing:

Your corporation buys some corporate bonds with a yield of 9% and some preferred stock, also yielding 9%. Assuming that your business is in the 46% tax bracket (the highest bracket for corporations), we can calculate the after-tax return on the bonds this way: 100% − 46% = 54%, the rate at which the bonds are taxed × 9%, the bond yield = an after-tax yield of 4.86%.

For the preferred stock: 100% − 6.9%, the rate at which common or preferred stock is taxed = 93.1% × the 9% stock yield = an after-tax yield of 8.38%. The after-tax yield of the preferred stock is almost double the after-tax yield of the bonds.

If you concentrate your corporate investments in preferred stock, which offers assured dividends each year, you'll have a steady cash flow of income into your business.

It sounds almost too good to be true, but it is—within limits. If a corporation derives more than 60% of its income from dividends, interest, rents, royalties, and other "passive" sources, IRS may decide to relabel it a personal holding company, and it will lose its 85% dividend exclusion tax advantage. Holding company income is taxed, by the way, at a rate of 70%.

Tax Shelter Hybrid—The Subchapter S Corporation: By now you see some of the advantages of incorporating, but you see a couple of disadvantages too—among them the lack of flow-through of profits and losses, and the element of double taxation, whereby the corporation is taxed on income, which is passed on to the shareholders as dividends and taxed again.

If bypassing these disadvantages interests you, you might want to consider setting up a Subchapter S corporation, a kind of hybrid business entity that combines many of the advantages of a "regular" corporation with special features of its own.

As a shareholder in a Subchapter S corporation your amount of liability is limited—as it is in an ordinary corporation—to the amount of your capital investment in the business, and does not extend to your personal property or assets. But in a Subchapter S corporation profits are not taxed at the corporate level but flow through directly (and are taxed directly) to you as shareholder.

Losses also flow through the "Sub S" and are taxed directly to you. This may appear to be a disadvantage, but just the opposite is true if you are in a high tax bracket. That's because you can use losses to offset your other income and thus save taxes. It is this special feature of the Subchapter S corporation that makes it an attractive tax shelter vehicle to many high-bracketed business people.

Another advantage of the Subchapter S corporation—one it shares with ordinary corporations, but which is lacking in partnership and sole proprietorship arrangements—is that the Subchapter S corporation can select its fiscal tax year.

How is this an advantage? The Subchapter S corporation distributes all undistributed profits to the shareholders on the last day of the corporation's fiscal year. Let's say the fiscal year ends January 31 and all stockholders are on a calendar year basis. The stockholders don't have to pay tax on the distribution for 11 months!

The procedure for setting up a Subchapter S corporation is similar to that of creating an ordinary corporation. However, shareholders must file a form indicating that they have elected to be taxed at the shareholder level rather than at the corporate level. The form must be filed in the first month of the year of incorporating or in the last month of the year before incorporating. Other requirements for favorable tax treatment as a Subchapter S corporation are as follows:

1. The number of shareholders must be limited to 15. (A husband and wife can be counted as one shareholder.)

2. Shareholders must be individuals (or couples); under

certain circumstances an estate or trust may own shares in a Sub S corporation (if the need arises, check with a lawyer or an accountant to find out the extent to which this is permissible; corporations may not hold shares.

3. Only one class of stock may be issued; only issued and outstanding stock may be counted.

4. The Subchapter S corporation must not have more than 20% of gross receipts from passive income sources (interest, dividends, rents, etc.) or from sales of securities (stocks and bonds).

5. No more than 80% of the sales income of the Subchapter S corporation may be derived from sources outside the United States.

How to Get a Couple of
Good Tax Breaks for Your Business

If you're a corporate bigwig, self-employed, a sole proprietor of a business, or a member of a partnership, there are a couple of good ways to shelter some of your business income—strategies that are neither very complicated nor very esoteric, but which, nevertheless, you may not have known about till now.

Equipment Leasing as a Tax Shelter Strategy for Your Business: If your company needs certain equipment, and if you set things up right, Uncle Sam will allow you some substantial tax breaks; enough, maybe, so you get back more money than you spend.

You can get these tax breaks by taking advantage of four concepts in the Tax Code: accelerated depreciation, the "class life" system of depreciation, the extra "first-year" allowance, and the investment tax credit.

Let's take an example: Your company buys a new computer with (according to IRS guidelines) a useful estimated life of nine years. (Your computer may actually be useful for 15 years or more, or go berserk in a couple of years. No matter.) The computer costs $10,000. Your company puts up $1,000 in cash and finances the balance.

As you already know, you're not allowed to deduct as a business expense the entire cost of a computer (or any other big-ticket equipment) in the year you buy it. Instead, you depreciate it and claim deductions based on that depreciation each year, usually over the number of years IRS has designated as the estimated useful life of the item.

But by using the "class life" system, you can write off the cost of your computer in seven years instead of nine! The class life system was authorized by IRS so that a taxpayer could estimate the useful life of each asset and use that life to determine depreciation. The class life system provides a broad range of guidelines within which to estimate the useful life and attempts to keep conflicts over useful lives to a minimum.

By using the 200% double declining balance method of depreciation you can get more than twice as much write-off in the first year than if you used straight-line depreciation. (In straight-line depreciation you deduct $10,000 ÷ 9 = $1,111 each year for nine years.)

In the better method you take 80% of the $10,000 cost of the computer—or $8,000—and divide by 7 (years of accelerated depreciation), then multiply by 2 (the 200% from which the method gets its name), and the result is a first-year depreciation deduction of $2,285.71! This is 206% of what you could claim using straight-line depreciation.

You can also claim a bonus depreciation deduction of 20% of the cost of equipment that has a useful life of six years or more. Since your $10,000 computer has a useful life of nine years, it qualifies for bonus depreciation of $2,000. Bonus depreciation can be claimed only in the year new equipment is purchased; but that's an extra $2,000 to add to the $2,285.71 you can claim in the first year if you use the 200% double declining balance method of depreciation. In all, then, your first-year depreciation deduction *so far* amounts to $4,285.71!

Note: You can treat equipment installed or placed in service any time during the first half of the year as if it were in service from the first day of the year. Thus, for any equipment installed up to June 30, you can claim a full year's worth of depreciation deductions when you file your tax return for the year. However, if you make this election, equipment you buy and have installed *after* June 30 of the same year cannot begin to be depreciated until January 1 of the following year. Therefore, it's always a good idea to have major equipment purchases installed before June 30.

Now back to that computer. You can claim a 10% investment tax credit on equipment or machinery that has an estimated useful life of seven years or more. Again your computer qualifies. An investment tax credit, or any tax credit, is not a deduction. It's something much better. Tax credits can be subtracted dollar for dollar from the total amount of taxes you owe for the year.

To see what the deductions plus the investment tax credit are worth to you we have to assign your business a tax bracket. Let's assume that your corporation is in the 46% tax bracket. Accelerated 200% double declining balance depreciation plus bonus depreciation gives you a deduction of $4,285.71, which in the 46% tax bracket will lower your tax bill by $1,971.43. Add to that the 10% investment tax credit, which on an item costing $10,000 is worth $1,000, and your tax savings for the first year you have the computer are $2,971.43!

And you achieved that saving by putting up only $1,000 of company money in cash—which means you've been able to get an almost 3-to-1 write-off. It's as if you were getting an interest-free loan from Uncle Sam. I call it a loan rather than an outright giveaway, because later, of course, your depreciation deductions will be less by the same amount you increased them in the first year. However, you will have had the use of the money in the meanwhile without having to pay a penny of interest.

More About the Investment Tax Credit: An investment tax credit is available on Section 38 property—new, tangible business property, including office and factory equipment and machinery as well as trucks, elevators, escalators, and certain research and storage facilities such as wind tunnels and silos. Added-on components of most buildings, such as central heating and air-conditioning systems, do not qualify; neither does real property in general, such as buildings and land.

Rehabilitating Buildings and the Investment Tax Credit: The cost of renovating or rehabilitating *older* commercial or industrial (not residential) buildings such as office buildings, retail and wholesale stores, factories, and warehouses qualifies for investment tax credit. Included among the rehabilitation or renovation procedures that are eligible for investment tax credit are installation of new wiring, flooring, plumbing, interior walls and ceilings, and heating and air-conditioning systems.

To qualify for the full 10% investment tax credit with this type of rehabilitation, the improvements must have an estimated useful life of at least seven years. You get two-thirds of the credit if the improvement has a useful life of five to seven years, and no credit if the useful life is less than five years. Also, the rehabilitation costs must have been incurred after November 1, 1978; the building must have been in use for at least 20 years before the renovation; and at least five years must have passed since the building or parts thereof were last renovated.

Closely Held Corporations: How to Take Money Out of the Company and Get Capital Gains Treatment: Let's look at a closely held family corporation. You've been in business for over ten years. The corporation has been accumulating a substantial amount of capital. You want to keep full control of the corporation and you want to get the capital out of the company and have it taxed at capital gains rates. Can it be done? Yes, and here's how:

You have set up a family business in 1968, and you own 60% of the stock, your spouse owns 20%, and your two children own 10% each. Cash has been accumulating. Your children need money for college. How do you distribute the cash and get capital gains treatment besides?

Get the corporation to purchase your children's stock. That way they realize a capital gain. The corporation must (1) purchase all of their stock, (2) the children must have owned the stock for at least ten years (if not, the distribution is taxed as a dividend), (3) your children must not reacquire stock in your corporation for the next ten years, and (4) they must give up all interest in the corporation, including being officers, directors, or employees.

Your children get their money for college, and you have not diluted your controlling interest in the corporation.

A word of caution: IRS requires your children to notify them if your children acquire any stock in the corporation within ten years from the date of the redemption. They must also file a return in the year of redemption. Otherwise the tax break will be lost. Of course, be sure to obtain professional advice.

If the children's stock is sold to another party instead of to the corporation you get the capital gains treatment, but you dilute your ownership interest and you may end up with active partners you don't want.

New Law: Corporate Rates Reduced: The corporate tax rates for taxable years beginning in 1982 will be reduced from 17% to 16% on the first $25,000 of income, and on the next $25,000 from 20% to 19%. In years beginning in 1983 and beyond, the 16% will decrease to 15%, and the 19% will be lowered to 18%.

Taxable Income	Tax Rate in Years beginning in 1981	1982	1983 and thereafter
0–$25,000	17%	16%	15%
$25,001– 50,000	20%	19%	18%

New Law: Changes in IRA and Keogh Plans: See Chapter 9 under "New Laws."

New Law: Subchapter S Corporation Shareholder Increase: For taxable years after 1981 Subchapter S corporations can increase the number of shareholders up to 25 from the past limit of 15.

New Law: Accumulated Earnings Amount Increased: Certain corporations, for the year 1981, can accumulate earnings up to $150,000 without fear of a penalty for unreasonable hoarding. For taxable years beginning in 1982, the accumulated earnings amount is increased to $250,000. However, this increase does not apply to service corporations in accounting, actuarial science, consulting, engineering, health, law, or the performing arts.

New Law: Deductions for Investment in Equipment: Taxpayers in 1982 will be able to deduct immediately up to $5,000 of equipment purchases, rather than follow a longer write-off schedule. This applies to new and used property up to the following amounts:

Year	Amount Deductible Immediately
1982 & 1983	$ 5,000
1984 & 1985	$ 7,500
1986 & on	$10,000

There is no Investment Tax Credit ("ITC") or installment sales eligibility on property expensed in this manner. Married individuals filing separate returns can expense 50% of these amounts. Gains on sales of property expensed under this provision cannot be deferred by installment sales treatment. Recapture is imposed on a disposition under the rules that apply to personal property depreciation.

New Law: Equipment Purchases for Your Business: The new tax law provides a faster method of recovering the cost of business equipment, called the accelerated cost recovery system ("ACRS"). This applies to capital expenditures for property acquired or placed in service retroactive to January 1, 1981, and up through 1984.

Most equipment will be eligible to be written off in three or five years, with some items being written off in ten years. The three-year property consists of such items as automobiles, light trucks, equipment used in research and experimentation, and other assets (such as special tools) with a guideline life under the Asset Depreciation Range ("ADR") of four years or less. The yearly deductions are 25% for the first year, 38% the second, and 37% the third.

Five-year property consists of most other equipment and machinery, as well as furniture and fixtures, single-purpose agricultural structures, and petroleum-product storage facilities. The yearly write-offs are 15%, 22%, 21%, 21%, and 21%.

The ten-year property consists of public utility equipment with a class life of 18-25 years under the old ADR guidelines as well as railroad tank cars. The yearly deductions are 8%, 14%, 12%, 10% for 3 years, and 9% for 4 years.

Class of Property	Deductions/Year									
	1	2	3	4	5	6	7	8	9	10
3-year	25%	38%	37%							
5-year	15%	22%	21%	21%	21%					
10-year	8%	14%	12%	10%	10%	10%	9%	9%	9%	9%

The entire cost can be depreciated. Salvage value is not taken into account.

In addition there is an investment tax credit of 6% for eligible property in the three-year class and 10% credit for all other eligible property (except for the 15-year class real estate to be discussed later, which does not qualify for the investment credit).

All depreciation under ACRS is subject to recapture. However, a 2% credit is earned on each year that the property is held. If you have taken the 6% ITC on a three-year class of property (a car, let's say), and sell it in the second year, you will have earned 4% credit (two years' credit of 2%), and would have to repay only 2% (6% ITC less 4% credit).

New Law: Used Property Investment Credit Limitation Raised: For taxable years beginning in 1981 through 1984, the amount of used property that can be eligible for the investment credit is increased to $125,000. From 1985 and thereafter the limit is increased to $150,000.

New Law: At-Risk Provisions Related to ITC: The ITC is limited under the new tax law in most activities to the amounts "at-risk" (except for real estate). To claim the ITC a minimum "at-risk" investment of at least 20% (25% for energy property) of the property's basis is required to receive the credit. The credit isn't allowed on amounts invested in qualifying property to the extent that the invested amounts aren't "at-risk" (as in nonrecourse financing). This applies only to property placed in service after February 18, 1981.

There is an exception allowing credit against basis acquired with nonrecourse loans from certain qualified lenders (that are unrelated to the borrower), and from direct or guaranteed federal, state, or local government loans, if the taxpayer has a minimum of 20% "at-risk" in the property. Qualified lenders include banks, insurance companies, savings and loan companies, credit unions, pension trusts, and unrelated third parties engaged in the business of loaning funds.

For solar or wind energy property, recycling equipment, qualified hydroelectric generating equipment, etc., in order to qualify for the ITC a taxpayer must have a minimum of 25% "at-risk." Any nonrecourse financing of the property must be a level payment loan (other than financing by a qualified lender).

New Law: ITC Carryover: If you have unused ITCs arising in years ending after December 31, 1974, you may carry them over for 15 years.

New Law: Lessor's ITC and Depreciation: In order to distinguish when a lease of investment property would be treated as a lease (thus allowing the credit and depreciation to go to the lessor) and not as a loan or a sale (which would disallow the ITC and depreciation), IRS had imposed severe guidelines. The new law makes it easier to insure that leases of property placed in service in 1981 would be characterized as a lease to the lessor, provided certain requirements were met:

1. Both the lessor and lessee must characterize the agreement as a lease and elect to treat the lessor as the owner of the property.

2. The lessor must be a corporation, a partnership composed of corporations, or a grantor trust in which the grantor and the beneficiaries of which are all corporations.

3. At the time that the property is placed in service, and at all times during the terms of the lease, the lessor must have a minimum "at-risk" investment of not less than 10% of the adjusted basis of the leased property.

4. The lease term (including all extensions) cannot exceed the greater of (i) 90% of the useful life of the property, or (ii) 150% of the existing ADR class life of such property.

New Law: Net Operating Loss and Investment and Other Credit Carryovers: For net operating losses ("NOL") in taxable years ending after 1976, the NOL carryover period is increased to 15 years after the loss year.

The carryover period for investment and WIN credits in years ending after 1973 is extended to 15 years. The carryover period for the new employee credit is extended to 15 years for unused credit years beginning after 1976. The alcohol fuels credit is extended to 15 years for unused credit years ending after September 30, 1980.

New Law: Optional Recovery Period: If you want, however, to defer your deductions for later years (when profits may be higher), you can depreciate the property by using the following optional recovery periods:

Class of Property	Optional Recovery Period
3-year	3, 5, or 12 years
5-year	5, 12, or 25 years
10-year	10, 25, or 35 years
15-year	15, 35, or 45 years

In the optional recovery period, depreciation is based on the straight-line method.

New Law: Investment Tax Credit for Rehabilitation Expenses: The new law eliminates the 10% investment tax credit for rehabilitation of qualified nonresidential buildings as well as repeals the 60-month amortization election for historic structures, and replaces them with the following credits, effective after December 31, 1981:

Classification	Credit Percent
Nonresidential	
30-year building	15%
40-year building	20%
Certified historic building	25%
(residential or nonresidential)	

The credit is available only if straight-line depreciation is elected. There must be a "substantial" rehabilitation during the 24-month period ending with the close of the taxable year. Except for historic structure credits, the tax basis of the building is reduced by the credit. The credit is available, however, for the portion of a rehabilitated building leased to tax-exempt organizations or governmental units after July 29, 1980.

"Certified" historic structures means that they must be certified by the Secretary of the Interior prior to taking the credit.

New Law: Low-Income Housing Rehabilitation Expenses: The amount of low-income housing rehabilitation expenses eligible for 60-month amortization was raised to $40,000 from $20,000 per dwelling unit effective for expenditures (paid or incurred) after December 31, 1981, under a program that permits responsible tenants to purchase their units at a price limiting the seller's profit. On other low-income housing expenses the $20,000 ceiling remains.

To qualify for the $40,000 limit, a low-income rehabilitation program must: (1) be certified by the Secretary of Housing and Urban Development or by a state or local government, (2) be occupied by tenants whose units are their principal residences, and (3) allow tenants who show home-ownership responsibilities to purchase their units at a price that limits the seller's profit according to a prescribed formula.

New Law: Deductibility of Corporate Gifts and Awards: The present law allows a deduction of up to $25 per year per person for gifts or awards.

However, the new law allows the deductibility of awards made for productivity, for length of service, or for safety achievement of up to $400 per award. If the award is for more than $400, it must be a "qualified plan award." A "qualifying" program is a permanent written plan that doesn't discriminate in favor of officers, highly paid employees, or stockholders. These awards can't *average* more than $400 per award, and no single award can exceed $1,600.

New Law: Corporate Charitable Deduction: A corporation's charitable contribution deduction limit was raised to 10% from 5% of taxable income, effective for tax years beginning 1982.

> Put not your trust in money, but put your money in trust.
> —OLIVER WENDELL HOLMES

11

Tax Shelters That Shelter Your Family

People give for any number of reasons, not the least being the pleasure of doing something nice for someone they care about. Then there's giving to show appreciation, giving to impress, giving to help out the needy, giving to put property out of the reach of creditors, giving to fulfill a business or political obligation, and I could probably think of 92 other reasons to give, but why bother?

The focus of this chapter is on a special kind of giving: tax-oriented giving, we'll call it.

A Lesson in the Joys of Giving: Uncle Sam says that each year you can give gifts tax-free up to $3,000 per gift (or its equivalent in real estate, stocks, bonds, and other assets). You don't have to pay a special gift tax and you can give to whomever you please—a child, each of your children, near or distant relatives, the guy behind the counter at the local dry-cleaning establishment—anyone.

During your life you can give away up to $175,625 tax-free. In addition, your husband or wife also can make any number of gifts up to $3,000 each tax-free year. Between the two of you, you can get rid of a total of $351,250 in a lifetime completely tax-free, plus $6,000 each year.

But why would you do such a wild and crazy thing as to

give away thousands of dollars a year to your children, let alone hand money over to a perfect stranger? We're talking after-tax dollars here, so even a tax-free gift is money you've already paid taxes on.

There are a couple of reasons. You're allowed to pass on up to $175,625 (or $351,250 as a couple) to any person completely tax-free, either (1) over a lifetime or (2) at death. So it might make sense, plus give you a lot of pleasure, to give *before.* you go. Note: If you give away $175,625, you do lose your estate tax exemption.

Second, you want to shift the interest the money in your gift can earn from your presumably high tax bracket to your children's presumably lower or zero tax bracket(s).

The important thing is to put your assets—some of them, anyway—into the hands of people you care about and out of the reach of IRS. In this chapter we're going to consider some techniques for achieving this goal. But first I want to take back what I said about giving to the guy at the dry cleaners. You *could* do it, but why not keep it all in the family?

Giving to Your Kids—
Whether They Deserve It or Not

When you give money or other assets to your children, you are in effect shifting income from a taxpaying donor (yourself) to nontaxpaying donees (your children).

Let's say you're in the 50% income-tax bracket and you have income-producing assets (real estate, stocks, whatever) that generate an additional $1,000 per year. You get to keep only $500 of it; the rest goes to IRS.

If you gave these assets to your child, who, let's say, is a minor, student, zero tax bracket with a personal exemption of $1,000, the child can keep every penny. Do this over a number of years for all your children and the savings becomes BIG MONEY.

Don't Be an Indian Giver (Giving the Way Indians Were Given To): When you make a gift, especially for tax reasons, the gift must be bona fide. Legally this means you have irrevocably transferred legal title, and are barred from having control over the gift, to which you have given up all rights and interest. If you attach strings, you risk the gift being considered incomplete, and losing your tax benefits.

Therefore, before you decide to give to your children or, say, to aid aging parents, consider carefully whether you can truly afford to sign away your rights to the assets, permanently. Once they're given, they're gone.

How to Simplify Giving to Children: There are a few potential problems. For one thing the child, assuming he or she is old enough to amble over to the bank and sign a withdrawal slip, can use the money as he or she pleases. The kid wants a moped, the kid gets a moped. You can express displeasure and forbid the child to ride it (you have not signed away *all* parental rights), but you cannot bar the withdrawal of funds or the purchase.

Also, by law minors cannot sell stock or real estate; they can be stuck with a dead horse if assets keep declining toward zero.

The Uniform Gifts to Minors Act removes some of these problems. The donor (you), or another adult, or perhaps a trust company, functions as custodian of the child's assets. The custodian can invest, reinvest, or spend the assets prudently for the support, education, or benefit of the child. When the child attains majority, assets and accumulated interest pass directly to him or her.

It may be tempting to name yourself custodian. If you do, you retain a certain amount of control over the money or property, and you may well believe that no one is more concerned about nurturing and developing these assets for your child than you are.

That may be so. However, should you die before the child

attains majority your custodianship will become a liability, since your gift or gifts will revert to your estate and can be taxed accordingly. This can be avoided by naming as custodian another family member, such as your brother, sister, an aunt or uncle—whoever's sharpest or most amenable to your suggestions for managing the income.

Also, if you are custodian of your child's assets, and you turn around and use the money to discharge ordinary parental obligations such as buying clothing or food for the child or paying the rent or the mortgage, you've attached strings to the gift, and the taxes revert back to you.

Under the act, interest and income to the child are taxable to the child, who like grown-up taxpayers is allowed the $100 dividend exclusion and a $1,000 personal exemption to offset taxes on his or her assets. However, if this is done, the child may not also claim the benefit of the $2,200 zero tax bracket exemption.

Before giving your child assets or money according to the Uniform Gifts to Minors Act (which, incidentally, has not been accepted by some states, Georgia and South Carolina, for example), check with your lawyer or accountant about the income-tax, estate-tax, and gift-tax implications.

Putting a Gift in the Child's Name: All too often this phrase is considered a euphemism meaning *temporarily* shifting assets.

IRS, unfortunately, doesn't look at it that way. To IRS gifts, like diamonds, are forever!

A Common Gift Strategy to Avoid: Some of my clients have made the mistake of "giving" to their children by putting real estate and other assets in joint names with them. This bollixes everyone up and is probably the worst way to give. You can't sell or trade the assets without the consent of the child—who, being a minor, is not eligible to give such consent. (You can sometimes get around this with a court order, but who needs the hassle?) Also, as a joint owner you continue to owe taxes on your share of the income. And finally, if you die the *entire* gift will be included in your estate and taxed accordingly. The child will have to stand in line with all the others, behind IRS, to get his or her share of what's left.

How About a Little Trust for Your Child?: If there's a large amount of money involved, you should investigate the possibility of setting up a trust for your child or children. Among the advantages of trusts, you as parent or guardian retain control over the following:

1. How the trust income is to be managed
2. How the income is to be distributed and/or accumulated
3. Duration of the trust
4. When the principal of the trust is to be made available to the child
5. How the principal is to be distributed
6. Who the trustee will be
7. Who, in the event that the first trustee dies (or if you are unhappy with the advice and decisions made on behalf of your child) will be named successor

The first step is to consult with a lawyer who specializes in trusts and estates, or to sit down and discuss the matter with the trust officer of a bank.

Family Trusts You Should Know About

There are at least 21 kinds of trusts, plus, as one estate-planning expert has said, "multitudinous variations on these basic categories."

We will concentrate on the trusts that further the financial security of your family and at the same time offer tax-sheltering benefits. Most of them can help provide the money for your children's college education if that's an important part of your planning. Or, failing college (get it?), they can give the kids a nice nest egg to start out with.

An Education in Short-Term Trusts: Imagine this: You have a seven-year-old son and already you're biting your nails down to the quick trying to figure out how you're going to swing a college education for the little fella. Tuition costs are running neck and neck with inflation (if not ahead) and you estimate you're going to need at least $7,500 per year— or about $30,000 in all—to send your son through four years of a good, not necessarily top-drawer, university.

One of your options is to set up, with the aid of a lawyer experienced in trust and estate planning, a short-term or "Clifford" trust. Such a trust is noncancelable and must be in force for at least ten years. Money accumulates for your son each year via income-producing property, such as stocks, bonds, and real estate, which you have transferred to the trust. (Be sure to include enough stock so that your son can make use of the $100 tax-free dividend exclusion.)

Over the years, the income earned by your contributions will earn more income—enough, if the trust is managed wisely and the income is invested in a safe, high-yield savings account or other money market instrument—to provide the necessary college money when your son turns 17. You will need to give your son, through the trust, enough property to generate $2,000 per year in income. Your son, again through the trust, pays taxes on the income. You don't.

Your son can't take advantage of the zero bracket amount (standard deduction), since it applies only to "earned" income and not to interest income, which is what your son is getting. So the unutilized zero bracket of $2,300 is added to his income; however, he can apply the $1,000 personal exemption deduction and the $100 dividend exclusion against it.

In the first few years the trust is in force he'll have a total taxable yearly income of $4,300 ($2,000 in interest income plus the unutilized $2,300 zero bracket amount), less $1,100 (the $1,000 personal exemption, plus the $100 dividend exclusion) or $3,200. This will cost about $126 a year in taxes. This will rise in future years as interest income accumulates. Even so, he will have an average of $1,874 each year for ten years, which, with the savings interest from the bank, will give him enough for college.

Now what's in this for you, besides peace of mind?

Let's assume you're in the 50% tax bracket, which means that in order to get the extra $30,000 to send your son to college, you'd need to earn an extra $60,000. A short-term trust relieves you of that necessity.

In addition, by removing $2,000 in income from your income each year, you're slicing $1,000 a year from your tax bill.

But that's not all. As long as the money your son receives from the trust is not spent on his support, he remains your dependent and you are eligible to claim him as one at least until he is 19—longer, if he continues as a full-time student.

And, oh yes. When the trust period is over, your property comes back to you.

There is one pitfall you must avoid if the short-term trust is going to accomplish its twin goals: college money for your son and tax benefits for you. You must not allow any of the trust income to be used to feed, house, and clothe your son. You will be taxed on any trust income used to assist you in meeting these basic parental obligations.

Be especially wary about signing any agreement that states you will be responsible for your son's expenses, such as the agreement usually included in applications for college enrollment. If you sign such an agreement you may be hit with a bill for taxes on the trust income, even though the trustee paid for all of the boy's college expenses. No, Virginia, the world is not always fair.

Ideally you should bow out of the financial picture the moment the trust has been set into motion. After that, don't sign agreements, don't pay bills, don't respond in any way to your son's creditors should he turn out to be a wastrel. Instead, refer requests for money to the trustee (which will probably be a pleasant change)!

If a trust is set up early enough, as in our example where

the child is about seven—even earlier would be better—by the time the money is needed for college the trust can be dissolved. The question of using trust income to discharge legal obligations should not even arise.

The Multiple Payout Trust: If you have more than one child, consider a multiple payout trust, really a system of separate trusts usually administered by a single trustee. If you need to provide college income for several children, the multiple payout trust makes more sense than a single short-term trust. That goes double if there is a lot of money involved, because in a multiple payout trust each child is considered to be a separate taxpayer and can shelter up to $1,100 a year by using his or her personal exemption and dividend exclusion.

But don't set up a multiple payout trust for one child. The income from each trust increases the child's tax burden to the point where returns are diminished.

2503(C)—Trusts or Accumulation Trusts: Believe it or not, a 2503(C) is not a *Star Wars* robot, but the code name of another kind of short-term (ten-year) trust—named after the tax regulation, 2503(C), which defines it. This "accumulation" trust salts away tax-deferred money and can be very useful in family financial planning.

You set up the trust (or rather, you have a lawyer or bank trust officer set it up for you) in the name of your child, and immediately begin to transfer income-producing assets to the trust. But the trust, instead of distributing the income, retains or "accumulates" it. As a result no tax is paid on income during the accumulation period.

A trustee is appointed to reinvest the earnings, and then, at the expiration of the trust, the trustee distributes the income accumulation in a lump sum to the child. The assets revert back to you. (Or you can have the child retain the assets too.)

If the child is under 21 when the ten-year trust period expires, the accumulated income (as well as the property assets, if that's the option you choose) is transferred to the child tax-free! However, if your child is 21 or older when the trust expires, the income is taxed. Obviously, to avoid the tax, it's better to get this kind of trust going when your child is ten or even younger.

You should also know that the income generated by a 2503(C) trust is not necessarily frozen until the expiration date: The trustee can take income out of the trust to pay for things that the child may need, such as orthodontia work or summer camp. And finally, the accumulated income can be taxed if the trust has been in effect for more than ten years. However, taxes are billed to the trust (that is, paid out of trust funds) and not to you!

What If You End Up a Recipient of a Trust—and Don't Need It? Let's look at you as the beneficiary of a trust. You appreciate the extra money, but as you already are in a high tax bracket, you want to give the income to a family member and then pick it up for yourself when you retire.

You can make an irrevocable assignment of the income of the trust to whomever you choose, by which you part with control over the trust for not less than ten years. The person assigned the interest in the trust pays any taxes that the trust generates. Thus you create a short-term trust out of your interest in your own trust.

Be sure you satisfy all the rules for a short-term trust. You must surrender all control of the income, or you will have to pay taxes on that income. Seeking professional advice is a must.

2503(B) or "Income" Trusts: This trust variation requires that income be distributed annually to the child or other beneficiary. The advantage of this trust over the short-term and accumulation trusts is that the principal and income do not have to be distributed at age 21. The trust is open-ended in that it has no built-in expiration date. It can distribute income once a year to your child for the rest of his or her life, or you can have it terminated in 15 years or 25 years or 38½ years for that matter. It's up to you as grantor.

This kind of trust is also more flexible in that the principal you contribute doesn't automatically revert to you or to the beneficiary; you can name a third party to receive it.

Because the trust is structured to require annual income distribution, gifts to it qualify for the gift-tax exclusion not available in the other trusts. That's the good news.

Now here's the potential bad news: The annual income distribution must be made to the child, who—depending on how "childish" he or she is in your estimation—may spend it in ways you consider foolish. (However, better to have the *income* going to the child than the *principal*, right?)

This risk can be gotten around to some extent by having the income placed in a custodial account for the child's benefit. Remember, when the child turns 21, the account must be handed over to the child.

Annual income distribution to the child is taxable to the child, who, of course, can offset the tax with the $1,000 personal exemption and the $100 interest exclusion. However, if you use the income to discharge ordinary parental support obligations, you pay the taxes.

Crummey Trusts May Be Best: A Crummey trust really isn't crummy, or it would be spelled that way. Actually, it is named after a Mr. Crummey, who sort of figured it out all by himself. Crummey trusts, I might add, are the rage now.

The mechanics allow you and your spouse to combine your individual annual $3,000 tax-free gift allowance and contribute it all to the trust for as many years as you like— or until you've used up your combined gift-tax exclusion of $351,250. You can include in your contributions both income- and nonincome-producing assets.

There's no mandatory annual distribution of funds to the child. He or she can make withdrawals or not, depending on how you set up the trust.

The trust has no specified expiration date; it can stay in force for any number of years after the child reaches 21;

income from the trust can accumulate indefinitely. There are taxes on the income, but these are billed to the trust.

Some of the best things in life are Crummey!

Discuss all your trust options with a lawyer experienced in trusts and estate planning or with a bank trust officer, asking for an explanation of the pros and cons of each. Take notes and collect available printed information. I guarantee that the figures and seemingly endless details will give you a headache, but don't make a snap decision just to get the whole thing over with. Sleep on it. Maybe several nights in a row. Then try to reach a decision based on what's best for you and your family's financial circumstances.

Do-It-Yourself Trust Alternative:
An Interest-Free Loan to Your Kid(s)

How's this for a corker of a tax-deferring strategy? Draw up a note giving your child an interest-free loan. The loan is not considered a gift, and it shifts income, and thus taxes, from your presumably high tax bracket to your child's lower one.

Here's how my Uncle Charlie did it: He made out an interest-free demand note, lending his son $50,000, payable at the end of seven years—at which time Steve will have graduated from college.

The $50,000 was invested in a high-yield money market fund that earned interest at 10% annually, generating $5,000 of income per year. Steve is taxed on the $5,000, but at a lower tax level than Uncle Charlie would pay.

When Steve graduates, Charlie will demand payment on the note and retrieve the $50,000 from the money market fund. He has a lower tax bracket, avoiding gift tax, and retaining control of the money.

If you choose this kind of do-it-yourself trust, don't forget to draw up a note clearly indicating the terms of the loan. You may want to have a lawyer take a look at it to check for any ambiguities; you may have it notarized. Not that you don't trust your son. It's just that IRS has this craving for documentation.

Another Alternative: Help Your Child Start a Business

Your son or daughter wants to start a business. The cost is $25,000. Here's a way to do it that maximizes your tax break if the business goes under.

Set up a Subchapter S corporation with you holding the stock in the company. In such a corporation profits and losses are passed on directly to the stockholders. If the business fails you will be able to deduct the loss on your own personal return. (Subchapter S corporations are explained in detail in Chapter 10.)

Have the stock issued be Section 1244 stock, that is, stock of a small-business corporation (capital and paid-in surplus under $1,000,000). If the company goes out of business you can deduct up to $50,000 per year on a single return, or up to $100,000 on a joint return against ordinary income. If the business is successful—about time we mentioned this possibility—you will get capital gains treatment on the profits when you sell.

Take care not to give your son or daughter the money directly. Then if the business fails, the loss will go to your child, and not to you! Chances are he or she would not be able to make good tax use of it.

New Law: Estate and Gift Tax Changes for Spouses:
The new tax bill provides a major reduction in estate and gift taxes (see Chapter 13), which will greatly alleviate the burden of these taxes on small- and medium-sized estates. After 1981 the new law eliminates the tax entirely for gifts and bequests between spouses. You can leave your entire estate without any limits to your spouse and not pay a penny tax.

New Law: Maximum Tax Reduced: The maximum limits of gift and estate taxes have been reduced from 70% to 65% in 1982, 60% in 1983, 55% in 1984, and 50% thereafter. Those individuals with large estates should postpone dying for a number of years.

New Law: Increase in Annual Gift Tax Exclusion: You can, beginning in 1982, give up to $10,000 a year (up from $3,000) to any individual donee each year without paying gift tax. A husband and wife may transfer up to $20,000 per donee every year absolutely gift tax free. Also provided are unlimited exclusions for amounts paid for the benefit of a donee for medical and school tuition expenses.

New Law: Current Use Valuation: Real property ordinarily must be included in a decedent's estate at its highest and best use. However, family farms, timberland, and real property used in an active trade or a closely held business may be valued, if certain conditions are met, on the basis of their current use. The resulting reduction in the taxable estate based on current use valuation prior to 1981 could not exceed $500,000. In 1981 this limitation has been increased to $600,000, in 1982 to $700,000, and in 1983 and thereafter to $750,000.

New Law: Transfers Made Within Three Years of Death: Most gift transfers made within three years before death are no longer included in the gross estate. However, for the purposes of determining qualifications under current use valuation, deferred payment of estate tax, and

qualified redemptions to pay estate tax, the gifts made
within three years of death are included.

The trouble with being a breadwinner nowadays is that the government is in for such a big slice.

—MARY McCOY

12

Tax Advice for the Single, Widowed, or Divorced Woman

We've had a strong women's movement in this country for a good 15 years now. The focus has been on erasing sex bias in education, attaining equal opportunities for jobs and career advancement, and then, of course, there is the ongoing battle to secure abortion rights. It seems to me too little attention has been paid by the women's movement to what should be a major concern in anyone's life: creating and preserving financial resources and capital.

I see indications that the situation is beginning to change, especially for many single, widowed, and divorced women. More and more they have the responsibility of being the breadwinner and are seeking financial advice. As they do, financial experts are responding by offering sound guidelines for effective money management geared specifically to the woman who is on her own.

I dislike generalities, but it seems to me that the woman on her own tends to have a greater interest in security than that of the average man or married woman. Maybe that's because women are not usually brought up to think of themselves as future earners and managers of money, and the novelty of the situation unnerves them. Faced with the responsibilities of being breadwinners—whether for themselves only, or also for their children or other dependents—there is a tendency for many women to be conservative in their approach to investments, to be somewhat less willing to take risks than many men. That's not a bad thing.

Here are some solid, commonsense, taxwise guidelines.

Life Insurance: If you have no dependents, you may not need to spend money on life insurance except as it affects business matters. (For this see Chapter 8.) If you are financially responsible for others, you should investigate the kinds of policies available, beginning with Savings Bank Life Insurance (SBLI), which offers good benefits at the lowest rates.

Health, Disability, and Accident Insurance are musts. They can keep the financial bottom from dropping out in emergency situations. To find out more about your options, consult an experienced life insurance agent.

Fire and Theft Insurance for your home and possessions is another must—one that is, unfortunately, often overlooked by single women. The common thinking seems to be "I have so little of any value, why bother with insurance?" But there's another way to look at the matter. Think of the *replacement* cost of all those "valueless" things you own. One apartment break-in, for example, could result in the loss of most of your wardrobe, your TV and/or stereo, and your small appliances, not to mention any jewelry or cash lying around. It adds up. Without insurance you're either going to have to live without your lost possessions or spend quite a bit of money (possibly earmarked for other purposes) to replace them.

It doesn't make sense not to have fire and theft insurance. Rates tend to be low and the coverage, rather generous—depending on the company you deal with and where you live.

Medicare and Social Security Benefits: If you're anywhere near retirement age you should acquaint yourself with the range of benefits offered by the federal government via Medicare and the Social Security Administration. For complete information, call or write your local Social Security office. You'll find the address in the phone book under the U.S. Government listings.

Tax-Deferred Retirement Programs: There are many alternatives. Many employers offer company-sponsored pension plans. If you're not sure about your company, make a point of asking the person in charge of employee benefits. If your employer doesn't offer a retirement program, consider setting up one of your own. (See Chapter 9.)

How and Why to Establish a Line of Credit—Even if You Don't Need Credit Now: In building a financial identity of your own it's important to develop a reputation for credit worthiness so you'll be able to borrow money if you ever need it. It's much easier to negotiate a loan if you've had loans in the past and paid them back on time. In fact, that's one of the major criteria for obtaining a loan. If you've never borrowed and have no credit history, it may be difficult indeed to scare up extra cash when you want it.

You may want to use this technique to establish a good credit rating: Go to a bank, sit down with one of the loan officers, and ask him or her how much the bank is willing to lend you, based on your current earnings, expenses, and so on. Chances are they won't trust you for much. But whatever the amount, borrow it, then quickly pay it back.

A few months later you can apply for another loan for a somewhat larger amount. Again take the money, put it in a savings account, and quickly pay it back.

I've known several people who've successfully used this technique to establish a good line of credit. Some of them have negotiated as many as four or five "trial loans," each one greater than the last; now they can borrow substantial sums if they ever really need to.

Another way to establish a credit history is to open a couple of department store charge accounts and apply for a major credit card. Use your new charging privileges sparingly, being sure to pay the balance in full when due. (Avoid installment payments if you can; finance charges can amount to 18% annually.)

Don't overdo your new credit power. Try to hold your indebtedness (not including mortgage payments) to less than 20% of your yearly income. (Traditionally, people have been advised to spend no more than 25% of their income on housing, including real estate taxes. But no one has to remind you that in recent years this rule has become increasingly difficult to follow. In areas like New York City you're lucky if you can hold it down to 30%.)

Know Your Credit Rights: As a woman, you should be aware of your rights:

1. Banks and other lending institutions *must* count as income any alimony and child support payment being made to you by a former husband.

2. You cannot be refused credit solely on the basis of your sex or marital status.

3. A potential creditor has no legal right to ask your intentions about bearing children.

4. A potential creditor has no legal right to ask about your ex-husband or his credit history unless he is directly involved in the loan negotiations, either as cosigner or as the owner of assets used to secure the loan.

How to Check Up on Your Present Credit Rating: You can obtain a copy of your current credit profile by calling either of the following companies for information: TRW Credit Data, (212) 233-8569; or Transunion Credit Bureau, (212) 239-2000.

Savings: Alternatives to the Traditional Savings Account: Reserve funds are important. Only you can determine how much you can or should keep on hand for emergencies. Whatever the amount, don't "borrow" from it for vacations or luxuries. You may be better off opening two or more accounts for money left over after everyday expenses have been met. One can be your emergency fund, and a second, straight savings for future purchases. A third can be started to accumulate money to be used later for investment purposes.

About the alternatives to stashing your money away in a regular account at a savings bank, it's not that I'm knocking savings banks; it's just that the interest rate on an ordinary account is so low—about 5¾% currently.

A good alternative is to keep money in a money market fund. The rate of interest can be 10% or more. Many of the funds offer check-writing privileges so that some or all of your money can be withdrawn instantly and used to pay bills, and so on. Money market funds are also known as SLY investments because they provide Safety, Liquidity, and a good Yield.

To find out more about these funds pick up a copy of the *Wall Street Journal*; almost all of them advertise there regularly. Or you can check *Forbes* or other financial magazines.

Certificates of deposit—CDs for short—are another alternative to think about. Offered by most banks, they pay interest rates equal to or even higher than those of the money market funds. The trouble with CDs is that they lock up your funds for at least six months—and up to three or even five years! You can touch your money during that time, but a heavy penalty will be charged. (Note: The penalty is tax-deductible!)

You may want to consider saving via U.S. Treasury bills; the interest is exempt from state and city income taxes. Check with your local banker or stockbroker.

If you have money available for investment purposes or tax shelters, consult with qualified investment advisers. The best way to locate them might be to ask friends who have had experience or dealings with them.

While you're discussing your overall financial situation with an investment adviser, you might bring up trusts.

Sometimes a trust can help a single person save on taxes and at the same time provide additional security. If you're supporting a parent or child(ren), a short-term trust can be an excellent tax-saving, income-stretching vehicle. Be sure you understand all the implications of a trust before committing yourself. (See Chapter 11.)

Special Tax Tip for Widows: If you have been widowed very recently—within the last tax year—you may file a joint tax return with your deceased husband if you have not remarried. (If you have, you can file a joint tax return with your new husband.) If you file jointly with the deceased, you compute your taxes as though he had lived through the year. However, only the portion of the decedent's income received before his death is included on the tax return.

In addition to your filing a joint return in the year in which your spouse died, you can use the joint return tax rates, if you qualify, for two additional years. Here's how: (1) stay unmarried, (2) maintain a household that is the principle home for your and his children or stepchildren, and (3) have been entitled to file a joint return with your spouse for the year of his death. You do not actually file a joint return, but are allowed to use the tax rates that apply to a joint return.

Every newly widowed woman should call her local Social Security office to explain her circumstances and find out whether any special provisions are available to her. If your deceased husband was a veteran, don't neglect to mention it: You may be entitled to receive additional benefits.

A Few Suggestions for Planning Your Estate: Taxes can be particularly hard on the estates of single people—whether never married, divorced, or widowed—since the marital deduction that allows half of an estate to be passed on tax-free to a spouse doesn't apply.

If you plan to leave everything to your children, or have some other beneficiary in mind, do everything possible in years to come to minimize taxes on your estate. (See Chapters 11 and 13.) However, don't give away now what you may need later just to avoid estate taxation at your death.

Consider setting up a life-insurance policy that will provide for the payment of taxes on your estate, leaving the estate itself more or less intact.

An attorney who specializes in estate planning can help you plan your estate so that the major portion goes to your beneficiaries and not to IRS.

Divorcing the Government Out of Taxes If You're the One Paying Alimony: If you're reading this chapter as a woman contemplating divorce or legal separation, but not yet unhitched, I urge you to consult with your lawyer and to have him or her point out all the tax consequences of the proposed action before you sign anything.

If you happen to be in the situation of some of the more successful young women I know, who are bucking tradition and planning to pay alimony to their ex-husband-to-be, keep in mind that you can't deduct a lump-sum financial settlement. You can deduct periodic alimony payments if they conform to any one of the following requirements:

1. The payments are made under a decree of divorce or separate maintenance, or are made under a written instrument "incident" to divorce or separation

2. The payments are made under a written separation agreement

3. The payments are made under a court-ordered decree of support

Don't agree to a settlement where you pay alimony at regular intervals for less than ten years, and it is possible to calculate the exact sum of the payments promised. This leads to loss of tax deduction because the payments will be treated as installments of a lump-sum settlement and will be disallowed.

If your husband and his lawyer insist on such an arrangement, you should insist on a contingency agreement that payments will terminate if he remarries. Then you may get the deduction, since the sum of the installment to be paid can be changed by his remarriage.

If for some reason you must pay a specific amount, arrange to pay it over a period of more than ten years. Then your payments are deductible if the installments you pay in any one year don't add up to more than 10% of the total amount.

Alimony payments are not an itemized deduction; they are deducted from your gross income. This is fortunate for you, because if you take the standard deduction you can subtract the alimony too.

One of the more bizarre strategies being tried by some couples with separate incomes is to divorce near the end of one year so one of them can pick up alimony deductions, and then remarry at the beginning of the next year. This no longer works. IRS doesn't recognize these "divorces" but considers the couple to have been married all along.

If you are serious about divorcing, it is important that you transfer your property interests under a written separation agreement and then obtain a final decree of divorce within two years. If you do not act within the time limit, the transfer will not be exempt from gift tax.

Property settlements may have other, unexpected tax consequences. Keep in mind that property settlements can be treated as a taxable event. When property is transferred according to a divorce decree or separation agreement, the transferor will have a realized gain or loss, which often comes as a surprise. Gain or loss will be determined by the difference between the adjusted basis of the property and its fair market value.

In community property states (Arizona, California, Idaho, Louisiana, Nevada, New Mexico, Texas, and Washington State) there is an execption to the rule recognizing gain or loss on transfers of property between divorcees: The divorced parties make an equal division of community property. Under Oklahoma law, "jointly acquired" property (similar to community property) is treated much like community property. This does not apply under Kansas law. Under Florida law, community property has been applied in the case of property held by the spouses as "tenants by the entirety."

Who Gets the Deduction? Custody battles are horrifying enough without the added hassle over who gets the dependency deduction for a child. There's a lot of legal mumbo jumbo on the books, but basically it boils down to this:

The parent who contributes the greater amount to the child's support (and who can prove it if necessary) is entitled to claim the child as a dependent. An exception is when the separation agreement or divorce decree specifically states that one parent may claim the child as a dependent regardless of how much that parent contributes to the child's support.

An interesting tax fact about child support payments: Unlike alimony, which is deductible by one spouse and taxed as income to the other, child support payments are neither deductible nor treated as income.

New Law: Contribution by a Divorced Spouse: A divorced individual is allowed to take a deduction for contributions to a spousal IRA established by her or his former spouse at least five years before the divorce, if the former spouse contributed to the IRA under the spousal IRA rules for at least three of the five years preceding the divorce. These contributions are limited to the lesser of (1) $1,125, or (2) the sum of the divorced spouse's compensation and alimony includable in their gross income.

He that dies pays all debts.
—SHAKESPEARE

13

Keeping the Feds at Bay
When You Die

How about projecting yourself way, way into the future? There you are, a fat cat with a big estate that you've worked your tail off to accumulate. What other tactics, besides the ones we've already discussed, can you use to make sure that your family gets more and the feds get less of what you leave behind?

For a better understanding, you need to know about how estates were taxed in the past and how the important changes resulting from the Tax Reform Acts of 1976 and 1978 affected estate taxation.

New Estate-Tax Basics

The estate tax is an excise tax levied on the transfer of property of the deceased. The first federal estate tax ("death tax") was created by the Tax Reform Act of September 8, 1916. With modifications, the act has been part of our tax laws ever since.

The biggest changes came with the Tax Reform Act of 1976. Before the Act there was a $60,000 estate-tax exemption—meaning no tax on the first $60,000 of the estate. There was also a one-time $30,000 gift-tax exemption: Once in a lifetime you could give away assets worth up to $30,000 in one year without having to pay gift tax.

The Act of 1976 unified estate and gift taxes. In over-simplified terms, taxable estate equals gifts of property and other assets during the life of the deceased plus assets transferred or "gifted" at death. Gifts on which taxes were paid during the life of the deceased are subtracted.

Unified Estate and Gift Tax Rates

Taxable transfer more than—	But not more than—	Tax on amount in col. (1)	Rate of tax on excess of amount in col. (1)
(1)	(2)	(3)	(4)
$ 0	$ 10,000	0	18%
10,000	20,000	1,800	20%
20,000	40,000	3,800	22%
40,000	60,000	8,200	24%
60,000	80,000	13,000	26%
80,000	100,000	18,200	28%
100,000	150,000	23,800	30%
150,000	250,000	38,800	32%
250,000	500,000	70,800	34%
500,000	750,000	155,800	37%
750,000	1,000,000	248,300	39%
1,000,000	1,250,000	345,800	41%
1,250,000	1,500,000	448,300	43%
1,500,000	2,000,000	555,800	45%
2,000,000	2,500,000	780,800	49%
2,500,000	3,000,000	1,025,800	53%
3,000,000	3,500,000	1,290,800	57%
3,500,000	4,000,000	1,575,800	61%
4,000,000	4,500,000	1,880,800	65%
4,500,000	5,000,000	2,205,800	69%
5,000,000		2,550,800	70%

Before the Tax Reform Act of 1976, when gift and estate taxes were separate, gifts made within three years before death were included in the gross estate if IRS felt there was good reason to believe that the gifts were made in contemplation of dying. The rule led to endless haggling, since it was usually impossible to prove one way or the other. The "contemplation of death" criterion no longer exists. All gifts and transfers of assets made within three years before death are now treated as part of the decedent's gross estate.

The Reform Act of 1976 increased the marital deduction for lifetime gifts to a spouse and for property passing from a decedent to a surviving spouse from 50% of the value of the gift and the value of the adjusted gross estate, to the greater of $250,000 or 50% of the adjusted gross estate. This allowed more property to pass to the surviving spouse tax-free on estates under $500,000 than before. Let's see how this works:

On an estate worth $400,000, the pre-1977 rules said that 50% would be eligible for the marital deduction; $200,000 would go to the surviving spouse tax-free. Under the new rules $250,000 would go to the spouse tax-free.

There is now an unlimited gift-tax marital deduction for the first $100,000 in gifts given to a spouse. Gifts over $100,000 up to $200,000 given to a spouse are taxed fully. Gifts over $200,000 are taxed after 50% marital deduction.

The concept of a unified gift and estate tax credit was new. A tax credit is subtracted from taxes due (not from the estate), so it counts for more. The unified credit was phased in as follows:

In 1977 a $30,000 credit was allowed, equivalent to $120,000 worth of exemptions.

In 1978 a $34,000 credit was allowed, equivalent to $134,-000 in exemptions.

In 1979 a $38,000 credit was allowed, equivalent to $147,333 in exemptions.

In 1980 a $42,500 credit was allowed, equivalent to $161,563 in exemptions.

And in 1981 and thereafter (or until estate-tax laws are modified again) a $47,000 credit is allowed, equivalent to

Death Costs and Taxes Levied on the Estate of a Decedent

Category of Cost or Tax	Definitions	General Information	Valuation and Deductions	Costs and Calculations
Probate	A legal "receivership" over which the probate court has jurisdiction. An executor (by will) or an administrator (under intestacy) is appointed to manage the probate estate. He is responsible for paying all obligations, and distributing the balance to the beneficiaries.	Obligations of the estate consist of: debts; executors', attorneys', accountants', and appraisers' fees; court costs; bonds; casualty insurance premiums; preparation of tax returns; publication fees; title search fees; etc.	Costs are levied on the general assets of the estate and constitute a lien on the assets. Costs are generally computed on the gross values of assets subject to testamentary disposition; life insurance not payable to estate and jointly held property do not pass through probate.	In general, probate expenses will approximate 5% ($5,000 minimum) of the gross probate estate. The rates and fees will vary from one court jurisdiction to another. Obligations must be paid before the probate proceedings can be concluded.
Federal Estate Tax	A tax on the privilege of making a transfer of property, at death. In general, the tax is imposed on the value of all property in which the decedent had an interest at the time of his death.	Value includable in the gross estate: extent of ownership held in property; income in which the decedent had vested interests; joint tenant property; powers of appointment; annuities and life-insurance proceeds.	Valuation is "fair market" at death or alternate date of six months. Deductions: probate costs; claims and indebtedness; marital deduction (allowed for up to greater of $250,000 or ½ adjusted gross estate	Tax rates scale from 18% to 70%. EXAMPLE Gross estate $2,200,000 Less probate costs − 200,000 Adjusted gross estate $2,000,000 Less marital deduction −1,000,000 Taxable estate (tentative tax base) $1,000,000

	ceeds in which the decedent had "incidents of ownership."	tate passing to a surviving spouse either outright or as a life interest with a power of appointment); charitable bequests; credit for state and gift tax; orphans' exclusion.	Tentative tax $ 345,800 Less: Unified credit — 47,000 State death tax credit — 33,200 Estate tax payable $265,600
State Death Taxes: Inheritance and Estate	Inheritance taxes are levied on the right of a person to receive property. Thirty-nine states have inheritance taxes. Nine states have a state estate tax similar to the federal estate tax. Most states have an additional tax which brings the total taxes up to the amount of credit allowed against the federal estate tax.	Generally the property taxed is that which the decedent owned at his death and which passed to others by his will or the laws of intestacy. 1. Life-insurance proceeds paid to insured's estate are generally taxed. 2. Life-insurance proceeds paid to named beneficiaries are usually wholly or partly exempt from tax.	Most inheritance taxes are graduated and levied against each heir's share separately. The exemptions and tax rates vary depending on the relationship of the beneficiary to the decedent. Generally, the closer the relationship, the greater the exemption and the lower the tax rate. Tax rates and exemptions are different for each state. Refer to your state's death taxes.

$175,000 in exemptions. This means there are no taxes due on estates that do not exceed $175,000!

The Tax Reform Act of 1976 created new rulings on joint property. The entire value of jointly owned property used to be included in the decedent's estate—and was thus subject to estate taxes—except for whatever part of the property the surviving spouse could prove was directly attributable to him- or herself.

But now 50% of joint property is included in the decedent's gross estate, the other 50% being retained by the surviving spouse, with no consideration being given as to which of them had earned, inherited, or accumulated the property in the first place.

Joint bank accounts are an exception. The reasoning is that since each spouse can make withdrawals from a joint bank account at his or her discretion, the account can't be nailed down as joint property. Or so says the IRS.

Funds in joint bank accounts are apportioned according to who contributed what. If the spouse is to get half without paying estate tax on it, the spouse must have contributed half.

Estate-Tax Strategy Based on a Marital Deduction Trust: Now that you know some of the basics of the recently revised estate- and gift-tax laws, you may want to consider strategies for using the new rules.

One such strategy starts where the marital deduction ruling leaves off. It can go a long way toward making sure that your family will be well provided for and your estate managed efficiently when you're no longer around to see to it yourself.

Have two trusts set up. The first will be a marital deduction trust. The marital deduction provides that the greater of $250,000 or half your adjusted gross estate goes to your spouse tax-free. Whichever is the greater amount provides the start-up funds for the trust. Don't name anyone but your spouse as lifetime beneficiary of the income from this trust, not even your children—your spouse should be the sole lifetime beneficiary, otherwise you'll be wasting the marital deduction.

Your spouse should have the power to appoint new beneficiaries of the trust when he or she dies. Your children will be the new beneficiaries. (If your spouse does not exercise this power of appointment, you can do it yourself. Name the children.)

The second trust, the nonmarital trust, should include your spouse and your children as beneficiaries. Start-up assets for this trust come out of the taxable portion of your estate. This trust should be structured so that when your spouse dies, its assets are not included in his or her estate, but instead pass tax-free directly to the children. The property in this trust will have been fully taxed at your death. Hence, if it is set up to provide income for your spouse for the rest of his or her life and then the property is distributed to your children, estate taxes are effectively avoided.

When you set up the two trusts, appoint a trustee, someone whose business sense you know is sound and who can be relied upon to give good, solid financial advice to your spouse and children when they need it.

The trustee must understand that if payments of principal are necessary to your spouse, funds should be taken from the marital deduction trust. The reason: When your spouse, its sole beneficiary, dies, the property will be taxed as a part of his or her estate. In depleting the assets of the marital deduction trust (rather than the nonmarital trust), the amount of taxes due on it when your spouse dies will also be lessened.

How to Make Sure You Get an Estate-Tax Break on Jointly Owned Property: The 1976 Tax Reform Act makes joint ownership of property advantageous: Since only half the stocks, bonds, real estate, boats, cars, and other jointly owned assets changes ownership at death, the surviving spouse has to pay tax on only half its value without having to prove he or she actually contributed the other half.

There is a potential problem: The new rulings apply only to property acquired by purchase or credited between spouses after December 31, 1976. IRS says property you acquire before 1977 is not jointly owned—unless you take corrective steps. You can re-create the joint ownership.

Jointly owned property must meet the following qualifications:

1. Joint ownership must have been created after December 31, 1976.

2. Joint ownership of personal property must have been created as a "completed gift"—as a transfer of property reported as a gift to IRS, and subject to gift taxes if the transfer is large enough.

3. The spouse who acquired real estate must have created joint ownership as a taxable event, with the transfer or "gift" reported to IRS and taxes paid if required.

4. The joint owners must be husband and wife.

You have to sever or partition the preexisting joint interests, then re-create them according to these requirements.

A lawyer or accountant can help you, but you can probably do it on your own by applying directly to IRS for information and forms for completing the procedure. Check with your state department of taxation, too, for special state requirements for re-creating joint ownership.

A special provision allows the donor-spouse (who is making the property transfer, or "gift") to report the transfer in a gift-tax return filed for any calendar quarter in 1977, 1978, or 1979. For tax purposes the donor-spouse is considered to have made the gift in the calendar quarter for which the return is filed. The value of the gift is reported as the dollar amount of the donor-spouse's half of the property at the time joint tenancy was first created, plus half of any appreciation of the property since then. Then prior joint ownership (predating 1977) doesn't need to be severed and re-created. You will have to order back tax forms to do this. Both ways take some effort—it's six of one and half a dozen of the other, if you ask me.

In re-creating joint ownership of stocks, bonds, and other personal property, the transfer will be subject to gift taxes, the amount of which is usually based on one-half the value of the property in question.

When you report transfers of property in order to establish joint ownership, you may not actually have to pay gift taxes, thanks to the marital deduction that allows gifts valued up to $100,000 to pass from one spouse to another tax-free, plus property up to $3,000 per year, plus gift-tax credits under the unified estate and gift-tax rulings.

You have two options with real estate, including your home.

1. You re-create joint ownership by filing a gift-tax return; one-half the value of the transferred property is immediately taxable. If the donor-spouse dies before the recipient, only the donor-spouse's portion is subject to estate taxes. And if the recipient-spouse dies first, only the recipient-spouse's portion is subject to estate taxes. The goal is to eliminate the need for the donor to pay taxes on the recipient's half of the property and on the appreciation, if any, of the recipient's portion.

2. If your real estate holdings are small and/or limited to a modest home, you assign joint ownership to you and your spouse, but do not file a gift-tax return. There is no taxable event and you avoid all gift taxes. However, the property automatically becomes part of the estate of the spouse who dies first and is subject to estate taxation at its full value. Not to worry. If the estate is small the marital deduction and the unified gift and estate tax credit would probably shelter it from heavy taxation.

Three-Generation Tax Break That Keeps More in the Family Longer: Once upon a time, not so long ago in fact, some of our larger, wealthier families kept their fortunes intact by means of a "generation-skipping trust."

It was possible then to set up special trusts whereby only income was passed on to one's children; the principal was passed on to one's grandchildren (who in turn would have income distributed to *their* children and bequeath the entire principal to their children's children).

In these families estate taxes were paid, at most, every other generation, when all the beneficiaries of a trust corpus (principal)—and there might be several of them—had died. The deaths of beneficiaries of income interest were not considered taxable events.

The sweeping tax reforms of 1978 changed this. IRS, seeing too many rich families passing along too many dollars tax-free for too many years, stepped in with new rulings. Now, a generation-skipping trust has few tax advantages.

The new rules define the death of a beneficiary of income as a "taxable termination." When there are two or more beneficiaries of interest income, the taxable termination occurs when the last beneficiary dies. Then transfer taxes are imposed.

In contrast, "taxable distribution" is any transfer of principal from a generation-skipping trust to any beneficiary belonging to a younger generation than that of any other beneficiary. That sounds like double-talk. An example will clarify:

Suppose you've set up a trust that provides income to your child for life; the remainder is to be passed on to your grandchild. Either can invade the principal. But any distribution of principal to your grandchild during your child's life is a taxable distribution. Distribution of income only to your grandchild during your child's lifetime is not considered a taxable event.

Since the 1978 Act, taxable terminations and taxable distributions are subject to taxes similar to the estate and gift taxes that are imposed on less baroque property transfers.

There is a detail of these new rulings that you might be able to use to keep your family fortune more or less intact, though it lacks the elegant simplicity of the old generation-skipping trust. The detail excludes from taxation the transfer of principal up to $250,000 through each of your children (the "deemed transferors") to their children.

You still have the new $250,000 limit to contend with. But if you have four children, $1 million ($250,000 for each child) can be transferred tax-free through them to your grandchildren. The number of grandchildren has no effect on taxes.

Flower Bonds: Or, How to Come Up Smelling Like a Rose: I don't know where flower bonds got their name unless it was from their "flowering" at death, but they represent one of the most interesting estate-tax breaks going.

Flower bonds, if owned by the decedent at the time of his or her death, can be redeemed immediately at death at face or par value and used to pay estate taxes, even though the bonds are far from maturity date. Only certain bonds issued on or before March 3, 1971, qualify. They can be purchased at any time by anyone, even the terminally ill. The only requirement is enough cash.

Some flower bonds can be bought at an invitingly substantial discount from par value, say at $850 for each bond with par value of $1,000. If you have 20 of these bonds in your portfolio, worth $17,000, and you die suddenly, even a day after purchase, each bond can be redeemed immediately at face value to pay estate taxes, yielding $20,000 in cash.

Here is a complete listing of flower bonds that can be used to pay federal estate taxes. The bonds, of course, are included in the decedent's gross estate at par value (not cost).

Important: For maximum estate tax advantages, flower bonds must be purchased when the market is well below par.

Series	Treasury Bonds* Dated	Due
3 ¼'s 1978–83	May 1, 1953	June 15, 1983
3's 1995	Feb. 15, 1955	Feb. 15, 1995
3 ½'s 1990	Feb. 14, 1958	Feb. 15, 1990
3 ¼'s 1985	June 3, 1958	May 15, 1985
4's 1980	Jan. 23, 1959	Feb. 15, 1980
4 ½'s 1980	April 5, 1960	May 15, 1985
3 ½'s 1980	Oct. 3, 1960	Nov. 15, 1980
3 ½'s 1998	Oct. 3, 1960	Nov. 15, 1998
4 ¼'s 1987–92	Aug. 15, 1962	Aug. 15, 1992
4's 1988–93	Jan. 17, 1963	Feb. 15, 1993
4 ⅛'s 1989–94	April 18, 1963	May 15, 1994

A Special Tax Break for Orphans: The Tax Reform Act of 1978 allows a tax break on amounts passed to orphans from an estate. On any interest in property passed to an orphaned child there is a deduction from the gross value of the estate of $5,000 multiplied by (21 minus the child's age).

A child who is orphaned at the age of 15 is allowed a maximum deduction from his or her parents' estate of $5,000 × (21 − 15) = $30,000.

IRS defines an orphan as any child of the deceased, whether natural or legally adopted, who has not attained the age of 21 years before the death of the parent and has no other known living parent.

"Actual Use" Tax Break for Real Estate: Certain classes of real property (real estate) should, if possible, be valued according to their "actual use," rather than their highest "potential and best" use.

The actual use of a plot of land where turnips are grown is turnip-growing. The potential best use of the plot may be to turn it into a drive-in movie or trailer park, or to construct garden apartments on it. Naturally, estate taxes on this basis will be much higher.

If certain conditions are carefully met, the executor of

* Chart reproduced with permission from *1980 Federal Tax Guide Reporter*, published and copyrighted by Commerce Clearing House, Inc., 4025 W. Peterson Ave., Chicago, Illinois 60646.

the estate can elect to value real property at actual use. IRS will disallow this valuation, however, if it reduces a gross estate by more than $500,000.

To qualify for special actual use valuation, property must be used as a farm, or in connection with a trade or closely held business (defined as a business with no more than ten partners, or in which the decedent owned at least a 20% interest). There are several other stipulations:

1. The decedent must have been a resident of the United States and the property must be located in the U.S.

2. The property must constitute at least 50% of the gross estate.

3. The property must be passed on to "qualified heirs": a spouse, children, or close relatives. (It can be passed on via the trust route.)

4. The property must have been used as a farm or in connection with a trade or closely held business for at least five of the last eight years of the decedent's life; during this period, the decedent or a family member must have been an active participant in running the farm or business.

5. At least 25% of the adjusted value of the decedent's gross estate must be in the form of real property (as opposed to personal property).

6. An actual use valuation agreement must be filed with IRS.

Before the executor applies for special actual use valuation, everyone should be aware that this places limitations on future use of the property. If the property is sold or transferred by family members to nonfamily members, or ceases to be used for farming, trade, or small business, IRS may leap back into the picture to recapture the tax money lost to it through granting actual use valuation. (There's no danger of recapture if the heir or heirs die and others to whom the property is transferred convert it to other uses.)

You should also know that a government lien is placed

on property for which estate taxes have been reduced by actual use valuation. This lien is in effect for 15 years, when the potential liability period ends, or less if the heir or heirs die, or tax benefits have been recaptured as a consequence of selling the property or altering its use.

Another key point of the Tax Reform Act of 1976 states that rather than forcing the sale of the farm or closely held business to pay estate taxes (usually due within nine months after death), the government allows estates to stretch out estate-tax payments over a 15-year period if the farm or closely held business is at least 65% of the adjusted gross estate.

How to Get an Installment Payment Break on Certain Estate Taxes: If a farm or closely held business is a large portion of an estate, the executor can apply for the privilege of paying estate taxes in equal annual installments for ten years, which gives extra time to accumulate money to pay the taxes.

To qualify, the farm or business must represent at least 35% of the gross value of the estate or 50% of the taxable value. Only taxes due on the farm or business portion of the estate are eligible for installment payment, and the privilege ends when or if 50% of the decedent's interest is sold or disposed of in any manner. Application for installment privileges must be made on or before the date taxes are due.

There's a special low (4%) interest rate on taxes due on the first $1 million of farm or closely held business property. If a property's value exceeds $1 million, the regular interest rate, currently about 12%, applies to the excess. This is another tax break in itself.

Some Annuities and IRA and Keogh Plans That May Provide Estate Tax Breaks: When one spouse dies, the other may obtain some exclusions from the gross estate through deductions connected with payments from retirement annuity contracts and from IRA and Keogh Plans. Possible exclusions:

1. Annuity payments from an employees' trust or paid under a contract purchased by the trust, made after death, if such payments are intended for a beneficiary other than the executor of the estate

2. Payments made to the decedent under a retirement annuity contract bought by the employer

3. Payments to the decedent (up to certain limits) received from a retirement annuity contract bought for its employees by an educational, charitable, or religious organization

Note: If the decedent contributed any part of the purchase price of the qualified annuity, that part will be included in the decedent's gross estate.

The Tax Reform Act of 1976 provides that benefits paid to the decedent by an Individual Retirement Account (IRA) and HR-10 benefits may be excluded to the extent that the decedent's contributions to the plan were deducted during life from his or her income tax.

Refusing an Inheritance; or, the Best Way to Look a Gift Horse in the Mouth: You won't believe it unless it happens to you, but there are circumstances where you're better off refusing an inheritance or gift. What if a relative leaves you an apartment building that's running hopelessly in the red and it will cost you more time and money than you care to spend to put it in the black? Or what if you inherit Great-Aunt Bertha's thoroughbred with the stipulation that the horse cannot be sold or given away, and you hate horses and can't afford the upkeep anyway? It's time to look the gift horse in the mouth.

IRS will recognize and honor a disclaimer: a refusal to accept property. No title has been transferred, so you'll owe no gift tax.

Your disclaimer must make it clear that you refuse the gift, and that whoever eventually gets stuck with the gift horse won't have gotten it from you as temporary owner. To avoid misunderstandings:

173

1. Put the disclaimer in writing.

2. Be sure your disclaimer is received by the person attempting to transfer interest in the property to you no later than nine months after the day interest was created.

3. Accept no part of the interest or its benefits before making a disclaimer.

4. Do not attempt to direct transfer of interest to anyone else.

New Law: See Chapter 11.

New Law: Estate and Gift Tax Liberalized: The new law allows for the following increase for gifts or for estates, effective January 1, 1982 (except if otherwise indicated):

Calendar Year	Unified Estate and Gift Tax Credit Increase to:	Equivalent Exemption from Estate and Gift Transfers of:
1982	$ 62,800	$225,000
1983	79,300	275,000
1984	96,300	325,000
1985	121,800	400,000
1986	155,800	500,000
1987 on	192,800	600,000

Thus, a person dying in 1982 can give up to $225,000 tax free from federal income taxes. This will undoubtedly help more people to live, and rest, in peace.

New Law: Unlimited Marital Deduction: The new tax law allows you to leave your entire estate, without limit, to your spouse and not pay any tax on the gift.

> The income tax has made more liars out of the American people than golf has. Even when you make a tax form out on the level, you don't know, when it's through, if you are a crook or a martyr.
>
> —WILL ROGERS

14

Tax Shelter Essentials

Now we come to the *real* tax shelters. I mean fairly high-risk investment ventures that offer potential (that word *potential* is important; it doesn't mean "surefire") profit payoffs while at the same time allowing you to take tax write-offs and deductions that not only reduce the cost to you of your original investment, but can save some of your other income from being sucked into the yawning maw of the Treasury Department. These are the ventures into oil and gas drilling, real estate, equipment leasing, cattle feeding and breeding, coal mining, and farming, as well as Broadway show and movie backing, lithographs, books, and other "exotics" that you've been reading and wondering about. These are the capital T Tax Shelters that satisfy the Wall Street purists' definition of the term. These are also the tax shelters that require you to be in at least the 50% tax bracket.

As different as a purebred Black Angus bull is from an oil well, as different as a lithograph is from a coal mine, these investment ventures have many elements in common—elements that allow you, as investor, special tax-reducing privileges, among them depreciation deductions, depletion allowances, and the conversion of ordinary income into less heavily taxed long-term capital gains.

In this chapter we'll examine some of these elements. But first:

We Interrupt This Book for Some Words of Caution!: Tax shelters tend to look good on paper, but what looks good on paper doesn't always work out in real life. For each kind of tax shelter there are dozens or hundreds of variables that can make the difference between success and failure. (Later on we'll discuss the primary risks associated with each category of tax shelter investing.)

Another thing: The government wants to encourage certain investments which are good for the country. To attract investment capital into these areas, Uncle Sam offers special tax treatment, but the government is understandably wary of investment that offers no conceivable benefit to the economy and appears to be contrived to allow a few already fat cats to avoid paying taxes. So IRS keeps a wary eye on all tax-sheltering deals.

One of the most important principles to keep in mind about any deal is its economic function. Your desire to avoid taxes and keep more of your money for yourself and your family to enjoy is as normal and natural as the instinct for sex, and you needn't feel defensive about it; but this only makes it truer that deals with no apparent purpose other than to help investors reduce their tax burdens are deals you don't want to touch with that proverbial ten-foot pole. If the slightest whiff of mismanagement or other questionable conduct arises, you stand to lose the special tax privileges and your entire investment.

Don't let the prospect of high tax savings lure you into any old deal. Give yourself time before you decide.

The prospectus (or offering documents) are the starting point for finding out about an investment. (That doesn't mean you're in the clear just because there *is* a prospectus.) Learn how to read a prospectus. If you don't understand every word and its implications, get an accountant or tax shelter specialist to translate for you. You can't make a sound decision about investing unless you understand exactly what's being offered, the tax-reducing mechanics of the venture, what you stand to lose and why, and the potential for profit. If there's no profit potential, there's no point going into the deal, no matter how tempting the tax write-offs are.

There are no risk-free tax shelters. Don't let anyone talk you into believing otherwise.

If I've succeeded in convincing you that every tax shelter that comes down the pike isn't going to work out to be the greatest thing since sliced bread (though some may come pretty damn close), that's fine.

What Makes a Tax Shelter Work?

Let's conjure up an imaginary investor named Joe. He's in the 70% tax bracket because so much of his income is from dividends, interest, and other "passive" sources. (Anyone below top-bracket taxation—50% or higher—probably should stay away from the capital T Tax Shelters; but you never know when somebody's going to score big in a lottery or poker game, or will inherit a bundle and want to do something interesting to reduce the tax bite on the windfall.)

Joe is a savvy, experienced investor who is going it alone this time—investing as an individual rather than in a partnership. (We'll get to partnerships in Chapter 15.) Aiming for profits-plus-shelter, Joe has invested in a commercial building whose cost is $50,000.

A Lesson in Elementary Depreciation: Joe knew that if he bought the building and held it for a while, he could claim depreciation deductions. The deductions, based on the theory that a building deteriorates with time (though its market value may be increasing), require no cash outlays. Joe kept the building for a couple of years, during which he claimed $10,000 in depreciation deductions. His gross ordinary income was reduced by the $10,000 deduction, which meant a big tax reduction.

However, his depreciation deductions lowered the "basis" of his building. "Basis" is the price paid for a property plus capital improvements on the property minus depreciation and other deductible expenses. It is used for tax purposes to determine one's gain or loss when the property is sold or exchanged. Basis is also used in computing depreciation.

Joe sold the building for $50,000, the same price he paid for it. Sounds like he didn't make a profit; but since his basis had been lowered to $40,000 by the $10,000 he took in depreciation deductions, for tax purposes he had made a profit of $10,000.

Now he has to pay taxes on his $10,000 profit, so his depreciation deductions deferred taxes rather than avoiding them. But for two years Joe has had interest-free use of the money from the depreciation deductions. Being a canny investor, he put that money to work making more money.

Deferral of taxes by depreciation deductions is a feature of many tax shelters. The longer you can defer tax payment, the better.

Long-Term Capital Gains Taxation Rates As a Tax Shelter Advantage: Joe knew that any profit from the sale of his building would be taxed at a maximum long-term capital gains rate of 28% if he held on to the building for more than a year, which he did. That's $2,800 in taxes on his $10,000 profit.

If Joe never bought the property, or had made the blunder of holding the property for a year or less, instead of $2,800 he would have paid 70% of $10,000 in taxes, or $7,000. The difference, $4,200, is significant even to a high-income guy like Joe.

Conversion of ordinary income into long-term capital gains is an important element common to most capital T Tax Shelters.

The Leverage Principle; or, How to Use Other People's

Money to Do All the Work for You: Leverage means using borrowed money to finance part of an investment. Joe used leverage when he bought his building; he paid $20,000 cash and obtained a mortgage (borrowing) for the other $30,000.

Joe got $5,000 a year in rental income from his property. If he had put up the whole $50,000 in cash, his return would have been 10% per year ($5,000 divided by $50,000). But since Joe invested only $20,000 of his own money, his return was 25% ($5,000 divided by $20,000).

The principal of leverage, as we'll see later, is an important component of many tax shelter deals.

Depletion Allowances and How to Gain by Losing: Depletion is applicable as a tax-sheltering device only to natural resources that are irreplaceable, such as oil and gas. As mineral resources are extracted and depleted in oil and gas drilling, coal mining, or timber cutting, the investor's property decreases in value. IRS allows the investor to receive part of his or her income tax-free as a sort of compensation for depletion. The concept is somewhat similar to depreciation in real estate and equipment-leasing ventures, where the investor claims deductions on the basis of theoretical (or real) wear and tear on the property.

The depletion allowance is in a sense a return of capital. The total amount of money that escapes taxation via the depletion allowance may eventually exceed the amount originally invested. At that point the investor has found a true respite from taxation.

A Short Course in Advanced Depreciation

Let's take a closer look at depreciation and how it is used by knowledgeable investors.

Depreciation deductions can be claimed only on investment property or property that is used in *business* or a *trade.* Your pleasure car and your home are not depreciable; their wear and tear is not connected with income-producing activity. (However, if your car and home were essential to your business activities, IRS would allow claims for depreciation deductions to the extent of their business use.)

Whenever property is bought for investment purposes or used for business, somehow, somewhere there are probably some highly advantageous depreciation deductions to be claimed. For example, when you amortize the mortgage on a piece of commercial property, the depreciation deductions may be large enough to shelter some of the income, and result in a tax-free cash flow. At the same time, as amortization reduces the amount of the mortgage, you are building up equity. But remember: The cash outlay for amortization is not deductible.

Straight-Line Depreciation: This is your everyday method of depreciation, and it couldn't be simpler. The annual deduction is cost of property divided by years of useful life, less salvage value. A small office building that costs $100,000 and has a useful life of 20 years suffers straight-line depreciation of $100,000 ÷ 20 = $5,000. We assume that the building has no salvage value after 20 years. (Depreciation of improvements you make on the property is computed separately.)

Accelerated Depreciation: You can accelerate depreciation (deducting more sooner) on some types of property. Accelerated depreciation, which can shelter not only the income from the property but part of your other income, lets you claim larger deductions in the first few years of "useful life," and smaller deductions later on. There are two kinds of accelerated depreciation: declining balance and sum-of-the-years digits.

Declining-balance depreciation. Under this method, depreciation is greatest in the first year, then declines each year.

In the chart, the first year's depreciation on a computer,

using 200% declining balance, is 200% of straight-line depreciation. Straight line is $10,000 ÷ 10 years = $1,000, so 200% declining balance is $2,000. (150% declining balance would be $1,500; 125% declining balance, $1,250.)

There is $10,000 − $2,000 = $8,000 left to depreciate. The second year you depreciate 200% ÷ 10 years, or 20% of $8,000 = $1,600; and you will see that each year's depreciation is 80% of the depreciation the year before.

Note that the total write-off is over $1,000 less than the $10,000 for straight-line depreciation. This is inherent in the declining-balance method.

If your computer has any "salvage value" after ten years, only cost minus this "junking" value can be depreciated to figure straight line (or sum-of-the-years digits) depreciation. But it isn't necessary to subtract the salvage before using declining balance.

The following chart summarizes the results of using various depreciation methods on a property having a $10,000 cost, a 10-year life, and no salvage value.

Year	Straight Line	200% Declining Balance	Sum-of-the-Years Digits	200% Declining Balance with Switch to Straight Line
1	$ 1,000	$2,000	$ 1,818	$2,000
2	1,000	1,600	1,636	1,600
3	1,000	1,280	1,455	1,280
4	1,000	1,024	1,273	1,024
5	1,000	819.20	1,091	819
6	1,000	655.36	909	655
7	1,000	524.29	727	655
8	1,000	419.43	545	655
9	1,000	335.54	364	655
10	1,000	268.44	182	655
	$10,000	$8,926.26	$10,000	$9,998

Sum-of-the-Years Digits Depreciation. In the chart, the sum of the ten years, $1 + 2 + 3 + 4 + 5 + 6 + 7 + 8 + 9 + 10 = 55$, is used as the denominator in calculating depreciation. The first-year factor is 10 years ÷ 55 = 0.1818. Multiplying by $10,000 gives $1,818.

The second-year factor is 9 years ÷ 55 (depreciation $1,636), the third-year factor is 8 years ÷ 55 (depreciation $1,455), and the last year is 1 year ÷ 55 (depreciation $182).

It's an arbitrary method that does have the virtue of adding up to the same $10,000 as the simple straight-line method. IRS won't let you switch back from sum-of-the-years digits to straight-line depreciation. But to make declining balance add up to $10,000 like straight line, you can switch back to straight line for the concluding years (see chart). Consult a knowledgeable accountant if you are considering a switchback method. And don't forget: The 200% declining-balance method gives you the largest first-year tax write-off. However, by the second year sum-of-the-years digits has more than caught up.

Let's look at another chart, which shows how the depreciation piles up for all four methods. After five years, you've depreciated exactly 50% by straight line, about 67% by 200% declining balance, and about 73% by sum-of-the-years digits. This is what accelerated depreciation means.

Recapture: Uncle Sam's Revenge: When you sell property that you've been depreciating at an accelerated rate, IRS is going to swoop down and recapture some of your depreciation deductions. Namely, Uncle Sam will recapture the difference between the depreciation you received at accelerated rates and the depreciation you would have received if you used the straight-line method. If you use the straight-line method, there can be no recapture.) The amount recovered by Uncle Sam will be taxed as ordinary income rather than at long-term capital gains rates.

Even without recapture, IRS has a way of taking a bite

Cumulative Depreciation

Year	Straight Line	200% Declining Balance	Sum-of-the-Years Digits	200% Declining Balance with Switch to Straight Line
1	$ 1,000	$2,000	$ 1,818	$2,000
2	2,000	3,600	3,454	3,600
3	3,000	4,880	4,909	4,880
4	4,000	5,904	6,182	5,904
5	5,000	6,723.20	7,273	6,723
6	6,000	7,358.56	8,182	7,378
7	7,000	7,902.85	8,909	8,033
8	8,000	8,322.28	9,454	8,688
9	9,000	8,657.82	9,818	9,343
10	$10,000	$8,926.26	$10,000	$9,998

out of some of your depreciation tax savings: The new *preference items.*

Tax Preferences—Items You'd Prefer IRS to Leave Alone: Preference items create additional taxes for you and more revenue for IRS. It's IRS's way of saying, "We're still gonna get you!" They include:

1. Excess accelerated depreciation on real or leased personal property

2. Itemized deductions in excess of 60% of your adjusted gross income (but not medical expenses or casualty losses)

3. Percentage depletion (to be discussed)

4. Productive well intangible drilling and development costs (to be discussed in Chapter 17)

The tax on preference items is 15% of the total amount of your preference items for the year over and above the greater of $10,000 or half of your tax liability.

Say you've invested in an office building and you take $20,000 more of accelerated depreciation than you would have taken straight line. Your taxes are $15,000 before taking preference items into account.

Tax preference item	$20,000
Minus the greater of $10,000 or half the tax liability (in this case the tax liability is $15,000, one-half of which is $7,500, so we use the greater $10,000)	− 10,000
	$10,000
Minimum tax rate	× 15%
Additional tax owed	$ 1,500

Tax preference items don't cancel good tax shelter opportunities, they just eat into them. But they should be analyzed and reckoned with *before* you invest, if you're smart.

Investment Tax Credit—Top Tax Breaks If You Can Get Them: You take depreciation deductions from your gross income before computing taxes, but tax credits can be subtracted right off the tax bill. For every dollar of investment tax credit you can subtract a dollar from the taxes you owe. If you're in the 50% tax bracket—or above—a tax credit is worth twice as much as a depreciation deduction of the same amount.

For example, if you're a married taxpayer filing jointly, with an income of $55,000, your taxes would be about $18,000. A deduction of $10,000 would reduce your tax bill by about $5,000, to $13,000.

But if an investment made you eligible for an investment tax credit of $10,000, you could deduct $10,000 from your $18,000 tax bill and end up having to pay only $8,000 in taxes.

For some depreciable property—computers, for example—an investor is allowed a credit for a percentage, varying with the type of property, of his or her investment. If the property is disposed of before the end of its estimated useful life, the credit is recaptured.

To qualify for investment tax credit, property must be

depreciable, have a useful life of at least three years, be placed in use by the investor on or before December 31 of the year for which credit is claimed, and be one of the following:

1. Tangible property—excluding buildings and their structural components such as machinery or equipment
2. An elevator or escalator
3. A single-purpose agricultural or horticultural structure
4. Qualified rehabilitation of a building more than 20 years old.

Note: For a tax credit, waiting until December 31 is OK; but for most deductions, including depreciation, investment must have been made significantly before December 31 of the year in which the deduction is claimed.

The usual investment tax credit rate is 10% of the cost of the *qualifiable* investment. If the property has a useful life of three to five years, one-third of its cost qualifies; five to seven years, two-thirds of the cost; seven or more years, 100% of the cost.

If you invested in a property with a useful life of three years and it costs $100,000, then a third ($33,333) qualifies for a 10% investment credit, which is $3,333 you can subtract from your tax bill.

There are limits to the amount of tax credits you can take. In one year you can subtract $25,000 on new property, plus 50% of your tax liability in excess of $25,000. On old (used) property, the one-year limit is $10,000 in tax credits. However, the excess can be carried backward or forward.

Suppose you've just purchased a new oil rig for $400,000. It has an estimated useful life of seven years. Your tax liability for the year, before investment tax credit, is $50,000. All of the rig's cost qualifies for a 10% investment tax credit of $40,000. But you don't save quite that much.

Your limit for one year is $25,000 plus 50% of your tax liability in excess of $25,000, so you have to do some calculating. The excess is $50,000 − $25,000 = $25,000, and 50% of it is $12,500. Add that to your $25,000 for your maximum investment credit: $37,500 is the amount of investment tax credit you can claim for your oil rig.

Allowing Uncle Sam the Privilege of Paying Part of Your Tax Shelter Investment: Given the "iffy" nature of capital T Tax Shelters, you may wonder why an investor would go into oil, coal, cattle breeding, or any other sheltering arrangements.

There are a couple of reasons. A good tax shelter—one worth investing in—offers the possibility of high profits as well as shelter for income. Also, the tax write-offs available in a sound shelter deal tend to reduce, sometimes significantly, the cost of your investment to you, and to shift some of the burden over to Uncle Sam. And if that's not a switch, I don't know what is .

Suppose your income is $55,000 a year and you have invested $10,000 in an oil and gas tax-sheltered investment, allowing you to take 100% deduction on intangible drilling costs. Compare your taxes with and without the tax shelter. (The savings shown in the table would be even greater if we included state and local income taxes. When considering a real deal, you'll want to calculate the state and local tax savings as well.)

	With a Tax Shelter	Without a Tax Shelter
Net income	$55,000	$55,000
Minus intangible drilling costs deduction (100% of $10,000)	− 10,000	− 0
Taxable income	$45,000	$55,000
U.S. tax	13,000	18,000
Tax savings	$ 5,000	0

Your tax savings are 50% of your investment. Looked at

one way, Uncle Sam kind of picked up the tab for $5,000 of your $10,000 investment, cutting your risk in half.

Now you know why so many canny investors are thinking and talking capital T Tax Shelters these days.

New Law: Depreciation Changes: See Chapter 10.

New Law: Tax Preference Items: For leased personal property and for all real property, the tax preference is any excess of the depreciation allowed under ACRS (see Chapter 10) over straight-line depreciation calculated using predetermined recovery periods for each property class. Such tax preference is subject to the add-on minimum tax, and, for 1981 only, it also reduces dollar for dollar an individual taxpayer's personal service income subject to the "maximum tax" rates.

15

Organizational Structures
of Tax Shelters

Without a structure, all business entities would be chaotic. Which structure is chosen depends on the number of investors and what kind of business activities they're engaged in; the amount of involvement in business decisions and control they desire; the amount of personal economic exposure they want to risk; the amount of money necessary to get the business going and to keep it going; and, of course, the tax factors.

The structure (or vehicle) most often favored for tax shelters is the *limited partnership*, which offers (1) limited liability, meaning that the economic exposure of an investor is limited to the amount of his or her investment in the venture; and (2) profits, losses, and tax credits that flow directly through to the investors, allowing the limited partnership's tax-sheltered benefits.

In a *corporation*, which also offers limited liability, there is no pass-through of profits or losses directly to investors. Profits are doubly taxed, first to the corporation, then to the stockholders.

Another kind of business vehicle, the *general partnership*, is a contractual relationship of two or more persons who have agreed to engage in business activities together. It exposes the investors (partners) to unlimited liability. In a worst-possible case, if you operate an oil-drilling program under a general partnership arrangement and the well explodes and suddenly there is no more Houston, you and your partners are legally responsible in full. But you do get a direct pass-through of profits and losses.

A *sole proprietorship* gives you unlimited liability and direct pass-through of profits. You run the show, and all losses, no matter how large, are yours personally.

The *Subchapter S corporation* (see Chapter 10) is a kind of little brother to a regular corporation. It avoids the double tax bite a regular corporation faces.

In a year of losses, stockholders of the Sub S corporation can choose to take the loss as individuals and deduct it from their other income. In a year of profits, the corporation can pay the taxes.

However, as Chapter 10 points out, a Sub S corporation has limits and drawbacks.

The Limited Partnership: Preferred Tax Shelter Vehicle: All things considered, the limited partnership is often the most suitable business arrangement for ventures in which tax sheltering and profitability are the primary aims.

A limited partnership has a *general partner* or partners, and the *limited partners* who are the investors. The general partner is the sponsor, syndicator, oil operator, or real estate developer who manages the partnership's business and is responsible to a large extent for partnership debts.

A limited partner (investor) contributes capital to the business. Liability for partnership indebtedness is limited to the amount of the investment. Gains, losses, deductions, and tax credits flow directly through the business to each limited partner in proportion to the amount invested.

Losses can be used as deductions from other personal income. All earnings passed on to the investor are taxed only once, and that once to the investor. (This is different from the corporate arrangement, in which losses are retained at the corporate level and profits are doubly taxed, first to the corporation and again when they are distributed as dividends and taxed to the stockholders.)

The limited partnership is distinct from a partnership in which each partner has general liability for debts of the partnership, and which is dissolved by the death of any of the partners.

Disadvantages of the Limited Partnership: There is no absolutely perfect investment vehicle.

An interest in a limited partnership, for example, is not liquid. There isn't much of a market for such interests, and you can't convert your interest readily to cash. I've known several unfortunate investors who were forced to liquidate at prices far below what their partnership interests were worth. In a way they were lucky: They might not have found a purchaser at any price.

Limited partnerships structured for maximum tax sheltering also tend to last 10 to 20 years or more. They're not for you if you want to make quick money.

Limited partnerships must be structured carefully to avoid being classified by IRS as "associations," which are taxed like corporations. The IRS uses four tests, of (1) continuity of life of the business; (2) centralization of management; (3) free transferability of interest; and (4) limited liability of the investors. All of these are characteristic of a corporation.

1. Continuity of life is a corporate, not a partnership, characteristic: A corporation doesn't dissolve because of anyone's death or resignation. A partnership does dissolve upon such death or resignation.

So the business will not be considered to have the corporate characteristic of "continuity of life." One point for the partnership.

2. On centralization of management, another corporate characteristic, IRS takes the position that there is central-

ization of management if management is "substantially" divorced from ownership.

Usually, in a limited partnership, the investors supply the greater part of the capital, and the general partner runs the operation without any say from the "limiteds." Thus, most limited partnerships that function as tax shelter investment vehicles do have the corporate characteristic of centralized management. The score is now one point against the partnership, and one for!

3. Free transferability of interest is a characteristic of corporations that enables corporation shareholders to sell stock without the approval of management. This is why a limited partnership usually imposes restrictions on transfer of interest of a limited partner, such as needing the approval of the general partner. Score: Two points for the partnership, one against. We could stop here and the entity would be treated as a partnership. But let's go further.

4. In the matter of limited liability, IRS holds that if a business does not have any member who is personally liable for debts incurred by the business, it can be viewed as a corporation. But in a limited partnership, the general partner is personally liable for debts and obligations (as a limited partner, you will want to be sure that the general partner has enough assets to meet such liabilities); thus the corporate characteristic of limited liability does not apply. Score three points for the partnership, one against.

This is more than enough. The tax laws give some leeway. The limited partnership need only score as a partnership on two of the four tests to qualify for favorable tax treatment.

A Corporation as General Partner? Why not? In fact, in most limited partnerships a corporation is the general partner.

The idea of a corporate general partner may raise questions: "Hey, didn't this guy Ober just say that a partnership can be treated as a corporation if no member is personally liable for the debts of the venture? And now he's saying that a corporation, where shareholders have no personal liability, can act as general partner in a limited partnership. What gives?"

IRS, too, casts a wary eye on this idea, but it's issued a number of private rulings saying that the arrangement passes muster if the following requirements are met:

1. If total contributions are less than $2,500,000, the corporate general partner must have a net worth at all times of at least 15% of the total contributions of the limited partners, or $250,000, whichever is less.

2. If total contributions are $2,500,000 or more, the corporate general partner's net worth must at all times be at least 10% of the limited partners' contribution.

3. In computing its new worth for these two conditions, the corporation cannot include its interest in the partnership or accounts and notes receivable from the partnership.

4. If the corporation acts as general partner for more than one limited partnership, it must meet the net worth requirements for each of the partnerships.

5. The limited partners may not own more than 20% of the stock of the corporation that is general partner, or its affiliates.

6. Purchase of a limited partnership interest must not carry with it the right or obligation to purchase a share in the general partnership/corporation or its affiliates.

These IRS rulings are "private": they do not carry the weight of the law. Still, a limited partnership risks being treated as a corporation and losing tax benefits if it does not comply with these rulings.

As a potential limited partner, one of your main concerns is the advice of an accountant, a financial adviser, or a tax attorney, who has checked the details of the venture to see that it qualifies in all respects as a legitimate tax shelter.

The All-Important "At-Risk" Rule: The good ole days are gone. Before 1976 investors could use leverage (borrowing power) to the hilt. You could invest in a movie deal by putting up $10,000 of your own money and signing a non-recourse note (an IOU for which you would not be personally liable and which could not be called) for $90,000. Then you would be eligible to depreciate $100,000 (your $10,000 plus the borrowed $90,000) from your income taxes although your liability in the deal was only $10,000!

The Tax Reform Act of 1976 put an end to all that. To discourage schemes whose sole purpose was avoidance of taxes, Congress set up at-risk rules, which limited the deductions an investor could take to amounts for which the investor was actually "at risk" (personally liable) in the following activities:

1. Oil and gas
2. Motion pictures and videotapes
3. Equipment leasing
4. Farming (not including growing of timber)

These restrictions do not apply to corporate investors, but, according to a second provision of the 1976 Tax Reform Act, apply to partnership use of non-recourse loans.

Loopholes in the Tax Reform Act of '76: No sooner had the ink dried on the 1976 act than alert promoters discovered loopholes and began to structure deals that could be squeezed through them.

The act specifically mentioned the four activities listed above prohibiting nonrecourse borrowing. Promoters argued that nonrecourse borrowing could be used to finance investments in other areas, such as cattle breeding and feeding, racehorse ownership, and coal mining. They and their accountants also reasoned that when assets were owned directly, limited partnership at-risk borrowing restrictions could be circumvented by structuring deals as sole proprietorships or unincorporated one-man businesses. A sole proprietorship, they claimed, would be eligible for deductions through nonrecourse borrowing, They came up with lithographic, record, and book deals.

To further curb abuses, the Revenue Act of 1978 extended the at-risk rules to all activities—other than real estate. The Act repealed the 1976 partnership at-risk rules as redundant, in view of the broader scope of the '78 law, and extended at-risk requirements to closely held corporations.

"At-Risk" Rules Today: The rules in effect now specify that investors in tax shelter deals take tax deductions of up to, but not more than (1) the amount of money (or the adjusted basis of property) they have actually invested in a venture plus (2) money borrowed for which the investor is personally liable (recourse borrowing, that is: money that will have to be repaid eventually). Real estate is exempted from the "at-risk" rules.

An investor would not be considered at-risk for any amount that he protects from loss by guarantees, insurance, stop-loss agreements, guaranteed repurchase agreements, or similar arrangements.

Those fabulous 3-to-1, 4-to-1, and sometimes (incredibly!) 10-to-1 tax write-off deals that you may have read about are things of the past. Legally, that is. There are still a few promoters operating as though the Tax Reform Acts of '76 and '78 had never been passed, signing recourse notes right and left and covering their tracks by telling investors that the notes they sign will never be called. Well, maybe. But what if the promoter dies and the recourse notes are enforced by his estate? What if? Remember, the investor is contractually obliged to pay up on such notes.

One Way to Get Around the At-Risk Rules: The '76 and '78 acts do not prevent corporations (other than closely held corporations) from investing on a nonrecourse basis in oil and gas, motion pictures, equipment leasing, and farming. If you've taken the trouble to incorporate yourself, you qualify as a corporate investor and can engage in nonrecourse borrowing. The money you raise by nonrecourse borrowing can be invested in a tax shelter deal if you continue to act as a corporation, rather than investing the money yourself, as an individual.

What to Do Before You Invest in a Limited Partnership: Don't put money for which you're personally at risk into any investment deal that isn't fundamentally sound. You have to find out what you're getting into before you get into it.

The investment should be carefully screened. You or a financial adviser need to find out as much as possible about the general partner. Ask for references—banking, business, personal, accounting, legal—you may even want to check police records to find out if any of the principals have been charged with criminal misdeeds or offenses.

Find out where the general partner's headquarters are. If the deal you're considering is an oil-and-gas drilling venture and the general partner has headquarters in Texas, make a few long-distance calls to the competitors. I've found this to be a good screening strategy. The competition can generally be counted on to give a fair evaluation: exactly because there may be no love lost between competitors, if the competition says your general partner is on the up and up (even though, as one oil driller said to me of another, "we lock horns at least once a week, and I'd like to kick his ass all the way to Alaska"), it's probably true. If the competition expresses more than dislike and hints at shady dealings, keep digging for more information and follow up on it.

Look at the prospectus to see if the deal is fairly structured from the investor's point of view. Be clear about the tax consequences of the deal. If you need help deciphering the language of the prospectus, take it to a financial consultant, a tax attorney, or an accountant. Yes, this may cost you a bit, but it's better than flying blind.

The fact is, only about 5% of the deals going around are worth your investment money.

To repeat: Don't go into deals that have tax benefits but no profit potential; these are the deals IRS scrutinizes most closely.

Don't go into a deal in a panic at the end of the year, hoping to cut your tax losses by investing before December 31. Investigate first.

Don't go into deals outside the United States. It's hard enough to check up on the ones here. And you may have trouble getting money that's owed you.

Avoid deals where the promoter offers pie in the sky—you will end up with egg on your face instead: money lost and no tax savings.

An Alternative: Pay Your Taxes: Agonizing as it is to give up 50% to 70% of your top dollars to the federal government, remember that you get to keep the other 50% to 30%. It's better to hang on to the remainder than to lose every penny in an ill-conceived investment strategy. Thirty cents on the dollar is a hell of a lot better than zero.

> Good fences make good neighbors.
> —ROBERT FROST

16

Shelters for Shelter: Investing in Real Estate

You may not know a Black Angus bull from a Guernsey heifer, a lithograph from an oil painting, a well casing from a drill bit, but you sure enough know an apartment house from an office building when you see one. Familiarity breeds more confidence than contempt, and maybe that's why so many people who'd be scared to invest in, say, coal ("because I don't know a damn thing about the stuff") feel more comfortable about putting money into real estate. That plus the fact that real estate prices in most parts of the country keep going up, up, and away. The common wisdom is you can't lose when you invest in real estate. That's obviously not true, but enough people seem to believe it to make real estate the most popular tax shelter investment.

Another plus for real estate is that it is one of the few investments in which nonrecourse borrowing (which allows you to borrow in the form of a mortgage large sums for which you assume no personal responsibility) is still allowed. Leverage, accelerated depreciation, and the potential for capital gains treatment of profits keep real estate deals looking good.

Now we'll consider the tax consequences of many kinds of real estate investment—from the single-family house to apartment complexes to shopping centers, office buildings, warehouses, and government-subsidized housing.

Let's start small and wave goodbye while the big fish swim

off after the office building, shopping centers, and apartment complexes (where we'll join them later). We'll stay in our little pond and look at the tax advantages of investing in a single-family house.

Starting Small: The Single-Family House
As an Investment

This kind of investment has been neglected by the biggies, and even the small investor tends to overlook it. Too bad. The small investor can do very well here.

When you invest in a single-family house, you're investing for a purpose, or rather for three purposes: tax write-offs, cash flow, and capital gains when you sell the house.

What kind of a house should you look for? Try to find one that gives you as many "yes" answers as possible to these questions:

1. Is the neighborhood desirable?
2. Is there a high percentage of owner-occupied houses in the neighborhood?
3. Is the house convenient to good public transportation? (This becomes more and more important as gas prices go higher and higher.)
4. Is the house on a par with other houses on the block—neither much more nor much less expensive? (If it's way off par you may have difficulty selling it.)
5. Are the exterior design and the interior floor plan appealing? (Few people want to live in a house that looks odd from the outside or is jerry-built or inconvenient on the inside.)
6. Has the owner of the house maintained it properly? (A well-maintained house naturally means less fix-up work for you and also provides a standard for your tenants to live up to.)

Once you've found your investment dream house, how do you work the deal? Let me introduce Carol and Howard, who have bought a single-family house for investment purposes.

Carol and Howard are married, have a combined income of $27,000 which puts them in the 35% tax bracket, and file a joint return. Their goal in buying a house was less tax write-offs than capital appreciation: They hoped to sell at a profit later. Three years ago they found a good house in a stable residential neighborhood, priced at $40,000. They put $10,000 down (25%) and got a $30,000, 25-year mortgage at 9%. Before buying the house they figured they could charge $400 a month in rent and they were right. The tenants pay for all utilities.

Here are the vital statistics of their venture:

Cash Flow

Gross possible income ($400 × 12)		$4,800
Minus: Allowance for vacancy	− $ 400	
Taxes	− 1,400	
Maintenance	− 400	
	− $2,200	− $2,200
Net operating income		$2,600
Minus: Mortgage payments		− 3,021
Net cash		− $ 421

Tax Shelter

Net operating income	$2,600
Minus: Interest payment	− 2,700
Depreciation[1]	− 1,875
Taxable income	− $1,975
Tax savings	$ 691

Cash Return

Net cash	− $ 421
Minus: Tax savings	691
Cash Return	$ 270

[1] As a used residential rental, the house qualifies for 125% depreciation over its useful life of 20 years. Carol and Howard figured that their depreciation base was $30,000 for the house, attributing $10,000 to the land (which is not depreciable). Depreciation is $30,000 ÷ 20 years × 125% for the first year.

199

Howard and Carol make a meager $270 profit the first year on their investment house. Since their net operating income doesn't cover the mortgage payments, they have to lay out their own money every month and wait until tax time to realize their tiny profit.

But remember, their goal was neither immediate income nor tax savings, but capital appreciation. Their situation looks a lot more impressive when they sell the house. They hung on to their investment house for just over a year. Then they put an ad in the newspaper stating that the sale price was a firm $50,000. Within a couple of weeks they had a buyer. Here's how the vital statistics of their investment looked after selling:

Sales Proceeds

Sales price		$50,000
Minus:	Mortgage balance	− 29,700
	Selling expenses at 8%	− 4,000
Gross proceeds		$16,300

Tax Consequences

Sales price		$50,000
Minus:	Selling expenses	− 4,000
	Adjusted basis ($40,000 − $1,875)	− 38,125
Taxable gain		$ 7,875
Minus:	Depreciation recapture ($1,875 − $1,500)	− 375
Capital gain		$ 7,500

Net Return

Gross proceeds		$16,300
Minus:	Capital gains tax (35% bracket × 40%)	− 1,050
	Ordinary income tax (35%) on recapture	− 131
Net proceeds		$15,119
Minus:	Original investment	− 10,000
Net (after-tax) return		$ 5,119

The after-tax return on selling their house is $5,119. To compare their return with returns on other kinds of investments we have to look at their cash and capital returns in terms of their present value using a 10% discount:

Present value of annual cash return (.90909 × $270)	$ 245
Present value of net return (.90909 × $5,119)	4,654
Total return	$ 4,899
Return on $10,000 investment	49%

A 10% discount is used because if Howard and Carol invested their $10,000 in an alternative investment such as treasury bills or a certificate of deposit for one year, they would have received a 10% return, or $1,000. It's easy to see that Howard and Carol came out way ahead on real estate.

Tips for the Single-Family House Investor: If you'd like to follow the same route to capital appreciation, keep these pointers in mind:

1. Don't rush into buying. Take your time and find good property that is affordable, but still easy to rent and easy to sell.

2. Death and divorce often dictate quick sales. Though you may bridle at the thought of profiting by someone else's misfortune, reality is reality. Offer less and see what happens.

3. If possible, assume the existing mortgages; they will probably save you significant interest costs. You will really luck in if you can assume a VA or FHA mortgage; interest rates are much lower than the rates of conventional mortgages.

4. Get good tenants. Many people avoid renting to singles, roommates, people with pets, and families with very young children. The reasons are obvious. Discriminating on the basis of income, credit ratings, and references from former landlords is not illegal, as long as you're consistent in screening *all* applicants who apply.

5. Set up a well-designed lease. It wouldn't hurt to have a real estate lawyer go over it before anyone signs up.

6. Don't invest unless you're sure you can carry the cost of the house and have funds set aside for emergencies. Vacancies occur. Boilers break down and need to be replaced. Plumbing pipes spring leaks. Faulty wiring can cause fires. Even though you've had your investment house inspected before buying, be prepared for surprise disasters by maintaining cash reserves.

How to Make Sure IRS Won't Tax You As a Dealer: Being involved in one real estate deal doesn't make you a dealer. Take precautions against the possibility of IRS misconstruing your real estate investments as "dealing." If you are a dealer your real estate profits can be taxed as ordinary income. (If you're in the 50% bracket, that's how profits will be taxed.) But if you maintain your status as an investor and hold on to your property for at least a year, when you sell you are taxed at more favorable capital gains rates (28% maximum).

The U.S. Supreme Court has ruled that your reason for buying a piece of property dictates whether you will be taxed as a dealer or an investor. Investors buy for investment purposes. Dealers buy for a quick resale.

Here are some of the activities and aims that define a dealer:

1. Property is purchased primarily for resale.

2. Property purchases and resales are frequent.

3. Property is sold to realize a quick gain.

4. Profits are quickly reinvested in more real estate.

5. Many improvements are made, to maximize profit on resale.

6. Properties are listed or advertised in newspapers and other publications.

7. Property bought is not used in business or trade.

8. Property sales are depended on for a major source of income.

9. Property isn't income-producing.

An investor's activities and aims are characterized as follows:

1. Property is originally acquired for rental or income-producing purpose.

2. Property is bought and sold infrequently.

3. When property is sold, it is to liquidate the investment.

4. Profits are not always quickly reinvested in more real estate.

5. Improvements are not made in order to effect quick resale.

6. Property is not bought or sold through advertisements.

7. Property is bought for use in business or trade.

8. Property sales are not depended upon to produce a major source of income.

9. Property produces substantial rentals.

How to Get a Tax Break on Your Lawn Mower and Similar Property: You know by now that *only property used in a trade or business is eligible for depreciation deductions.* The dishwasher in your kitchen and the dryer in your laundry room are not depreciable. However, the dishwasher and dryer you purchase for your income-producing property are eligible for depreciation and bonus depreciation! How come? Because these items are connected with income-producing activity, in this case your rental house.

If a piece of property such as a lawn mower is used both personally and for business, you can claim a depreciation deduction based on the extent of its use in your business.

IRS also allows you to take "bonus" (extra) depreciation on tangible property in the year you buy it. Bonus depreciation can be claimed on 20% of the cost of the property, up to a limit of $10,000 on a single return (which means an extra $2,000 in deductions), and up to $20,000 on a joint return (up to $4,000 in extra deductions)!

If you've invested on a partnership basis, the partnership is limited to $2,000 in extra deductions; each partner's share can be deducted from his or her gross income at tax time.

Such items as lawn mowers, appliances, and room air conditioners (but not central air conditioning) used in connection with income-producing property are eligible for depreciation deductions as well as bonus depreciation. Buildings do not qualify, because they are real property rather than personal tangible property. Mobile homes are eligible for bonus depreciation as tangible personal property. Elevators and escalators are not considered tangible personal property for the purpose of 20% bonus depreciation, but they do qualify for investment tax credits. (See Chapter 15.)

Property that qualifies for bonus depreciation may be new or secondhand, but it must have a remaining estimated useful life (the time during which property can be expected to remain useful for income-producing purposes) of at least six years, and must not have been acquired from a relative.

How to Figure Bonus Depreciation Deductions: The 20% bonus depreciation deduction is figured with reduction for salvage value (the value of the property after it has been totally depreciated).

Bertha, who bought a mobile home in February 1980 for $12,000 and who has been renting it out since, calculated her 1980 depreciation deduction on the trailer, plus bonus depreciation. Her mobile home has an estimated useful life of ten years and a salvage value of $1,000.

Bonus Depreciation:	
20% of $12,000	$2,400
Regular Depreciation:	
10% of $9,600 ($12,000 cost of trailer less $2,400 bonus depreciation)	960
Total Depreciation, 1980	$3,360

For 1981 and thereafter, Bertha will be able to claim only the regular depreciation deductions of 10% of $9,600, or $960 per year. (This assumes there are no adjustments to the basis—cost value—of her mobile home.) Salvage value is disregarded when bonus depreciation is computed.

Had Bertha not known about bonus depreciation, her deductions would have $1,100 per year:

$12,000 (cost of mobile home less $1,000 salvage value)	$11,000
$11,000 divided by 10 (estimated useful life of the trailer)	$ 1,100

Thus Bertha receives $3,360 − $1,100 = $2,260 extra in total depreciation deductions in 1980 by taking the 20% bonus.

Real Estate Rules of Thumb . . . But Remember: No Two Thumbprints Are Alike: Before we go on to bigger (but not necessarily better) real estate investments—the kind that require more money than even a top-bracketed taxpayer can pay out by him- or herself; the kind where group investing via a limited partnership makes most sense— you should be familiar with a few old and new rules of thumb for investing in real property. These "rules" are just helpful guidelines that show how the old pros in real estate judge the soundness of investments.

Times change and so do rules of thumb. A real estate guideline that made good sense in 1975 might make no sense in 1980, and 1980 guidelines may be hopelessly dated by 1985. As Mary Wortley Montagu said, "Generalizations are generally wrong." Which itself is a generalization.

Anyway, for what they're worth, for houses and condominiums:

1. Annual income × 2.5: You can afford a house or condominium costing 2.5 times your annual income. This

is a rule familiar to practically everyone who ever thought of buying a house.

2. Old rule of 100, plus new updated rule: The old rule of 100 said that to determine the value of a house, multiply the monthly rent payments by 100. This rule no longer holds for single-family homes, as prices vary so widely.

The new thinking on condominiums, however, is that they should sell between 100 and 120 times their monthly rental costs.

3. Rule of 25% for mortgage payments: Another outdated rule. More realistic today is that mortgage payments should not exceed 35% of your net income, figured by subtracting long-term obligations such as auto loans, but without calculating in your tax deductions.

4. Rule of 6 to 7 times gross annual rent: Under this rule, it's unwise to pay more than 6 to 7 times what you could get in gross annual rent when buying income property.

5. Rule of 10 times net operating income: According to this rule, the yearly net income of a building times 10 gives a good estimate of the property's value.

6. Rule of 5% for repairs: The idea here is that investors should allow 5% of annual gross income on a building for repairs.

7. Rule of 5% for vacancies and collection allowances: Another as in (6).

8. Rule of 5% for cost of property management: Still another 5% of annual gross income on a building. Some real estate pros put the cost higher—7% management fees, for example, are often charged for medium-sized income property; 10% may be necessary to take care of a single-family home.

For further guidelines, an excellent book is *Real Estate Guidelines and Rules of Thumb* by Ronald Gettel. Once you get the hang of real estate, your own rules of thumb will serve you best.

The Special Tax Shelter Aspects of
Real Estate Investment

Whether you invest in income-producing properties on your own or as a member of a limited partnership, you can get special sheltering benefits at every step: when you buy property, while you hold it, and when you sell or swap it.

In real estate you can use leverage to the hilt, investing less of your money, and more—quite a bit more—of money belonging to someone else, usually a bank. Also, your properties may be eligible for fat depreciation deductions though their market value is significantly appreciating! As the years go by you or your group are building up equity in the property as you write off interest costs on mortgages and take those big depreciation deductions. When the property is sold (after a year or more), your profits are taxed at long-term capital gains rates instead of as ordinary income.

The great potential for tax savings in real estate is matched by large risks, to be discussed later.

A Lesson in Leverage: Leverage means borrowing to the hilt and letting other people's money do some (maybe most) of the work for you. Every home buyer with a mortgage has used leverage—though he or she may never have heard of the term. The leverage of a mortgage is nonrecourse borrowing: Your personal assets need not be put up as security for the loan, because if you default on payments the lender will simply take the house back and keep what you have paid. The property itself is the collateral for the loan. Let's set up two simple—in fact oversimplified—examples of leverage. In Venture A you, as part of a limited partnership, invest $10,000. Total investment is $100,000; it yields a profit of $15,000 the first year, which is to be distributed equally among the ten investors:

$100,000 × 15% = $15,000
$ 15,000 ÷ 10   = $ 1,500 return for each investor

In Venture B your group uses its $100,000 as a down payment on an apartment building costing $500,000 with 15% return per year ($75,000).

That doesn't mean you made $7,500 on your $10,000 investment! Your group has to pay interest on the $400,000 mortgage on the building. At 9%, interest is $36,000, which you must subtract from the $75,000 cash return. The difference, $39,000, is what gets split ten ways. Your share is $3,900—still a lot more than the $1,500 return of Venture A. And we haven't added in some more profit: Your share of the interest paid on the mortgage is deductible against the cash flow for the year!

What You Need to Know About Depreciation Deductions for Real Estate Investments: Chapter 14 told you something about depreciation, whether straight-line or accelerated.

In real estate you want and can often get accelerated depreciation with big deductions during the early years of your interest in the property. It has been said that accelerated depreciation is the equivalent of floating an interest-free loan from Uncle Sam, to be repaid when the property produces net taxable income or is sold.

What kinds of property qualify for accelerated depreciation? More than you might expect:

1. Newly constructed rental housing qualifies for all methods of accelerated depreciation, including 200% double declining balance.

2. Newly constructed commercial or industrial property qualifies for 150% declining balance.

3. Used rental housing qualifies for 125% declining balance, if it has a useful life of 20 years or more.

4. Used commercial or industrial property must be depreciated according to the straight-line method.

5. Rehabilitation expenses on existing low-income property can qualify for a special 60-month write-off. Yes, the entire rehabilitation expenses can be depreciated and written off in five years!

In Chapter 14 we also discussed recapture, which is the government's way of getting back the excess in those big early depreciation deductions if you sell the property soon after.

Real estate recapture is more complicated than, say, recapture when you sell a depreciated computer.

From 1964 through 1969, if you had held *any* kind of property for at least ten years there was no recapture.

On depreciation deductions taken after 1969 and prior to 1976, the amount of recapture depends on the type of property. All excess depreciation can be recaptured on commercial or industrial real estate, no matter how long you or your investment group has held the property.

On new or used income-producing residential property, if the property is not held for at least 100 months, all the excess depreciation is recaptured. If the property is held for 101 months, 99% can be recaptured; if held for 102 months, 98%; and so on. There is no recapture if the property has been held for at least 200 months.

But on income-producing residential property that has depreciated beginning in 1976, all the excess depreciation can be recaptured no matter how long the property has been held.

On low-income Federal Housing Authority Section 221(d)(3) and on Section 236 housing, excess depreciation taken after 1969 escapes recapture if the property has been held for 120 months. For 119 months, 1% is recaptured; 118 months, 2%; 20 months or less, 100%.

Excess depreciation taken on HUD Section 8 low-income housing and Farmers Home Administration Section 515 housing held for 200 months after 1969 would not be subject to recapture. But as is the case with some of the other property discussed in this section the less time the property is held, the greater the percentage of excess depreciation that will be subject to recapture. All excess depreciation claimed after 1969 for property held less than 100 months is subject to recapture.

Accelerated depreciation is legal in every way, but it can be risky. Recapture can wipe out all or most of the tax benefits of a real estate investment. If within the first few years the property is foreclosed, for example, and excess depreciation is disallowed as a result, the dollar-amount of the deductions will come back to you or your limited partnership as income taxable at a rate as high as a whopping 70% maximum. You can forestall these horrors, to some extent, by creating a special sinking fund in which money is stashed away for emergency situations.

Excess depreciation deductions when recaptured fall into that strangely termed category known as "tax preference items." Meaning IRS is crazy about them, but that you generally should be just as crazy about avoiding them.

If you're investing in real estate for the long haul rather than the quick kill, you don't have to worry much about recapture. The longer a property is held, the smaller the percent of excess depreciation deductions that can be recaptured.

How to Avoid Recapture: Use the Component Method of Depreciation: The component method is rapid and can be used for any kind of investment real estate: new, used, commercial, industrial, or residential. It uses straight-line deductions on various "components" of the property.

Say you or your group has bought an older office building for $300,000. It has an estimated useful life of 50 years; but because it is a used office building, only straight-line depreciation is allowed, which means a yearly tax write-off of $300,000 ÷ 50 years = $6,000. Nothing to get excited about.

Faster depreciation, with bigger tax write-offs immediately, can be obtained by assigning component parts of the building separate estimated useful lives and depreciating them separately. Some components eligible for separate depreciation are ceilings, floors, roof, elevators, ventilation and plumbing systems, wiring, and lighting. IRS assigns each of these components comparatively short life, which is the point.

Expert appraisers must be hired to evaluate the components. Here's how the figures might look:

Component	Remaining Life (Years)	Cost
Roof	10	$ 15,000
Ceilings	18	25,000
Plumbing	15	25,000
Heating	12	10,000
Elevator	10	30,000
Ventilation	10	5,000
Lights and wiring	12	15,000
Structure	50	175,000
		$300,000

In this case, $125,000 of the cost of the building is allocated to component parts and the remaining $175,000 is allocated to the basic structure. Because the components each can be depreciated on a straight-line basis over their own relatively short useful lives it is possible to (1) write off the cost of these items very rapidly, and (2) have no problem with recapture as well as minimum tax!

If you're constructing a new building, you can use an accelerated depreciation on the basic structure and component depreciation on the rest to get large write-offs in the early years. *Some* of the depreciation can be recaptured, but only some.

Real Estate Risks: Many types of real estate are available to the investor. We've talked about conventional real estate: new and existing shopping centers, office buildings, and warehouses, and income-producing residential units.

Investors in government-assisted housing are eligible for high initial tax benefits, offered by the government in order to direct the flow of investment capital into housing for the elderly and poor.

Rehabilitation investments, in which most of the capital goes toward improving and modernizing older structures (often inner-city buildings) so that they can be returned to profitable use, is a similar area for investors to explore.

Other types include raw land (and its development), and farms, orchards, and other agricultural land investments (see Chapter 19).

You will want to be able to compare the risks inherent in each category of real estate investment with the potential benefits in tax sheltering, cash flow, and capital appreciation. This chart (which is a modification of Lewis Mosburg's in his *Tax Shelter Desk Book*) roughly surveys the field, but is by no means the last word on the subject.

Type of Real Estate	Risk	Tax Shelter	Cash Flow	Appreciation
1A. Existing office buildings and warehouses with good tenants	Low	Moderate	Moderate	Low to moderate
1B. Existing shopping center with chain store as major tenant	Low	Moderate	Moderate	Low to moderate
1C. Existing multi-family residential units	Low to moderate	Moderate	Moderate	Moderate
1D. New multifamily residential units	Moderate to high	High	Good	Good
2. Government-assisted housing	Moderate	Very high	Low	Low (unlikely)
3. Rehabilitation of existing structures	Moderate	Very high	Low	Low to moderate
4. Raw land	High	Low	Low	Low to moderate
5. Farms, orchards, agricultural	High	High	Low to moderate	Low to moderate

Limited Partnership Real Estate: Limited partnerships have been discussed in deal in Chapter 15. Here, the specific applications to real estate will be considered.

A general partner can save the limited partners (often busy executives and professionals) a lot of time and effort by using his or her knowledge and a portfolio of properties to do all the searching for and selection of property—whether single-family homes or large, expensive buildings.

As in other limited partnership investments, you want limited liability without the double taxation inflicted on a corporation.

Your decision to invest should be based on an offering prospectus. If the deal is for existing property, study the current income and expenses of the property, check to see what the general partner plans for present tenants, and for reducing operating expenses, improving income, and so on.

If it's a new construction venture, consider the basic economics of the project, the construction plans, and the feasibility of the deal. If an office building is planned, check on rents of other new office buildings in the area, and consider whether the area *needs* another new office building. (One way to gauge this is vacancy rates in existing buildings.) Give some thought to what kind of tenants your building needs in order to be profitable. If construction costs dictate high rents, but the location is a depressed or semidepressed area, your nice new building may stay vacant for a long time.

A substantial part of the money raised—perhaps as much as one-third of the total invested by the "limiteds"—will go into "offering" and organizational costs, which include legal and accounting fees, cost of writing and printing the offering prospectus, and commissions to the people who sell the program to investors. Undoubtedly some of the money represents profit for the general partner. You and your tax shelter adviser should examine the prospectus to judge whether the general partner's profit is reasonable or not. Is there enough money left over for investment after preliminary costs? You will need money to acquire the property, pay finance costs (and construction costs, if the deal involves construction), and create a reserve fund for emergencies.

When you examine a prospectus, compare the offering and organizational costs with the amount to be spent on acquiring property, construction costs, reserve funds, etc.

I've seen deals where the total amount of money to be raised was near $1,500,000—but only $100,000 of it was slotted for property acquisition. Common sense tells you that a deal in which so little of the investors' money will be used for acquisition and/or construction costs is a rip-off. Remember, a prospectus is legally required to tell the truth, but it isn't required to offer something worth investing in!

The general partner will secure mortgage monies or construction loans. Here's where the partnership uses skillful leverage to pump outside money into the project.

However, leverage should be held within reasonable limits, or the whole deal may be jeopardized. If the prospectus indicates more than a 1½-to-1 tax write-off, be suspicious. When the building has acquired and/or construction is completed, the general partner will be responsible for renting space, collecting the rents, and supervision of the property. Rents and other income (such as laundry coin-op machines for apartment tenants' use) will be used to pay off the mortgage, to build up reserves, and to pay the general partner "management fees." The rest will be distributed to the limited partners.

The prospectus should promise regular (quarterly or semi-yearly) reports from the general to the limited partners, including breakdowns of expenses and other aspects of the partnership operations, plus the tax figures on the property (dollar amount of deductions allowed, amount of cash distributed, etc.).

When the venture has been operating for ten years and mortgage payments have substantially reduced the amount owed by the partnership to the lending institution, it may be possible to refinance the property. Then money not earmarked for repairs or maintenance may be passed on to the general partner and investors. Distribution of refinancing money is not what IRS calls a "taxable event." On the other hand, refinancing creates additional debt against the property, and it will eventually create rents and sales proceeds that are not distributed but paid to the mortgage (the partnership as a whole). These must be reported as taxable income by the investor.

Eventually the property will be sold. (Sale is a taxable event.) The mortgage will be paid off and any remaining money will be distributed among the general partner and investors according to their partnership agreement. If the property has been held for more than one year, the investor is entitled to capital gains tax treatment. Deficiencies in the annual cash flow to investors will usually be made up when the building is sold.

What Happens in a Foreclosure? Some deals don't end on such a happy note. That's why you should look for a guarantee in the prospectus that for a stated period the general partner guarantees to make up any negative cash flow, thus protecting the property from early foreclosure if mortgage payments cannot be met.

Foreclosure is possible when the guarantee period is over or if the guarantee is meaningless. IRS treats foreclosure as a sale in consideration of cancellation of the mortgage. There is gain (taxable at capital gains rates if the property has been held for more than a year) if the mortgage debt exceeds the adjusted basis of the property. If so, you will have to pay back to the government some of the tax savings you have taken.

How to Screen a Limited Partnership Real Estate Deal:
1. Beware of the shady or incompetent general partner! You want a person or organization with a sterling reputation based on integrity, honest dealing, and conservative business policies, with experience in managing building operations and/or construction plus the wherewithal to stand

behind guarantees and make good on financial obligations. You can feel somewhat reassured about the general partner if the prospectus says he, she, or it has also invested money in the deal.

2. It's easy to get into trouble if you insist on judging the merits of a deal all by your lonesome, especially if you have never invested in real estate. The investors who make the soundest decisions and who—usually—get the most in profits and tax write-offs are those who have all deals they are interested in analyzed by a professional who is familiar with similar transactions. The nice lawyer who negotiated your divorce or helped you incorporate your business may not have the real estate background necessary to evaluate a deal, and the same goes for the accountant who does your taxes every year. You need a specialist. If necessary, ask for recommendations from the local bar association and the local chapter of the American Institute of Certified Public Accountants.

Your expert lawyer or accountant evaluator should have no economic interest in the deal, either as a principal or agent of the general partner.

3. Screen a deal for good tax write-offs, but don't overlook the profit angle. Any deal worth your investment dollars has profit potential as well as tax benefits. Always check that the income and the expense projections are sound.

4. Besides consulting your expert adviser, you may want to do some price checking of your own to get a better "feel" for the business end of real estate investment. Study some or all of the following publications:

Annual Income and Expenses Analysis for Apartments, Condominiums, and Cooperatives. Institute of Real Estate Management, 430 North Michigan Avenue, Chicago, IL 60611. $30 or free if you are a builder or own and submit income and expense figures for inclusion. Statistics on apartment buildings.

National Office Space Mart. Communications Channels,

6285 Barfield Road, Atlanta, GA 30328. $32/year. Statistics on office building rentals.

National Real Estate Investor. Communications Channels, 6285 Barfield Road, Atlanta, GA 30328. $32/year. Statistics on general law developments.

Shopping Center World. Communications Channels, 6285 Barfield Road, Atlanta, GA 30328. $24/year; free to managers and owners. Statistics on shopping centers.

How One Smart Investor Screened a Garden Apartment Deal: Screening techniques may vary from deal to deal. I'll give you the step-by-step approach taken by an investor we'll call Paul, who was considering buying an interest in a garden apartment development. Knowing how Paul screened his deal may help you when the time comes for you to evaluate yours.

1. Figuring out costs, expenses, and rents per apartment: The development Paul was interested in is in Houston and has 75 units. It would cost $1,650,000, including mortgage and limited partners' contributions. Average price of a unit: $22,000 ($1,650,000 divided by 75 units). After a preliminary consultation with his lawyer, Paul made a few long-distance calls to find out how the $22,000 compared with unit prices of other garden apartments in the area. He got the information through local banks, local building inspectors, tax assessors, real estate brokers and appraisers, and the Houston Chamber of Commerce. He also used some of the periodicals we just listed. (You can take a similar first step, no matter what kind of property you are considering.)

2. Figuring out debt service: The group of investors would put up $412,500. The property had a permanent mortgage from a local bank of $1,237,500. The debt service is 12% per year on the mortgage, or $148,500 (12% of $1,237,500). Debt service per apartment is $1,980 ($148,500 divided by 75).

3. Figuring out operating expenses: These are items

like maintenance, utilities, repairs, insurance, security services, trash removal, lawn care, management, legal and accounting fees, and taxes; they can be taken from the prospectus, where they total $75,000 per year ($1,000 per unit).

4. Figuring out return on investment: Paul wanted to make at least 7% on his cash investment, or $28,875 for the group (7% of $412,500), or $385 per unit ($28,875 divided by 75).

Paul now had the hard figures needed to decide if the deal made sense. He also had to factor in a vacancy rate, which he roughly estimated at 5%.

Here are the expenses-per-apartment calculations:

	Per Apartment Unit
Debt service	$1,980
Operating expenses	1,000
Return on investment	385
Expenses per apartment	$3,365
5% vacancy factor (100% − 95%)	× 1.05
Rent necessary per apartment	$3,543

The monthly rent necessary is $3,543 ÷ 12 months = $295 per apartment.

Paul made some more phone calls to see if $295 per month was a realistic rent to charge in Houston. He took into account that new apartments rent for more than old and that for comparisons to be valid allowances would have to be made for amenities such as the location of the project and the kind of tenants it would be expected to attract. While he was on the phone, Paul took the opportunity to ask about the reputation of the general partner.

How to Figure the Value of a Property By Looking at the Permanent Mortgage Loan: The loan should be made by an independent third party, such as an insurance company or a bank, not by an individual. Insurance companies and banks are legally obligated to limit their loans—generally to 75% of the value of the property. An insurance company can offer a mortgage loan of up to $1.5 million on a property appraised at $2 million. Then the limited partners would have to invest about $500,000. That's 100% of the property—no less!

Here's the formula:

$$\text{Value of property} = \frac{\text{amount of mortgage loan by bank or insurance company}}{75\%}$$

How to Figure Out Cash Flow By Looking at the Debt Service (Payment of Principal and Interest): The bank or insurance company issuing a mortgage loan will figure that for a property to be economically viable, 75% of the cash flow should pay for the debt service on the loan.

On the mortgage loan of $1.5 million cited above, debt service of 11% is $165,000 per year. The cash flow generated by the property should be $220,000 ($165,000 divided by 75%) to meet the standards of the lender.

The formula:

$$\text{Cash flow} = \frac{\text{debt service by bank or insurance company}}{75\%}$$

You can use this formula and the figures in an offering prospectus to calculate the cash flow on almost any property. If the prospectus indicates cash flow much in excess of your calculation, be wary.

Section 8 Housing: Renting to the "Poor, Huddled Masses" for Tax Advantages: If you are looking for a tax shelter with a 2-to-1 or 3-to-1 first-year write-off, plus some later-year deductions, consider Section 8 housing. Tax deductions greater than your actual dollars "at risk" are still allowed in real estate, even though the '76 and '78 tax laws knocked out these big deductions in most other tax shelter deals.

The reason: You still get interest, real estate tax, and depreciation deductions on the full price of the property, even though you put up, say, only 15% or 20% in cash, and the balance is a mortgage. For example, on a $1 million property with an $800,000 mortgage, deductions apply on the $1 million—and are passed through to individual investors in a limited partnership tax shelter arrangement.

*What Is Section 8 Housing? It is a government-subsidized project designed for the elderly or for low-income families. The Department of Housing and Urban Development (HUD) will pay the owner, under a 20-to-40-year contract, the difference between the fair market value for rent and what a tenant can pay under a "25% formula." Those who qualify to live in such housing pay up to 25% of their income for an apartment, and HUD pays the owner a direct subsidy of the difference between what the tenant pays and the designated fair market rent for the apartment.

For example, if a tenant earns $10,000 a year, then under the 25% rule he would pay $2,500 a year, or $208.33 a month, in rent. If the apartment would normally rent for $250.00 a month, HUD will pay the owner the $41.67 difference.

It also pays the rent for unoccupied apartments for the first two months—important considerations during the rent-up period. In addition, HUD will pay the interest costs and principal for unoccupied apartments for the next 12 months. Finally, HUD will let you automatically raise rents every year and, if your costs start to soar, grant emergency rent increases.

But the main attraction of Section 8 housing to investors is the front-end write-offs of 2 or 3 to 1.

Example: An investor who puts $10,000 into a Section 8 housing deal might be able to write off $20,000 to $30,000

*This section is reprinted from the May 3, 1970 issue of *Executive Wealth Advisory*, copyright © 1979 by The Research Institute of America, Inc.

the first year, with additional deductions available in subsequent years. The leverage is excellent because you have to put up only 15% of the cost of the building or the renovation; the rest is financed. Hence, you enjoy tax deductions for interest payments as well as immediate tax deductions for carrying charges while the building is being built. It isn't possible to take these deductions on other kinds of real estate owing to the construction write-off limitations of the Tax Reform Act of 1976.

You can also take accelerated depreciation.

Finally, although the cash-flow return on the investment is not particularly interesting (from 2% to 5% generally), it is sheltered from taxes in the early years in most cases.

A checklist of what to scrutinize before you buy follows. Remember: The only reason for the attractively high write-offs is the high potential risk.

1. Check out the track record of the developer. The attractiveness of the high write-offs brings some unscrupulous operators into these programs. If complete information is not forthcoming, look for another deal.

2. Beware of "extra costs." The tax benefits are so good that investors may lose sight of charges, fees, etc., that are never mentioned in the beginning of negotiations but have a way of cropping up at the last minute. Are the fees reasonable? Remember that the government requires the investors to put up only 15% of the cost of equity. Probably anything over this amount goes into the pockets of the developer, the promoter, the attorneys, and the accountants.

3. Double-check the tax angles. Is the useful life for depreciation purposes realistic? IRS may later prove that a building has a useful life of 30 years, though the developer might try to get away with a 20-year life. Consult a tax attorney or an accountant who is familiar with Section 8.

4. Make sure the deal is economically viable. If the real estate venture proves unprofitable you will be hit with an income tax on the recaptured amount, the difference between the accelerated depreciation and straight-line de-

preciation. Depreciation that is recaptured is taxed as unearned income at a rate up to 70% as opposed to 50% on earned income.

5. Make sure the developer has the wherewithal to do the job. Have him post a performance bond.

6. Find out about the area in which the Section 8 project is to be located. Is it growing or declining? Will the building have any residual value at the end of 20 to 40 years, when the HUD contract expires? Can the building go it alone or be put to some other use?

7. Find out about the competition. Are there other similar types of housing in the area and how are they doing?

8. Determine whether the housing is designed for the elderly or for low-income families. Generally the elderly would be a better bet: (a) demand for elderly housing is strong; (b) most elderly people qualify for Section 8 housing; (c) turnover rate is lower, as the elderly move less frequently; (d) cash management is less of a problem because elderly people generally pay their bills on time and seldom skip out; (e) maintenance is not so much of a problem because there aren't young children or vandalism to contend with.

Real Estate Sale and Leaseback: One of the more popular methods of financing is the sale and leaseback: The owner of income property sells it and leases it back from the buyer. The seller must maintain and keep up the property. The buyer gets income without management hassles. This method of financing can be used for large commercial and industrial properties and for smaller office buildings, apartment buildings, and shopping centers.

The advantage to the investor is that as the seller takes over the maintenance and repairs, the investor has no administrative duties. However, the investor must be sure that the lessee has a good credit rating and can be counted on to make the payments. Otherwise the lessee may default on the sale and leaseback.

Because the investor is the owner of the building he or

she is allowed to take depreciation on the structure. This may result in tax-free income.

The lease should allow the investor to fully pay off the building at the end of the lease term. The ideal setup is a net lease where the tenant (lessee) pays all the maintenance and operating costs, including insurance and taxes on the building.

Why would the original owner of a building agree to this arrangement? For one thing it allows the owner additional cash and retention control over the real estate. If the owner took out a mortgage loan, he or she would get only two-thirds of the value of the property. With a sale leaseback the owner gets 100%. This new cash can be used for working capital or to increase profits through tax savings.

Here is a "do" and a few "don'ts" for negotiating a sale-and-leaseback deal:

1. Get an independent real estate appraiser to value the property.
2. Don't get a balloon mortgage (if you want to maintain future peace of mind).
3. Don't get a low-interest mortgage that comes due soon.
4. Don't get a mortgage with demand or acceleration clauses. These will ruin your peace of mind.
5. Don't have renewal or repurchase options. They only serve to tie up the property more.

Construction Deals: A Whole New Ball Game

Construction deals are very different from deals in existing property. In fact, there is no riskier real estate deal than investment in the construction of a new building. If you don't know what you're getting into, don't get into it.

Investors as well as developers used to be eligible for immediate deduction of interest and taxes during the construction period. This allowed fairly large initial write-offs, often large enough to shelter ordinary income.

Times change. Immediate deductions for taxes and interest on construction loans are no longer allowed; they must be written off over a period of ten years. You still get the deductions, but you have to wait for them.

Phase-in Rules of Construction Expenses: Here's how these are phased in over several years:

Nonresidential real estate: Half of the construction loan interest and taxes paid in 1976 were deductible immediately, the other half being deducted over a three-year period, beginning when the property began to bring in rental income or was put up for sale. Beginning in 1977, all construction loan interest and taxes were to be amortized (deducted) over a five-year period. The amortization period increased by one year every year; by 1982—and presumably for some time afterward—amortization will take ten years.

Residential real estate: Immediate write-off is still allowed, but beginning in 1981 construction loan interest and taxes must be amortized over four years, increasing by one year every year thereafter, then leaping to ten years in 1984.

Low-income residential property: Investors in low-income housing construction (FHA Section 221(d) (3), Section 236, Section 167(k), and Section 515), are eligible for immediate write-off of construction loan interest and taxes until 1981. Beginning in 1982, amortization must be deducted in yearly installments. According to the present schedule, in 1988 the amortization period will jump to a full ten years.

Whenever the construction period drags on for more than one year, each year's construction expenses must be treated separately, according to the rules above.

If a new building is constructed and sold at a profit, or exchanged for another property *before construction expenses have been deducted*, special rules take effect. In determining the profit or loss on the newly constructed building, construction loan interest and taxes that haven't yet been written off are added to the basis of the building. If buildings are swapped in a nontaxable exchange, the remaining construction loan interest and taxes are written off over the allowable period by the original investor, just as if they continued to own the building.

How to Get Investment Tax Credit on a Building (Even Though Buildings Don't Qualify for Investment Tax Credit: An investment tax credit, if your memory needs refreshing, can be subtracted directly from your tax bill. It is better than a deduction of the same amount from income.

I'll tell you how a guy named Ben, who knows all the angles but who's as straight as they come, managed an investment tax credit on a building under construction. To begin with, instead of having permanent walls put up, Ben had movable wall partitions installed. Permanent walls do not qualify for an investment tax credit but partitions do. Why? Partitions, being movable, are deemed by IRS to be business property and thus qualify for investment tax credit.

Ben was able to get investment tax credit on the elevators, which qualify for the credit in commercial or business property; you can't get the credit for an elevator or escalator in a residential building.

So that his tax credit claim would stand up if IRS questioned it, Ben had the contractor bill him separately for the movable partitions and the elevators.

No investment tax credit is available on property with an estimated useful life of less than three years. You can claim one-third of the maximum credit if the estimated useful life is at least three years but less than five; and two-thirds if it is at least five years but less than seven; and the maximum if it is at least seven years.

The property needn't be new to qualify for investment tax credit. The same rules apply to used property, with one important limitation: You can't claim on more than $100,000 worth of used property per year. If it looks like you're about to go over the $100,000 limit, see if you can't spread your purchases over two or more years.

How to Depreciate Land, Even Though Land Isn't Depreciable: Certain land *costs* are depreciable. Don't overlook them! To qualify, land costs must meet these requirements:

1. The costs must be directly associated with improvements made on the land.

2. The improvements must be "inextricably" bound up with the land.

3. The estimated useful life of the land improvement should be identical with the life of the income-producing asset it is intended to improve.

Courts have approved grading and graveling of private access roads for customer use in reaching a place of business, a tunnel built under a public road connecting two business buildings owned by the same taxpayer, and dredging as part of the construction of a pier as eligible for depreciation deductions.

The government may contest depreciation deductions claimed for land improvements that "outlive" the assets they are intended to serve or improve. Take your questions about this to an accountant, or query your regional IRS office directly.

New Law: Depreciation Changes: See Chapter 10.

New Law: Faster Write-offs in Real Estate: Real estate placed in service after 1980 can be written off in 15 years as part of ACRS (see Chapter 10), except for certain property such as theme park structures and certain residential manufactured homes that can be written off in ten years. You can use an accelerated method based on the use of the 175% declining-balance method (200% for low-income rental housing), switching to straight line to maximize deductions. IRS is presently developing a table for this depreciation. You may, however, elect a straight-line method of depreciation. Taxpayers will no longer be allowed to depreciate components separately, but must use a composite method of cost recovery for the entire structure. No salvage value is taken into account for the purpose of calculations.

New Law: Depreciation Recapture: On *nonresidential* property all depreciation under ACRS is recaptured if the general recovery period is utilized. There is no recapture, however, if the optional straight-line depreciation has been elected.

On *residential* property the excess of accelerated depreciation over straight line is subject to recapture.

New Law: Tax Credit for Rehabilitation Expenses: See Chapter 10 under "New Law: Investment Tax Credit for Rehabilitation Expenses."

New Law: Construction Period Interest and Taxes: Noncorporate taxpayers are permanently exempt from having to capitalize construction period interest and taxes after December 31, 1981.

New Law: Current Use Valuation: See Chapter 11 under "New Law: Current Use Valuation."

I remember hearing the story of a man who made a million dollars in oil. The story would have been correct, except that it wasn't the man, it was his brother; it wasn't oil, it was gas; it wasn't a million dollars, it was a hundred thousand; and he didn't make it, he lost it.

—ANONYMOUS

17

Oil and Gas: A Major Leak
in the Tax System

You don't need me to tell you about the voracious appetite for oil and gas in the United States. We consume an astonishing 18 million barrels per day, which is 756 million gallons. The average American uses almost 4 gallons of oil per day.

A major new energy breakthrough during the next few years is unlikely, and we're going to continue using oil and gas far into the foreseeable future.

As more and more investors realize that they could be on the selling end of the oil business (the other end of the gas pump) instead of being mere consumers, there's a correspondingly greater interest in tax-sheltering oil-and-gas drilling ventures.

Why You Invest 50¢ Dollars in Oil and Gas: To compensate investors for the risk incurred when they put their money on the line in oil-and-gas exploration programs, IRS reciprocates with special tax incentives. You are offered the possibility of immediate deductions. If you're in a high tax bracket, 50% or above, the special tax treatment allows you in effect to invest using 50¢ dollars.

Assume that due to intangible drilling costs (these will be explained later) your investment allows you a write-off of 100% during the first year. If you invest $10,000 in the program, you can deduct a full $10,000 from your other income before taxes. If you're in one of those upper tax brackets and not invested in a drilling program, the government would have taken half of the $10,000, allowing you to keep the other half. Since this is the case, it's not stretching the point too far to say that in investing $10,000 in oil-and-gas exploration and taking the entire $10,000 as a tax write-off, Uncle Sam has actually given you half your investment, $5,000, for putting the other half into a drilling program.

You also get favored treatment in the form of the depletion allowance when (and *if*; it can be a big if, remember) your oil revenues start to come in. Thanks to the government's depletion allowance, about 30¢ to 35¢ of every dollar you get back is tax-free.

When you sell your interest in the program you get long-term capital gains treatment on the profit—assuming, of course, that you have held your interest for more than a year.

The economics of oil and gas have never looked better. Rising prices and rising demand have made this investment, when successful, more profitable than ever—even taking into consideration the increased drilling costs. With or without an oil embargo, the United States is in a serious energy crunch, which is going to get worse—with higher prices—before it gets better.

The investor may be motivated by self-interest, but in supplying some of the money necessary to drill new wells, he or she is wittingly or unwittingly acting for the public good.

Gas and Oil: What Are They and How Are They Found?
Contrary to popular belief, oil and gas are not found in pools or cavities beneath the earth's surface, waiting to be sucked

out by a strawlike device. Nor do they flow in rivers under the ground. Rather they are found in porous, usually sedimentary, rock or even sand.

These now precious resources were formed from the remains of plants and animals that lived millions of years ago. As the earth's crust shifted, some of the remains were displaced deep underground. Temperature, pressure, and chemical changes caused by bacteria changed the remains into oil—or so the organic theory holds. (When I explained this theory to a young relative, he responded brightly with: "You mean oil is something like pressurized bug juice?")

The oil and gas migrated upward until they were met and blocked by layers of nonporous rock. Often it is necessary to drill through nonporous rock to get to the oil-filled porous rock or sand underneath. Gas, which is lightest, forms near the top of the rock or sand deposits, oil is in the middle, and usually there is water underneath.

How do geologists know where to drill? They examine the rocks on the surface for clues about the rock structure below. They also try to define the beds of ancient seas which existed millions of years ago on the surface and are now deep below: Oil is most likely to have developed on or near these ancient seabeds. Geologists also look for a promising ratio of sand or shale to locate potential "oil traps" (reservoirs formed by geological barriers to oil migration.) Airplanes carrying gravity meters or magnetometers fly over the area, measuring the density and magnetic properties of the earth's surface.

Geologists use seismographic readings that measure the shock waves produced by explosive devices planted in shallow holes. Patterns in time and amplitude of the waves can indicate the probable presence of rock, shale, or sand that may contain oil. More oil has been found by seismic surveying than by any other means.

Another technique is to drill a well and run an "electric log" (not a log really, but a cable) down the hole; on sending an electric charge down the log it is sometimes possible to determine whether the sand below is oil-bearing and to what degree. This also helps decide where to drill the next wells.

Setting Up the Prospect: When a likely location has been found, a "land man" will go to the owners of the land and secure leases for the oil-and-gas mineral rights. (Most owners are quick to consent to drilling on their lands: If the drilling is successful, they will be richly compensated by royalties.)

After a prospect has been selected and the legwork of leasing, mapping, and surveying has been done, the only way to find out if there is pay dirt below is to start drilling. That's expensive, and that's where you, the investor, come in.

In a limited partnership oil venture the general partner, usually an oil company, provides the expertise, is responsible for the operation of the partnership, and makes the management and business decisions while assuming unlimited liability for debts and other obligations.

Either public or private offerings are made to attract investors. Characteristically, a public program, which must be registered with the SEC, is a "blind pool": The prospects to be explored are not specifically named.

When the necessary capital has been raised, at $5,000 to $10,000 per unit, the money (your money, if you are one of the investors) is used to finance drilling of the prospect.

Drilling is usually contracted for on one of these arrangements:

Footage arrangement: Payment to the contractor is based on price per foot drilled from the surface down to a preset depth of "geological horizon."

Per diem arrangement: Payment is the same each day.

Turnkey arrangement: For a fixed amount the contractor agrees to provide labor, equipment, and materials to drill to either the casing point (the depth at which the operator makes the decision to stop, or run and set a casing to keep the hole from caving in), or to completion.

A footage contract is the best for a limited partnership, which is not billed during delays, as it would be on a per diem contract. The turnkey contract costs most: The contractor has naturally jacked up his estimate to allow for almost everything conceivable that might go wrong. (He has to pay for costs in excess of the turnkey price.) If a limited partnership can get a contractor to drill turnkey for a markup of 12% or less over real cost, it is doing very well indeed.

If all goes smoothly with the drilling, there is "mud" to be analyzed. "Mud" is a kind of all-purpose heavy liquid which is circulated down the drill stem and back up the side of the hole to the surface, carrying drilling cuttings back up with it. The "mud" also lubricates the bit and plasters the sides of the hole to prevent caving in and to confine high-pressure gases or liquid so as to prevent a blowout or gusher. An analysis of the "mud" will indicate if oil and/or gas are present. If it's yes, the next step is to determine if there is enough of the stuff down there to make the well commercial. If all systems are go, the well is "completed." This means the final steps necessary to bring the well into production, such as running and cementing a casing, perforating, running tubing, acidizing, and swabbing. If the well flows naturally, the tubing is topped by an assemblage of valves at the top of the well, called a Christmas tree or wellhead. Otherwise a pumping unit is installed on the surface.

As the oil comes in it is run into a tank that separates out salt water. Pressure and flow must be carefully supervised.

Finally, the oil is transported by truck, train, or pipeline to refineries. Keep in mind, when examining a prospectus, how far the drilling area is from good roads or a pipeline. A field 100 miles from nowhere can be significantly less profitable to investors, even if the drilling is successful.

As natural pressure on a well diminishes, pumping is necessary, and when pumping becomes inadequate, "secondary recovery" methods—usually involving thermal procedures or the injection of water or miscible (mixable) fluids down into the well—will, it is hoped, increase ultimate recovery of the precious crude.

Tax Aspects of Oil-and-Gas Drilling Programs

Intangible Drilling Costs: The Reason for Your Large Initial Write-off: The large first-year write-offs available to oil-and-gas investors come from intangible drilling costs, which make up a substantial part of the expenses incurred in the search for oil and gas. They are the costs connected with drilling, testing, and completing a well that have no salvage value, such as cost of labor, fuel, repair work, and supplies needed for drilling, as well as money spent for hauling everything to the work site. Intangible drilling costs are deductible in the year they are incurred.

The percentage of drilling costs deductible by the investor as intangible are 50% to 80% for a successful well and 100% for a dry hole.

Expenditures for tangibles, such as well casing and tanks, are not immediately deductible, but must be capitalized and depreciated over the life of the program for 10, 20, or more years. Additionally, they may qualify for investment tax credit.

Rulings on tax treatment of intangible and tangible drilling costs have led to "functional allocation," the intangible/tangible sharing arrangement in many oil-and-gas ventures whereby the investor is charged only with the intangibles (which are immediately deductible) and the general partner is charged with the rest, including completion costs.

More About That Much-Discussed Depletion Allowance: The depletion allowance lets the investor receive a portion of the income, or profit, tax-free. Although the depletion allowance has occasioned cries of public outrage, the government's thinking is that the investor is the owner of the "economic interest" in depleting oil and gas reserves, and drilling decreases the value of his or her property. Thus he or she is entitled to some form of compensation.

Cost depletion allows you to deduct from your other income the cost per barrel of oil or per cubic foot of gas of every unit that is sold. The cost per unit is the cost of the property divided by the estimated reserves. If it costs a partnership $500,000 to obtain the rights to sell 50,000 barrels of oil, the cost per unit is $10, which can be deducted from the income on every barrel of oil extracted and sold.

Percentage or statutory depletion allows the investor to deduct a statutorily authorized percentage against the gross income. The current percentage deductible is 22% of annual gross income, not to exceed 50% of net or taxable income.

The Tax Reduction Act of 1975 repealed percentage depletion allowances for the larger oil and gas operators, but it is still available to small investors and producers whose production does not exceed 1,000 barrels of oil or 6 million cubic feet of gas per day.

If a well produces both oil and gas, the number of barrels of oil produced per day is multiplied by 6,000 cubic feet, giving a daily total in gas equivalent, on which the percentage depletion is based.

Under the Tax Reduction Act of 1975 the percentage depletion allowance will be reduced to 20% in 1981, 18% in 1982, 16% in 1983, and 15% in 1984, where presumably it will remain for several years.

The 22% figure applies to the partnership's gross rather than net income, and as net income is what's distributed, the investor still gets 30% or more of his or her profit from the venture tax-free!

For every dollar that the oil-and-gas company receives, let's say it has 34¢ of operating expenses, leaving 66¢ as net income to be distributed to the limited partners. You, as a limited partner, receive 22% of the whole dollar (not of 66¢) tax-free. But 22¢ is 33% of 66¢, so you are getting 33% of your net tax-free.

The percentage depletion allowance cannot exceed 65% of the investor's income from all sources; however, amounts in excess of 65% can be carried over and used as a deduction in the following year.

The general partner computes cost depletion allowance and percentage depletion allowance, and uses the larger of the two.

Windfall Profits Tax: Impact on Investors: On April 2, 1980, the Windfall Profits Tax Act was signed into law. This imposed an excise tax on the increases in crude oil prices, the so-called "windfall profit," which was a result of deregulation of crude oil prices and increases in the price of domestic oil as a result of the monopolistic actions of the Organization of Petroleum Exporting Countries.

You should keep in mind that this tax is only a part of an overall energy policy which allows for decontrol of domestic oil and gas prices. The effect of this policy is to make oil and gas investments more attractive than they had been in the past. For example, newly discovered oil that is sold at the decontrolled price of $40 per barrel, has a windfall profits tax of approximately $6, leaving $34 a barrel, which is far more attractive than the $2-a-barrel price in 1972 and the $13-per-barrel price at the beginning of 1979.

The act created three categories, or tiers, of domestic crude oil production (the windfall profits is the difference between the selling price of the oil and the base price which is adjusted for inflation and state severance taxes):

Tier I (All domestic crude oil that is not Tier II or Tier III—basically "old" oil.) The base price is $12.81 per barrel, and the windfall profit tax rate is 70%.

Tier II (Stripper oil or oil from wells that produce less than 10 barrels a day.) The base price is $15.20 per barrel, and the windfall profit tax rate is 60%.

Tier III (Newly discovered oil, not in production prior to December 31, 1978; certain "heavy" oil, and incremental tertiary oil.) The base price is $16.55, and the windfall profit tax rate is 30%.

The base price for all categories will be adjusted periodically for inflation. "Independent producers" (those who do not operate retail outlets for the sale of oil or gas with total sales in excess of $5,000,000 per year or operate a refinery with runs of more than 50,000 barrels on any day—in other words, most of you) qualify for rates of 50% for Tier I oil and 30% for Tier II, whose combined total does not exceed 1,000 barrels per day. All producers are subject to the 30% rate for Tier III oil.

Incidentally, the independent producer status is determined at the partner or individual level rather than at the partnership level. Most investors will qualify for the reduced tax rates.

To soften the blow of the windfall profits tax, investors have two tax benefits. First, the tax will be deductible for federal income tax purposes by each partner. In addition, each partner can claim a percentage depletion deduction calculated on the income of the gross selling price (not reduced by the windfall profits or severance taxes). This means the investor will receive a significant portion back of the windfall profits tax.

What You Should Know About Lease Acquisition Costs: Lease acquisition costs are incurred when you acquire a leasehold interest in oil-and-gas properties. The costs must be capitalized, being added to your basis for cost depletion, and recovered through the same cost depletion. You get no tax benefit: You would have rceived the same deductions through percentage depletion.

If a lease proves worthless and the project is abandoned, the cost of acquiring the lease is immediately deductible as an abandonment loss.

What Happens If the Hole Is Dry? If a project is abandoned through loss of mineral rights or because the well proves dry and the mineral rights are worthless, an immediate deduction is permitted. The cost of tangible property abandoned in such a venture is also deductible if it cannot be reused or sold.

Operating Expenses: Ordinary and necessary business expenses are deductible in oil-and-gas ventures as in any other venture. In addition, delay rentals, which are paid to the lessor to defer development of the property and thus buy more time for the partnership to develop the property, are currently deductible.

Royalties and rents must be excluded from gross income when determining the percentage depletion allowance. This is because the recipient of the royalties is entitled to use the depletion allowance to offset royalties.

Depreciation and Investment Tax Credits: Tangible property connected with drilling is eligible for depreciation deductions and for investment tax credit. New property qualifies for 200% declining-balance depreciation (Chapter 14) and used equipment qualifies for 150% declining balance. If depreciated property is prematurely disposed of, excess depreciation deductions and any investment tax credit are subject to recapture by IRS.

The Sale of Oil-and-Gas Property: At the end of an oil-and-gas program, if the limited partnership has held it for more than a year, profit on its sale is eligible for long-term capital gains tax treatment—offset somewhat by IRS recapturing some depreciation on intangible drilling expenses. The Tax Reform Act of 1976 required this. It also required that the gain made on a sale be taxed at ordinary income rates to the extent that the intangible deductions claimed exceed the deductions that would have been available had the partnership elected to deduct intangible costs through depletion.

Some public oil-and-gas drilling programs (as opposed to those that are privately offered) have "stock exchange" features. You can make a tax-free exchange of your drilling-program interest for the common stock of the corporate general partner, if the general partner is a corporation with stock that is publicly traded, as is often true. Eventual sale of the stock will usually be eligible for capital gains treatment.

How Long Can You Expect an Oil Well to Produce?
The average oil well has an economic life of about 10 years; the average gas well, 15 years or more. You are not necessarily locked into the program for the life of your well(s).

Over a Barrel; or, the Risks of Oil or Gas Investment:
The great economic and tax advantages of an oil or gas venture outweigh the risks. Consider these factors before you take such a risk:

1. Your financial position: If you're not in the 50% tax bracket, forget about an oil-and-gas investment. The tax advantages won't be worth it. The only exception to this might be if you have a net worth of at least $225,000.

2. Dry holes mean no profit. But if you're in the 50% bracket, at least the government will "pay" half of your losses.

3. Finding oil and gas doesn't ensure a profit. Delays caused by being "shut in" (a well that can't produce because it is too far away from good roads and transportation facilities, or a pipeline) may keep your investment from turning a profit for a long, long time.

4. The general partner or sponsor of the program may not act responsibly. (Chapter 15 tells you how to check up on him—in advance.) The general partner should know the business inside out and be prudent in all dealings.

5. Watch out for conflicts of interest.

6. Will you be able to hold out until cash flow begins? Oil-and-gas programs are long-term investments. If you need immediate cash flow, forget about them.

7. Diversification is important. Oil and gas is a numbers game: The more wells you have in more locations, the

greater are your chances for profits. Seek out a program with a number of wells—at least 20—in a number of areas.

A little background information is in order here.

Exploratory and Developmental Wells: Exploratory drilling programs are riskier. They include wildcat wells, which are drilled far from areas that are producing; field extension or stepout wells, drilled in unproved areas to determine the limits of a field that is already in production; deep test wells, which are drilled at unproved deeper levels, perhaps in an already proved field.

Exploratory drilling succeeds 1 out of 9 or 10 times, industry-wide. Developmental wells succeed in finding some oil about 8 times in 10. Naturally, the deal offered investors is much less favorable.

Most investors should seek a balanced program with both exploratory and developmental projects.

Limited Partnership or Joint Venture? Some drilling programs are structured as joint ventures. This means you are liable for losses in excess of your capital contribution, losses, for example, from "blowouts," fires, pollution, or offshore spills. My advice is to forgo the joint venture for the limited partnership.

Assessments, or "Overcalls": In some programs, if the general partner has spent all the original funds and needs more money to develop a newfound field, he can—if the prospectus so stipulates—call upon you for more money to continue and complete the drilling.

Choose a prospectus where your compliance with additional assessments is voluntary, with no penalty imposed other than dilution of your interest in the venture if you decide not to pay.

Contributing to an assessment, however, is usually to your advantage. Without these funds the general partner may resort to "farming out," or selling an outside party the rights to drilling on the acreage; then the partnership will only get a percentage of the third party's interest. By not contributing to an assessment, you and the other investors may be sacrificing a high degree of profitability.

An alternative to additional assessments is borrowing from a bank against reserves established by initial drilling.

Assessments are deductible, and as such provide additional write-offs for investors.

Sharing Arrangements: A fair sharing arrangement of profits between investors and the general partner is crucial. There are six types of sharing arrangement:

1. Overriding royalty: Here the investors pay all drilling costs and receive all income, except for a percentage of gross income, which is reserved by the general partner. Management shares in revenues from the beginning through a cost-free interest in production.

2. Net profits interest: Investors pay all costs and receive all profits except for a percentage of net profits paid the general partner.

3. "Carried" or "reversionary" interest: Investors pay all drilling costs and receive all income until costs have been recouped; then the general partner backs in for a percentage of the profits.

Check if the reversion is figured on a well-by-well, prospect-by-prospect, or whole-program basis. The most attractive, from your point of view, is whole-program basis, followed by prospect-by-prospect.

4. Disproportionate sharing: Investors and general partner share costs on a basis determined by formula, and share income on a different basis. Investors may contribute 100% of the costs and receive 50% of the revenues.

5. Proportionate sharing: Investors and general partner share costs and revenues on the same basis.

6. Functional allocation (also called intangible/tangible or noncapital/capital arrangement): Investors bear the cost of deductible intangible expenses and the general partner pays the tangible or capital costs. The investors assume the risk of finding oil and gas. If they are found, the general

partner shells out the money to complete the well. The general partner has no "dry-hole risks" and therefore may be overcompensated. Even so, most public oil-and-gas drilling programs use this arrangement because of the sales appeal of the immediate large tax deductions available to the investors.

Sometimes a drilling program combines two or more of the arrangements listed. One common combination is to use an override with a net profits interest, which ensures that the general partner gets a percentage of both net and gross income.

The most attractive arrangements, from the investors' point of view, are proportionate sharing, and next, functional allocation. The least attractive is the overriding royalty, which allows the general partner a share of the gross revenues even if the investors receive no income or sustain losses.

Evaluating the General Partner's Track Record: The prospectus will give you a kind of box-score roundup of the general partner's previous activities, with tables indicating the mix of exploratory and developmental drilling, the number of wells that came through with oil or gas, and the number of dry holes. (Oil- or gas-producing wells are listed as "productive"; but remember, "productive" is not always synonymous with "profitable.")

The box score should be used to gauge the scope of the general partner's prior activities rather than as a definitive rating of him or her. When I look at a box score, my primary concern is whether the general partner is attempting to bite off more than he or she has ever tried to chew in the past.

More useful indicators of past success are the "net cash" and "payout" tables in the prospectus. These indicate the dollar amounts expended on past ventures and the revenues received by investors in those ventures.

Some potentially useful information—estimates of the underground reserves of oil and gas in past programs—is generally not in the prospectus, because it is difficult to accurately estimate reserves until the producing history of a drilling program is complete. Early estimates often are followed by substantial revisions.

The SEC limits the right of prospective investors to request and review information about the quality of the leases, or prospects, that are in the inventory "portfolio" of the general partner right now. Release of such information would violate the SEC's "blind pool" rules for unspecified property offerings.

The SEC allows a broker-dealer participating in the offering to review such information. You can and should ask such a broker-dealer if a careful review of the leases has been made. (However, he or she cannot furnish you detailed information.)

If you're considering investing big money in an oil-and-gas venture it's definitely worth your while to seek the services of a reputable independent petroleum consultant to act as your representative and help you evaluate the past programs managed by the general partner. By studying the figures, he or she can judge whether the costs listed in the prospectus for the present program are reasonable.

What You Should Know About Conflict of Interest: Oil and gas deals, like other tax shelter investments, can be marked by conflicts of interest. These conflicts of interest are to some extent inherent in the nature of a limited partnership. It is, however, a conflict of interest for the general partner to run more than one drilling program, or to be drilling somewhere else on his or her own account. Problems may arise in areas where a general partner may profit at the expense of the investors.

Most prospectuses include a section clearly labeled "Conflicts of Interest." Read it carefully. Be aware of the following conflict areas:

1. Sales or purchases of leases of producing properties: Sales figures should be supported by independent appraisals.

Purchases of leases by the program should be at cost (including cost of the lease) or market value (which can be judged by comparing the acreage with the cost of comparable land in surrounding areas)—whichever is less. Generally, you, as investor, get a break when an old lease is bought at cost, as it probably has appreciated.

2. An option to transfer fewer than all the drilling locations on a prospect or field should be viewed with suspicion. A general partner may be using investors' money to "prove up" wells for his or her own account.

3. Commingling of program funds with the funds of the general partner is to be avoided. Investors' money should be handled separately from the general partner's money.

4. Management services for the program should be billed at cost, with a reasonable margin of profit tacked on. The general partner should not be allowed unlimited management fees. Read the details in the prospectus and decide if fees are reasonable.

5. The general partner should not have the option of using program funds for his or her own account, nor should any loans from the general partner to the program be at unreasonable interest rates.

6. Redemption by the general partner of an investor's interest in the program should be paid for according to the value of the investor's interest as assessed by a qualified independent petroleum appraisal outfit.

7. General partners should not be allowed to set monthly management fees on wells. The temptation for the general partner is to continue operating a low-yield well that pays just enough to cover the monthly management fees, but not enough to provide any profits to investors.

What to Look for in a "Good Deal" in Oil and Gas: A "good deal" is simply a fair deal based on sound economics, with sound tax deductions a strong secondary consideration. It's a deal in which you'll get a good run for your money. Let's briefly review the main points:

1. Look for a program that includes a minimum of 20 wells, at least 35% of them lower-risk developmental wells.

2. Look for geological and geographical diversity, with wells drilled to different depths and wells in different parts of the country.

3. It's good if the general partner has an in-house lease inventory, a portfolio of prospective drilling locations already leased to the company. This allows for greater diversification, and means that once the general partner has accumulated investor funds, the program can begin right away. However, beware that "unlikely to hit" leases might be dumped in the program.

4. Find out as much as you can about the general partner.

5. If in doubt, get a tax attorney or tax shelter specialist to interpret some of the financial information in the prospectus.

6. Look for areas where conflict of interest can cause serious damage.

7. Study the prospectus to see how investor money is to be spent. At least 85% should be used for drilling and drilling-related activities.

8. If the prospectus indicates that an intangible/tangible sharing arrangement is to be used, check that the investors are to receive at least 60% of all revenues.

9. If the prospectus indicates that a reversionary interest sharing arrangement is to be used, check that it is stated clearly that the investors are to recover 100% of their money before the general partner backs in for a share (not over 25%) of the revenue.

10. Assessments should be voluntary, limited, and without penalty to those who do not participate.

11. Look for a deal that will give you a 2-to-1 minimum return over a ten-year period—say you contribute $10,000 and receive $20,000 back by the end of ten years. Distribution of cash back to the investors generally begins within 18

to 24 months after the program starts. On a 2-to-1 program, you should see your original investment come back within 3 to 5 years.

12. Other things being equal, look for a program slated to get started soon after January 1. This is when drilling rigs are easily available; your deductions are more likely to occur as projected; the quality of the prospects is likely to be better.

13. Other things being equal, look for a program with an oil company, instead of an oil fund management company, as general partner. You will be less likely to be "promoted," or taken advantage of.

14. Finally, phone—or better still, meet with—the general partner (or one of the higher-ups in the company if the general partner is a corporation). As a potential investor, feel free to ask about any arrangements in the prospectus that puzzle or bother you. Feel free to ask about matters not included in the prospectus. And if the general partner evades your questions, avoid the deal!

New Law: Royalty Owner Credit: The new law provides individuals, estates, and qualified farm corporations with up to $2,500 against their windfall profit tax for the calendar year 1981. This credit isn't available to royalty interest created after June 9, 1981 out of a proven operating mineral interest, unless the royalty was created according to a binding contract entered into before June 10, 1981. This credit is not available for any production for royalty interests transferred (including subleases) after June 9, 1981. This transfer rule does not apply to transfers at death, certain changes in trust beneficiaries, and transfers as long as the transferor and the transferee are required to share the $2,500 credit and where the production was qualified royalty production of the transferor.

New Law: Royalty Owners Exemption: Qualified royalty owners receive an exemption from the windfall profit tax of an aggregate of two barrels a day determined on a quarterly basis from 1982 through 1984, and three barrels a day thereafter.

New Law: Stripper Oil: Beginning in 1983, independent producers' stripper oil production is exempt from windfall profit tax, if four conditions are met: (1) oil must be removed after 1982; (2) oil must be produced by an independent producer; (3) oil must be attributable to the producer's working interest in the property; and (4) the property must not be a property transferred by a nonindependent producer on or after July 23, 1981.

Oil from stripper wells that does not qualify will continue to be taxed at the same rates that were in effect prior to 1983.

New Law: Newly Discovered Oil: The windfall profit tax rate on newly discovered oil has been reduced from 30% in 1981 to 27.5% in 1982, 25% in 1983, 22.5% in 1984, 20% in 1985, and 15% in 1986 and thereafter.

30% − 15% in 1986.

When your ship finally comes in, it's always docked by the government.

—ANONYMOUS

18

Equipment Leasing: Deferral Tax Shelter

Everybody knows about tax shelter investments in oil, real estate, coal, cattle, and horses. (At least everybody knows they exist; the details continue to be a mystery to most.) Equipment leasing is something else again. Few people have heard of it. Fewer have any idea of what it's all about. That's probably because it's suitable to taxpayers in the 60% bracket or higher, who can utilize the high write-offs leasing provides.

Equipment Leasing, Explained: Briefly, an equipment-leasing deal involves the purchase by an investment group of certain types of expensive commercial equipment, such as computers, railroad rolling stock, airplanes, barges, oil-drilling rigs, industrial machinery, pollution control devices, and some kinds of medical equipment; the list could include just about any commercial equipment you can get hold of with a cash down payment and a loan.

The investment group (the lessor) leases the equipment to a business (the lessee) that prefers to rent rather than buy its own equipment. Leasing may be more attractive to businesses in the long run; there's no need to assemble a cash down payment, no need to be burdened with finance charges, no need to be stuck with equipment that may become obsolete in a few years. Another big advantage of renting instead of buying: the lessee's working capital remains uncommitted and can be used for other projects. Leasing frees up the credit line. In renting, the lessee has used, in effect, "off-balance-sheet" financing. Leasing, you see, is a way of financing assets for industry.

The investment group (lessor) accepts the risk of owning and paying for the equipment and in return gets immediate, large depreciation deductions, tax write-offs for interest on loans secured to purchase the equipment and other "front-end" deductions. When the deal works out as planned, the rental fees paid by the end user of the equipment (the lessee) not only cover the loan payments but leave enough over to provide modest cash distributions to investors.

To make use of the deductions, the investors must be personally at risk for the amount of loans; if the lessee defaults on rental payments, the investors are liable for the balance due the lending institution; they also lose out on the tax advantages of the deal, which can go down the drain. Obviously, it's important that the investors lease equipment only to businesses with top-notch credit ratings as listed in Moody's and Standard and Poor's.

A Few Potential Problems of Equipment Leasing and How to Avoid Them: When all goes well, the benefit of equipment leasing is predictable, stable, partly tax-sheltered cash flow. But even when dealing with triple-A-rated businesses the investment group must protect itself from the consequences of default.

Suppose the creditors of a defaulting company came along and tried to repossess the leased equipment. A sure way to prevent this is for the partnership to have a "perfected security" interest in the equipment, which gives it prior claim to the property.

Another problem that may arise indirectly from default of the original lessee—especially if the default occurs a few years into the contract—is obsolescence. If the equipment has aged considerably, or if more efficient equipment has been introduced into the marketplace, the investment group may have a hard time finding another company to release or buy the equipment. Default or no default, obsolescence can affect the eventual disposition of the property when the lease terminates. This is why the partnership should go only into deals that have "full payout leases," that is, leases that specify rental fees high enough to quickly repay the loan.

A so-called "hell or high water" clause is another crucial element in safeguarding the interests of the investment group/lessor. This clause bars the lessee from prematurely terminating the lease; it also prohibits assignment of the lease to a third party. It should be a part of any leasing arrangement.

As an investor/lessor you have a certain measure of security if your equipment is leased to a triple-A company such as General Motors or ATT, which must literally go bankrupt before it can wriggle out of the terms of a lease. But there's a trade-off. With the vast resources of a General Motors backing the lease rather than Duck Soup Company, the return on your investment will be less, because the risk is less.

Why Go into an Equipment-Leasing Investment? Equipment leasing is essentially a deferral of tax liability. You deduct large amounts of depreciation (200% declining balance on new equipment and 150% declining balance on used) in the first years, along with interest and front-end expenses. After a few years the lease generates taxable income (because the depreciation and interest are less) and there is no cash income to the investor (because of the debt service on the borrowings). Then the investor has to pay taxes on "phantom" income (paper income that exceeds the amount of cash distributed).

The initial write-offs in equipment may be 3 or even 4 to 1 (This means that for every dollar contributed, investors can deduct $3 or maybe $4 from their ordinary income. Not bad!)

The deferral of tax liability is as if Uncle Sam said you owed him $100,000, which you could pay now or over a period of seven years if you went into a 7-year leasing program. You'd probably opt for the 7-year payment plan, and that's what equipment leasing is all about: a large write-off now and put off paying taxes until later.

What You Should Know About Tax Benefits: Instead of 200% declining-balance depreciation, investors in new property may elect to use the sum-of-the-years digit method of figuring depreciation, which, as explained in Chapter 14, starts off with less advantage over the straight-line method than declining balance has, but more than catches up later.

The asset depreciation range (ADR), a compilation of U.S. Treasury guidelines on estimated useful life of various items, gives relatively short lives for equipment: computers, 5 to 7 years; railroad boxcars, 12 to 18 years; and so on. This is good, because the shorter the life of the property, the faster the tax write-off can be.

On property that has a useful life of at least six years a "bonus" depreciation deduction of 20% more of the cost of the equipment is allowed during the first year, limited to $2,000 for individual taxpayers, and $4,000 for taxpayers filing a joint return.

About halfway through the lease period, a "cross-over" point is reached where accelerated depreciation deductions (high during the early years, but decreasing rapidly in later years) coupled with the gradual shift from interest to amortization of interest on loan payments no longer shelter income from tax. In fact, a negative ("phantom") income comes into being: Investors are taxed on income they do not actually receive. The excess write-offs taken in the early years catch up with you. Investors must plan for this before going into a venture, and should have funds available to deal with it.

Finally, if there is foreclosure or the equipment is sold, or even given away, all depreciation, not just depreciation in amounts in excess of straight-line deductions, will be subject to recapture as ordinary income to the extent of any gain over the adjusted basis of the property.

What About Investment Tax Credit? Corporate taxpayers can get investment tax credit but not a partnership lessor, unless:

1. The lessor manufactured or produced the equipment.

2. The lessor wants to take the risk of an operating lease. The guidelines on operating leases require, among other things, that the lease period, including renewal provisions, be limited to less than half the estimated useful life of the equipment. I don't recommend this arrangement, no matter how tempting the promise of investment tax credit; it exposes your group to the risk of being unable to release or sell equipment because of obsolescence. The trade-off is not to your advantage.

3. The business expenses of your group, including salaries and maintenance and repair of leased equipment (but not including depreciation and interest) exceed 15% of the income from the property.

How to Make Sure a Lease Works to Your Advantage: Your group must have a lease rather than a conditional sales agreement; the latter forfeits all excess depreciation deductions and investment tax credit. It is essential that the lessee not be permitted to purchase the property at the end of the lease.

The lessee is responsible for upkeep and maintenance of the equipment. The partnership should obtain warranties from the seller or manufacturer of the equipment stating that it is free from defects, and these warranties should be mentioned in the lease, which should also state that maintenance and/or repair work necessary to the proper functioning of the equipment is to be done by properly qualified technicians, using only first-rate replacement parts. Periodic inspections of the equipment should be made to see that the lessee is maintaining it according to the lease provisions. This is essential for later selling or releasing of the equipment.

The lease should not allow IRS to construe the transaction as a sale rather than a rental. IRS has provided guidelines for structuring lease transactions (*Rev. Proc.* 75-21, 1975-18 I.R.B. 15; *Rev. Proc.* 75-28, 1975-21 I.R.B. 19). The guidelines have not been enacted into law, but they touch on the points an audit—if it came to that—would cover, and they are well worth following:

1. At least 20% of the total acquisition cost of the equipment must be contributed by the investor(s) and be unconditionally at risk.

2. Fair market value at the end of the lease term and its renewal period must be at least 20% of the original cost.

3. The remaining useful life of the equipment at the end of the lease term, including renewal periods, must be 20% of the useful life, or at least one year, whichever is greater.

4. The lessee is limited to an option to purchase the equipment, based on the fair market value, at the end of the lease term.

5. The lessee is prohibited from improving (other than for maintenance and repairs) the equipment or paying for any of the cost of the equipment.

6. The lessee may not lend the lessor money on the equipment or guarantee any loans connected with its purchase.

7. The lessee must demonstrate that it entered the transaction for profit, independent of tax benefits.

The Lowdown on Interest: Interest paid on the purchase of property is usually fully deductible, unless it is considered to be investment interest. Then it is limited to $10,000 per year. Interest in a leasing venture becomes investment interest if either of these tests are met:

1. The business deductions of the lessor are less than

15% of the rental income from equipment for the year (excluding interest and depreciation).

2. Guarantees of a specific return against economic loss are given to the lessor.

It's not unusual to use investment interest in a leasing venture. After all, the interest not deductible in one year can be carried forward indefinitely and deducted in future years. You should know if investment interest is used, because it will affect the timing of your tax deductions.

In equipment leasing, corporations have it all over individuals, partnerships, limited partnerships, and Subchapter S corporations. The at-risk rule does not apply to corporations, so they can use nonrecourse financing when making purchases. Neither does a corporate lessor have the "investment interest" limitation.

Nonincorporated businesses can receive high first-year write-offs and modest tax-sheltered profits thereafter, if the leases are properly structured. For many investors the write-offs balance off the at-risk rule.

Equipment leasing is highly sophisticated. It should be entered into only with the help of highly knowledgeable legal and accounting professionals.

New Law: New Rules for Depreciation, Investment Tax Credit, and Leasing: See Chapter 10 under "New Laws."

New Law: Advantages for Loss Corporations and Taxpayers: Corporations, other than Subchapter S and personal holding corporations, may be assured of lease treatment with a 10% investment if the lease is not for more than 90% of the actual or 150% of the ADR class life of the property, whichever is greater. The lessor now has the certainty that the tax benefits can be passed on to the lessee, through reduced rental charges on the property. Loss corporations or individuals can take maximum advantage from the new capital recovery rules through reduced rents.

The art of taxation consists in so plucking the goose as to obtain the largest amount of feathers with the least possible amount of hissing.

—JEAN-BAPTISTE COLBERT

19

Down on the Farm: Agricultural Tax Shelters

So you always hankered after being a farmer, but never wanted to do that much work. Well, here's your chance to be a passive farmer and get the same kind of tax treatment as the real dirt-under-the-fingernails types. All you need to do is put up enough cash to get in on a good limited-partnership farming venture, step into a pair of overalls, sit back with a tumbler of Jack Daniel's and you're in business. Well, almost. Before you reach for your checkbook you should understand the profit potential of farm investment tax shelters.

For tax (and tax shelter) purposes, farming includes everything from raising crops, such as wheat or corn, to growing fruit in orchards, tending grapevines, and commercial flower gardening. You have to enter the venture "for profit," as required by Section 183 of the Internal Revenue Code. That means your major interest in the business is income, not tax avoidance. So it's important that the venture is run to produce income—that the land is efficiently managed, the crops are carefully tended and gotten to market on time, and all else that farming for profit implies. Otherwise, you forfeit the tax breaks.

You can profit from farming through sale of your produce and through appreciation in the value of land. Many agricultural ventures are the result of someone's (or some group's) having bought a large parcel of land in the hope it could be sold to a developer at a large profit. Farming was an afterthought, a way to defray the costs of carrying the land for a few years while its value went up. You too might eventually realize huge profits from the land you plan to farm if and when it attracts the attention of a large residential, commercial, or industrial developer.

Meanwhile, back on the farm, one major advantage of the investment is that you or your investment group can use the cash method of accounting, where you deduct expenses for seed, fertilizer, and other supplies and equipment in the year that the expenses are incurred. If the nature of the venture is such that several years must pass before income is generated—as may be true of an orchard, where trees must fully mature before they bear fruit—the costs of development, depreciation, and interest payments on loans will create losses for tax purposes. If you are a member of a limited partnership the losses can be applied to offset your ordinary income. Further deductions can be claimed for fencing, outbuildings, farming equipment, and so on. Deductions of 140% to 170% of your investment are not unusual, assuming leveraged recourse borrowings.

Limited-partnership investors need not report any unrealized appreciation of land value or livestock until the sale is actually made. Then your gains will be subject to capital gains tax treatment, provided that the livestock is held for draft, dairy, or breeding purposes.

Corporate investors do not fare so well in farming ventures. With the exceptions of small businesses or family corporations (gross receipts of $1 million or less), they must use the accrual method of accounting. Furthermore, start-up expenses (those incurred before sale of the first marketable crop) must be capitalized. An interesting chart supplied by the Institute of Energy Development (see below) shows how expenses are treated for tax purposes by the farmer, the investor, and the corporate farmer.

Initial Deductibility

Type of Expenditure	Total Amount	Full-Time Farmer	Farming Syndicate	Corporate Farmer
Partly consumed farm supplies (25%)—no crop sales	$10,000	$10,000	$ 2,500	0
Reproductive crop expenses—no crop sales	10,000	10,000	10,000	0
Reproductive grove or vineyard expenses	10,000	10,000	0	0
Harvested but unsold crops	10,000 cost	0	0	− 10,000
Crops sold, but revenue uncollected	10,000 selling price	0	0	− 10,000

Farm-Style Risk Factors: The risks of an investment in farming are similar to the risks in livestock breeding and feeding ventures: Bad weather can destroy crops totally or in part; so can plant diseases and insects. Market fluctuations can be a major problem. There can be disputes with organized farm labor and the possibility of a consumer boycott of crops. Water is increasingly scarce; lack of it will ruin certain crops just as surely as flood conditions will.

As in all investments, competent management is crucial. So is the need to establish a fair fee structure for management and removal or resolution of conflicts of interest.

Some farming operations entail a long start-up period and by nature will not become economically self-sufficient for years. It's quite possible that economic and tax climates will change during that time.

By all means check with an accountant or tax attorney

before entering a farming venture to make sure the tax deductions work the way you want them to.

Ranching as a Tax-Sheltered Investment

So you'd rather be a cowboy than a farmer. Fine. Like farming, a ranch investment offers the possibility of two kinds of profit: gain realized from the sale of cattle or horses or sheep or whatever, and/or the possibility of making a large profit from sale of the land.

Ranching too must be engaged in "for profit" rather than for pure tax avoidance. Investors in a ranching venture must make sure the operation is managed for optimum profit (even if losses, not profits, result); otherwise claims for deductions will be disallowed by IRS.

The tax-sheltered advantages of ranching are similar to those of cattle breeding and feeding. Expenses for current care and maintenance of livestock are deductible in the year they are incurred, which can result in long-term tax deferral. Other deductible expenses are associated with building dams, constructing drainage ditches, leveling or grading, land clearance, fertilization, and measures taken for conservation purposes.

Fences, buildings, and ranching equipment can be depreciated. Livestock held for breeding or dairy purposes, except for horses, is also depreciable. Risks? There's always the possibility that depreciation deductions taken on purchased livestock will be recaptured when you sell the beasts; loss of investment tax credit, if any, is also possible if animals have not been kept for the required period. If you have not owned the land for at least ten years before selling it, depreciation claimed for improvements and conservation expenditures may be recaptured.

In ranching you have a double-barreled chance to lose:

Your cattle/horse/sheep operation may be unprofitable, and you may have purchased land at a high price that no developer would care to match, meaning you may have to liquidate at a loss. But you can look at it the other way around: Maybe you'll reap big bucks from livestock sales plus sell the land for umpteen times what you paid for it. Maybe.

Farming and Livestock; or Give Me the Simple (Tax-Sheltered) Life

You don't have to give up your Fifth Avenue triplex and pack out to the sticks to take advantage of the tax-sheltering opportunities offered by farming and raising (or, in the case of cattle, simply *feeding*) livestock. All that has to move is your money.

What do you get in return for your investment in the agricultural well-being of the country? It depends on the kind of venture you have in mind. In general, farming and livestock investors get high tax deductions at the beginning, when start-up expenses are high. Later, as crops or animals are sold and the business begins to bring in income, taxes must be paid on profits. So, like many other tax-shelter investments, agricultural ventures result primarily in the deferral of taxes—deferral that allows you time-use of money you would otherwise have paid out to Uncle Sam. And that ain't hay.

The deductions that result in tax deferral are usually taken at least a year, maybe quite a bit longer (depending on whether your product is vegetable or animal), before you begin to see any income. You use the cash method of accounting, deducting your expenses in the year they are paid out; thus, initially, farming produces rather large tax losses.

As an investor you can deduct these losses from your other income, but the amount of write-off you are eligible for is limited to the amount you are at risk for. The at-risk amount is the total cash you have invested plus any loans you have negotiated for investment purposes and for which you are personally liable.

Nonrecourse financing, where the lending institution looks to the farm property as collateral to be used as a guarantee against default or foreclosure, is not considered to be at risk for the investor, who is not personally liable for repayment. You can use nonrecourse financing if you like, but your deductions are limited to the amount for which you are personally at risk.

Farm Deductions; When Timing Is All: The new tax laws have affected the time when some farm deductions can be taken. Individual investors or limited partnerships can now deduct expenses for seed, fertilizer, and other farm supplies only in the year that the supplies are used. In the past, partnerships could stock up on supplies in advance and get a big immediate deduction, but no more.

For the same reason, the tax laws make it unwise to go into a deal at the end of a year expecting to get big deductions for that year. Very little of the supplies can be used by year-end and thus deducted.

Other advantages to farming investments are that investment tax credits are often available and that ordinary income can be converted into capital gains.

Tax Credits for Livestockers and Farmers: A 10% investment tax credit is available on tangible property used in farming, including livestock raised as part of a breeding or dairy income-producing venture (but not horses), fences, wells, storage facilities, and so forth. If you invest in $100,000 worth of livestock and property that qualifies for the investment tax credit, you can subtract 10%, or $10,000, from the taxes you owe to the government that year!

How Capital Gains Fit into the Livestock/Farming Picture: If you hold your interest in the venture for more than a year and then sell it, you are entitled to capital gains tax treatment (which means a maximum tax rate of only 28%) on any profits.

Getting Fat Waiting for the Cows to Come Home

Some people swear by cattle-breeding tax shelters. These ventures are riddled with risk; but when they succeed, investors come out happier than a cow in clover (or a pig in slop, if porkers are the animal of choice).

A Quick Rundown of the Advantages of Cattle-Breeding Ventures: Why invest in cattle breeding instead of something more, well, cultured, like old masters or Chinese ceramics? Let me count the whys:

1. There's great demand for the product and a relatively short start-up time. (All you need are a few heifers and a lot of bull.)

2. You can get accelerated depreciation on animals once they reach maturity and start going over the hill. (Yes, it's true!) The 200% declining-balance method is appropriate if you purchased the animals to build up your herd. If the animals are part of an existing herd you purchased en masse (I suppose that means a "used" herd), you can use the 150% declining-balance method.

The estimated useful lives of these animals are short; your assessed depreciation range for livestock is 8 to 12 years. Offspring can't be depreciated, as there is no cost basis for them. (You didn't buy them—the stork brought them.) Still, the cost of feeding and raising calves is deductible.

You can use the 150% declining-balance method to

depreciate new farm buildings and other facilities. For used or existing buildings you must use the straight-line method.

3. Bonus depreciation is available for animals you buy for your herd if they have a remaining estimated useful life of six years or more. Bonus depreciation deductions can be claimed on 20% of the cost of the animal, not to exceed $2,000 for an individual or $4,000 for a married couple filing jointly.

4. A 10% investment tax credit is available for each animal (excluding horses) used for draft, breeding, or dairy purposes. A heifer or bull qualifies for full credit if its remaining estimated useful life is seven years or more. Selling cattle before the end of their estimated useful life can result in recapture of the investment tax credit that was taken on them.

5. You are eligible for capital gains treatment on the sale of cattle held for breeding purposes for 24 months or longer. On completion of the sale, excess depreciation is subject to recapture and taxation as ordinary income.

Here's where it gets a little complicated: The sale of off-spring of the original herd, if you have owned them for 24 months or longer, are taxed entirely at capital gains rates. There is no recapture, because they were not depreciated.

How Profitable Is Cattle Breeding, Anyway? Despite the long list of tax advantages, the risks associated with cattle breeding are formidable. Many ventures barely pass the break-even point. As for the failure rate, well, I personally know only a handful of investors who have made money in syndicated cattle-breeding programs that were offered to the public.

Cattle breeding can be commercial breeding or purebred breeding.

In *commercial breeding* the idea is to produce calves to supply the country's demand for beef, while at the same time building up the herd for eventual sale at a profit. So, the bigger the herd and the more they reproduce, the better. Many of the calves born are "culls," which means they are inferior and are marched off to the slaughter houses. They graze on grasslands until they weigh 400 to 700 pounds and are known as "feeders." Then they are sold to cattle feeders, who fatten them up on feedlots until they reach a weight of 1,000 to 1,100 pounds and are slaughtered. With the high cost of grain, many cattle may be pastured on grassland rather than the feedlot. Profits from the sale usually go back into the business. The trouble is, cattle are frequently sold to the investor at prices above their normal market value; feedlot costs may also be excessive. Expenses may be so high that the potential for profit is almost nil.

A bad ratio of male to female calves may prevent the herd from expanding. Too many bull calves and not enough females ultimately shrinks the herd. (One bull can effectively service a whole herd of cows.)

Tax-free swapping of your female calves for someone else's heifers (unbred females) is permissible. This can help build up your herd. But swapping a bull for a heifer is a taxable transaction!

In a *purebred breeding* program the goal is to produce a herd of cattle with superior genetic qualities that can be sold to commercial breeders to improve their herds. Breeders are at a disadvantage from the start, as it is hard to predict which breeds will be in greatest demand a year from now.

Premium prices must be paid for purebred cattle. An investment group should be prepared to spend between $1,000 and $3,000 per purebred cow (as opposed to $300 to $500 for commercial cows). It is not at all unusual for purebred bulls to sell for $10,000 each; some have been sold for $1 million. (Their commercial cousins go for a mere $500 to $1,000.)

Emergency liquidation of an entire herd of exotic purebred cattle would certainly depress prices for the breed, making them less valuable. So you can't bail out in a hurry without taking a big loss.

The speculative nature of cattle breeding in general, and

of purebred breeding in particular, should put you on your guard. Yet that handful of investors I mentioned made substantial gains. Probably you should not put more than a limited part of your tax shelter budget into a cattle-breeding venture (preferably commercial).

A few commonsense guidelines can minimize the risks:

1. Cattle are often sold to investment groups at inflated prices. Do your homework to find out the real going prices.

2. Check on the costs of feeding the animals. You can't win if it costs more to feed them than you get when you sell them.

3. If the deal is a limited partnership venture, check on the reputation of the general partner. (See Chapter 15.) Read the prospectus to determine whether the general partner's fees are reasonable. Watch out for meaningless guarantees. Try to figure out the down side or worst case analysis of the deal. An accountant or attorney who specializes in tax law will be valuable in judging a deal.

Cattle-Feeding Programs: The goal of a cattle-feeding program is to convert grain or grass into beef at a profit while taking advantage of tax deferral opportunities.

Tax Benefits of a Cattle-Feeding Venture: Cattle feeding works on a leverage basis. For each dollar that you or your investment group puts up, $2 to $4 are borrowed from a bank. About one-third of the money raised is spent on deductible items such as feed, feedlot service, and interest on the loan. The other two-thirds is not deductible and is spent on buying the feeder cattle.

Tax deferral is achieved by deducting your costs for feed and cattle maintenance as expenses are incurred. Five or six months later, when your fattened cattle are sold, you're taxed on the profits. If you don't stop there, but buy more feed and more cattle, you can roll over your tax liabilities as you wish.

Another advantage of cattle feeding is that it does not create items of tax preference, and thus in the year of investment there's no potential for minimum tax liability.

Cattle-Feeding Tax Addenda: The Tax Code no longer permits prepaid fees (for example, for feed) to be deducted in cattle feeding. This has eliminated most end-of-year cattle-feeding deals.

The Tax Reform Act of 1976 requires that corporate investors or partnerships having a corporate partner, who are engaged in a farming business, must use the accrual method of accounting, and must capitalize certain "pre-productive" period expenses (Internal Revenue Code Section 447).

Two Kinds of Cattle-Feeding Programs: Each type has its advantages and disadvantages to the investor:

1. The *agency* agreement is an arrangement whereby cattle are purchased in the name of the investor or investment group and are turned over for maintenance to an agent or cattleman. This reduces the risk of being audited, since your contract with the feedlot agent or cattleman assures your active involvement in the business. Administration costs of an agency agreement tend to be lower. And financing may be easier to get than if you're operating under a syndicate arrangement (discussed below).

However, an agency relationship does not spread the risks as a syndicate arrangement does. You don't have limited liability under an agency agreement as you would with a syndicate.

2. *Syndicate* arrangements are limited partnership deals, the syndicator serving as general partner. The partnership contracts with a feedlot operator who maintains and feeds the cattle. The result is greater diversification and limited liability for you as an investor. However, the tax risks are greater, as we shall see.

One Big Plus for Cattle-Feeding as an Investment: If you are looking for flexibility in planning your taxes from year to year, cattle-feeding programs may be uniquely advantageous. For example, if you need to transfer income from one year to the next, a short-term feeding program can work in your favor. Or if your master tax plan calls for long-term tax-sheltered investment of some of your money, a series of short-term cattle-feeding programs or a long-term program may suit your needs. However, because of the heavy use of leverage in cattle-feeding programs, changes in the price of grain or of beef can upset your planning.

. . . and an Equally Big Minus: Another risk is that fattened cattle cannot be withheld from market in the hope of getting a better price; this would result in increased feed and maintenance costs, and the quality of beef is affected if cattle are not slaughtered in good time.

The Stop-Loss Provision: No Way to Minimize Risk: To minimize the risk to the investor of widely fluctuating feed and beef prices, the syndicator or feedlot operator may offer to guarantee that the investors' losses per head will not exceed a certain amount. In return, the syndicator or feedlot operator takes a percentage of the profits—if there are any—and it may be as high as 50%.

This provision seldom does what it is intended to do. Usually the stop-loss is adjusted so that the syndicator or feedlot operator profits in "normal" markets. In bad markets, such as we saw in the mid-1970s, the guarantee may become meaningless when the syndicator or operator goes bankrupt.

Because the stop-loss provision is a form of guarantee, the investors' activity may be interpreted by the IRS as not being farming "at risk" and thus disallow the deductions.

Steer Averaging and Other Techniques to Buffer Cattle-Feeding Risks: Setting up a long-term cattle-feeding program so that market highs and lows tend to balance out is called steer averaging. It is, in a sense, similar to the dollar-averaging techniques used by many stock-market investors. The technique is often good, though it failed to protect many cattle feeders from disaster in the crazy (for cattle investments) years of the mid-seventies, when demand and prices for beef went down while the price of grain

265

soared; many hapless investors were whipsawed into ruination.

Another way to buffer risks (and profits) is to hedge on the purchase and sale of cattle on the commodities market. Skillfully done, this can help balance out price fluctuations. The flies in the ointment, however, are the commissions you will be charged on each futures contract. That, plus elimination of the chance of making a big profit, makes hedging less attractive than it at first seems.

Getting You Off the Horns of Dilemma: To deal or not to deal? If that is the cattle investment question, these pointers may help you decide which way to go in a tough business, and whether a breeding program, a feeding program, or *no* program makes the most sense:

1. You must enter a cattle program for profit, not just for tax benefits, or IRS will disallow your deductions. Stop-loss, hedging, or paying high fees can be overdone and invite trouble from IRS.

2. Hedging in the futures market can be very risky if you buy on margin.

3. Screen management—the cattle syndicator or general partner in a limited partnership—carefully for reputability and a proved track record. Can management stay abreast of scientific progress in cattle breeding, feeding, and health care?

4. Don't let the annual fee, if any, charged by the syndicator or general partner get out of hand.

5. Conflicts of interest may cause problems. If some of the cattle die, be suspicious if almost all of them turn out to be yours; see that your money isn't paying for grain to feed the feedlot operator's cattle; see that your animals go to market at the same price as his.

6. Have an independent agent monitor your cattle operations periodically.

7. Cattle feeding is a short-term investment. Price fluctuations affect it more than cattle breeding.

8. Check extensively on whether the prices you are

being charged for cattle are in line with prices being paid by other investors and professional cattlemen.

9.   Fraud is not unheard-of in cattle programs. You may be led to believe you have purchased premium cattle; then inferior animals are delivered. Games can be played with the scales when your animals are weighed at time of purchase and sale. And the cattle rustlers are still alive and rustling!

10.   When you invest in a number of feedlots in various sections of the country you take less chances with the weather—an important factor in raising cattle. Bad weather can affect the overall health, the amount of weight gained, and the mortality rate of cattle.

11.   A commercial breeding operation should rely on its own bulls or on artificial insemination for expansion. Purchasing the services of a premium male is super-expensive.

12.   To be profitable, the calving rate must equal the 85% historic industry average.

13.   It's important to the future of a herd that the mix between male and female cattle be right. Cull and slaughter male calves, aiming toward one bull and lots of cows to produce more offspring.

14.   Disease is a risk whenever animals are involved. The industry average of death loss by disease is 2%. To make profits your death loss should be kept below that.

15.   Insurance for death loss to the herd can be extremely expensive. Some syndicators will agree to indemnify investors against excess death loss, say, over 4%; but the guarantor must have sufficient liquid net worth to make the guarantee meaningful.

16.   Don't let the cattle operator make money just by your going into a cattle deal. The promotion fee should be kept to a minimum.

New Law: Current Use Valuation: See Chapter 11 under "New Law: Current Use Valuation."

Take care to sell your horse before he dies. The art of life is passing losses on.

—ROBERT FROST

20

Horse-Racing Syndications: Don't Get Taken for a Ride (Plus a Few Words on Other Livestock Investments)

A horse is a thing of beauty, no doubt about it. Especially thoroughbreds, the breeding and racing of which is the business of racing syndicates. There has been a surge of interest in horse racing and in syndicating racehorses, which is structurally similar to cattle breeding. A group of brood mares is acquired, and one or more stallion shares, to breed and sell yearlings. Some may be trained and raced. As in other agricultural ventures, land acquired for use may later be sold for real estate development.

The syndicator or general partner in a thoroughbred breeding venture manages the business, seeing to it that the horses are properly stabled and cared for, that regular veterinary services are rendered, and that promising yearlings are sold or placed in training for racing. In exchange, the syndicator receives regular compensation plus extra fees for brokerage, insurance, and arranging stud service.

Tax Breaks Available: Many of the tax laws that apply

to cattle breeding also apply to horse breeding, but there are exceptions:

Racehorse investment resembles other exotic investments in that the front-end write-off approaches the 300% to 400% level! Now you know you're dealing with high economic and tax risks.

Racehorse syndication is planned to produce long-term tax deferral. Deductions can be taken on interest payments on loans and on the maintenance and depreciation of the animal(s). IRS does not allow investment tax credit for racehorses.

The investors generally buy horses from the syndicator or general partner at a large markup, paying in installments through a recourse "balloon" loan (where the principal is due in a large final installment), payable upon termination of the partnership. This kind of financing allows for hefty front-end write-offs; it also creates more business and tax risks.

Because of use of recourse borrowing secured by chattel mortgages on the purchased animals, the at-risk limitations for investors are waived.

Long-term capital gains treatment may be available for the sale of a horse in stud service for not less than 24 months to the extent that stud fees exceed the depreciation previously taken on the horse and any balance in the investors' EDA (excess deductions account). An investor no longer needs to make additions to his or her EDA account for excess farm losses incurred after December 31, 1975, according to the 1976 Tax Reform Act; but to the extent the investor incurred such losses before 1976 in other agricultural activities, the balance in his or her EDA account is subject to recapture from the proceeds of post–'76 Reform Act agricultural investment.

Accelerated depreciation (150% declining balance) may be taken on horses bought for the venture, but not on the foals. *All* the depreciation taken is subject to recapture and subsequent taxation as ordinary income. Deductions for grain and other supplies are limited according to "farming syndicate" rules to feed, equipment, and supplies actually consumed during the tax year.

Your investment in thoroughbreds must be structured for profit potential, or IRS may attack and disallow your deductions. The Revenue Code states that breeding, training, showing, and racing of horses must have gross income exceeding deductions for at least two out of seven consecutive tax years.

Financially Stampeded—Don't Get Lassoed By Horses: Special risks go with investing in live animals: risks related to disease, accidents, or death of the animals; to weather and other environmental conditions; and to management. These risks are multiplied when the animal is a delicate thoroughbred racehorse. Expert management is even more important. You must rely on the judgment of the syndicator or general partner on which horses to buy for breeding purposes and on which yearlings to sell and which to train for racing.

Conflict of interest, common in cattle ventures, may be even more common in thoroughbred ventures. The animals may be sold to you at an unfair markup. Excessive fees may be demanded.

If the excitement and glamour of breeding thoroughbreds gets the better of you and you plunge in anyway, remember you are locked into a long-term investment. You would have an even harder time unloading a group of thoroughbreds in a hurry than a herd of purebred cattle.

A Few Words About Other Livestock Investments: A tax shelter that I always find rather amusing is purchase through a syndicate of hens for egg production.

The cost of poultry must be capitalized and deducted over a 12-month period (or over the poultry's estimated useful life if less than 12 months); it can be deducted only in the tax year in which the poultry are disposed of. Sale of poultry is not eligible for capital gains tax treatment. Poultry ventures are subject to the rules of at-risk financing.

Tax benefits are like those for other animal investments: initial tax deductions and fast depreciation. All depreciation deductions are subject to recapture and taxed as ordinary income when the animals are sold.

Risks? Chickens get sick and die; syndicators must be screened; and so on as for other animals.

Do your homework for any kind of livestock investment. Read everything you can find about your "animal of choice"; learn about proper care and feeding. And before investing, talk the deal through with a qualified tax adviser.

That popular Stage-playes . . . are sinfull, heathenish, lewde, ungodly Spectacles, and most pernicious Corruptions; condemned in all ages, as intolerable Mischiefes to Churches, to Republickes, to the manners, mindes, and soules of men. And that the Profession of play-poets, of Stage-players; together with the penning, acting, and frequenting of Stage-playes, are unlawfull, infamous, and misbeseeming Christians.

—WILLIAM PRYNNE

21

Be an Angel: Making It (or Breaking It) on Broadway; or, So Your Aunt Ethel's a Producer!

Backers of Broadway productions are called angels, but "martyrs" or "gluttons for punishment" would be better names. They invest plenty, but only rarely do they get their money back. And as for making a profit—well, everybody knows it happens *sometimes*, but it never seems to happen to someone anybody knows.

When there are profits, they're made not only from Broadway box-office sales, but from subsidiary rights if the show is made into a movie or a TV special, or if a musical is recorded. A successful show will go on tour, perhaps with a couple of touring companies working simultaneously.

What you should know is that even if a show is a box-office hit, the investors may never see a cent of profit. How come? It costs an awful lot to keep a show going. Salaries of stars, director, and choreographer may be astronomical. Feature players, understudies, wardrobe mistress, and second violinist also have to be paid. The author may get a large chunk in royalties, and the theater receives a percentage of gross receipts. The general partner/producer is cut in for a share of the net profits and receives a management fee payable out of *gross* box-office receipts. Beware of the producer who has never had a hit but who lives in the luxury you dream of! From 35% to 50% of gross box-office receipts may be skimmed off the top for stars and management alone. When it's time to divvy up the profits, the investor stands back toward the end of the line.

Just because you backed the play, believed in it, laid out money that made it possible, don't expect opening-night tickets, or *any* free tickets, *any* time. As for being invited to that glittering star-studded champagne and caviar opening night party, forget it.

There are consolations. You'll be able to deduct what you contribute when you file your tax return and deep down inside you'll have the satisfaction of knowing that you're a patron of the arts. That, mostly, is what "angels" are all about.

Of all our natural resources, the first one to be exhausted will probably be the taxpayer.

—ANONYMOUS

22

Timber: Seeing the Forest for the Trees

Timber investments offer distinct tax advantages plus what are often called "interesting economics":

1. Timber is constantly growing, but . . .
2. You don't pay any tax until you cut or dispose of it.
3. If you hold timber long enough—over a year—you receive capital gains treatment on the sale.
4. Current maintenance and operating costs are deductible in the year they are incurred.
5. You receive cost depletion (see Chapter 17).
6. Your timberland (if you own it) may appreciate in value, and you may be able to sell it at a large profit.

Hence, you get tax deferral on any realization of gain. When your timber is sold you get long-term capital gains treatment and receive cost depletion to boot. A very nice package of benefits.

The Workings of a Timber Venture: You or your investment group must obtain "economic interest" in the timber, either by purchasing timberland outright or by buying cutting rights from the landowner, which give you the privilege of cutting without an interest in the land.

If you're buying land you can use cash or borrowed funds,

either by recourse financing (where you or your group are liable for the debt if anything goes wrong) or nonrecourse financing (in which the lender accepts the property as collateral for the loan). The cost of the timberland must be capitalized; payments on the mortgage principal are not deductible as a business expense. However, cruising costs (evaluation of timber and land by a professional forester), costs of planting, spraying, clearing, culling (weeding out some trees so that others may grow better) and other land maintenance expenses, and costs of fire prevention measures and fire insurance are deductible in the year the expenses were incurred and paid for. Taxes and interest payments are also deductible for the tax year in which they were paid.

Tax Planning and Economic Flexibility—Added Advantages of Timber Investments: Trees take a while to grow and mature, but once past the sapling stage they don't spoil or go bad like a crop of peaches or even a feedlot full of cattle. This means you can time the disposition of your timber, cutting and selling when it best suits your tax or economic needs. The year you or your investment group wants income is the year to cut and sell. When losses make better tax sense, let the trees stand. If timber prices are down, postpone cutting for a couple of years and see if prices go up. (Then too, the longer your trees are allowed to stand, the taller and presumably more valuable they become.)

When timber you have held for over a year is cut, your gains are treated as long-term capital gains, and your losses are treated as ordinary rather than capital losses, according to Section 1231.

There are three ways to get capital gains treatment with timber:

1. Sale of standing timber: Timber held over one year is a capital asset and the investor is entitled to capital gain or loss, with long-term capital gains treatment.

2. Cutting of timber by owner: When you cut your own timber it can be treated as a sale under the Tax Code,

whether or not you sell it. The gain or loss is the difference between the adjusted basis of the timber and its value from the first day of the taxable year.

3. Section 1231 treatment: To treat gains as capital gains and losses as ordinary losses, the investor must retain an economic interest in the timber.

Depletion deductions are computed according to a complex formula (Section 611) that would take a book to explain. Depletion is allowable only on a cost basis on the timber felled during the year, not on the timber that is sold. Cost depletion is allowable. The tax laws are especially complex in this area, and obtaining professional advice is essential.

Risks: Bad weather can wipe out a whole stand of seedlings or stunt the growth of saplings; soil can be eroded by floods; disease, insects, and forest fires can damage or kill your trees. Good management can minimize some but not all of these risks.

A Few Guidelines:

1. If you are buying raw, undeveloped land, compare the price of comparable land in the area. A few long-distance calls or even a visit to the area is worth it if you are considering a sizable investment.

2. Whether you're buying land or just the cutting rights, prefer land carrying trees of varying maturity. This kind of investment automatically regenerates itself. As older trees are felled, seedlings can be planted to replace them and younger trees will be growing to maturity.

3. A "timber cruise" is crucial before buying. Only an independent professional forester can give you accurate information about suitability of land for future plantings and about the quantity and quality of the trees already standing. (A local agricultural college or university with a good agricultural department can help you locate a forester and can provide other useful information about the industry.)

4. The land you invest in should have at least one good

access road. The cost of building a road can add significantly to the total cost of your investment.

5. Management should know all the ins and outs of the timber industry and should be thoroughly screened. (See Chapter 15.)

Who knows? Maybe money does grow on trees.

New Law: Current Use Valuation: See Chapter 11 under "New Law: Current Use Valuation."

> The average taxpayer believes in only one kind of government handout—the kind that takes the government's hand out of his pocket.
>
> —Anonymous

23

Hitting Pay Dirt:
Investing in Coal

Coal has come into its own; rather, it's coming back into its own. Once in dominant use as an energy source, for years the value of coal was eclipsed by our preoccupation with low-priced oil and gas. The situation is changing, especially in this country. Coal is something we definitely do not have to import. The current estimate is that perhaps 4 *trillion* tons are buried on the North American continent, most of it in the United States. This is enough to supply our energy needs for centuries. No wonder coal is beginning to catch on with investors.

Though I'd prefer to accentuate the positive and eliminate the negative, as the old song goes, the truth is that coal mining is fraught with problems. In oil and gas the main problem is locating resources; in coal the main problems are environmental.

Coal burning pollutes the air. (Although pollution devices are expensive, we will see increased use of them as more and more industries turn to coal as fuel.) Deep coal mining is dangerous business that has jeopardized the health and safety of miners for centuries. Strip mining has been banned in certain parts of the West due to agricultural, aesthetic, and environmental considerations. Where strip mining is allowed, the mining companies are required to repair the devastation of the land by restoring it to its original contours, removing all wastes and replanting the land with grass and trees.

With all of its problems coal may be the fuel of the future, or at least the fuel of last resort. Gas and oil reserves are depleting; the implications of nuclear energy are terrifying; and the development of solar energy is still in its helpless infancy. What's left? Coal.

An interesting thing happened in 1976, when investors seeking large tax write-offs correctly anticipated that movie deals would receive adverse tax treatment. They suddenly switched from movies to coal, believing that mining investments would allow them to claim immediate 300% to 400% tax write-offs. The proposed deals were based on a lump-sum advance royalty payment secured by the investor through nonrecourse borrowing and paid to landowner or mining lessees for the right to mine properties. Investors believed, or were led to believe, that these lump-sum payments, whether or not any coal was produced, would be immediately deductible. The nonrecourse notes would presumably be paid off quickly when coal profits began rolling in.

These assumptions were almost immediately challenged by IRS, which on October 29, 1976, announced a proposed amendment to deny current deductions of lump-sum royalty payments and defer deductions until the year when the coal was actually sold. There was the additional threat that past lump-sum advance royalty deductions would be knocked out retroactively.

In 1977 many investors who had rushed into coal deals to get big immediate tax write-offs met with disaster. Because these investors knew nothing about coal and because of outright fraud, many coal properties produced much less coal for much higher costs than the investors expected. They got burned.

On December 19, 1977, the U.S. Treasury adopted the proposed regulations. A one-year prepayment of annual minimum royalties payable uniformly over the life of the lease, or for a period of at least 20 years (whichever is shorter), may be deducted in advance; but other deductions for payment of advance royalties to land or mineral rights owners must be deferred to the year when the coal is sold.

The Structure of a Typical Coal Deal: A limited partnership is formed and leases are secured, let's say, on acreage containing 1 million tons of recoverable coal. It is assumed that 100,000 tons of coal can be mined in a year, so the lease allows the partnership mining rights to the coal for ten years or until all the coal is mined, whichever comes later.

The partnership agrees to pay the land or mineral rights owner a royalty fee of $4 per ton of mined coal, and an advance minimum royalty payment based on 40,000 tons of coal per year, or $160,000, whether or not the coal is mined, the advance to be deducted from the regular royalty as the coal is mined.

If the rights to mine the coal were acquired on November 1, 1980, the partnership would pay the advanced minimum royalty payment of $160,000 on December 1, and deduct $160,000 for that year.

Let's suppose the partnership spent $15,000 for exploration procedures and $50,000 to build an access road. The estimated cost of mining the coal is $18 per ton. The mining cost includes labor, equipment, transportation, tippling (emptying loaded cars), land rehabilitation, taxes, management fees, and selling commissions. These are "ordinary and necessary" business expenses and are deductible as they are incurred.

Exploration expenses are also currently deductible, as are certain development expenses (such as tunnels, shafts, and roads), which are incurred after commercially exploitable quantities of coal have been confirmed, but before the beginning of commercial production. The partnership may choose to deduct such expenses over the period during which the coal is mined.

On the basis of these deductions, investors can expect to claim a 1-to-1 tax write-off on the amounts they have contributed to the venture.

The partnership makes contractual arrangements with a miner who will supply the labor and machinery necessary to extract 100,000 tons of coal each year, and with a utility company that agrees as an "end user" to purchase 100,000 tons of coal a year at $24 per ton for ten years.

As the coal is mined and sold, the partnership is eligible for a 10% depletion allowance deduction on gross revenues, not to exceed 50% of net revenues. Gross revenues of $500,000 should mean a depletion allowance of $50,000; but if the partnership nets only $90,000, the depletion allowance would be only half of this, or $45,000.

If the partnership buys its own mining equipment, depreciation deductions on the equipment, as well as investment tax credit, are available. For new equipment 200% declining-balance depreciation can be used; for secondhand equipment, 150% declining balance. Sale of equipment before the end of its useful life makes depreciation deductions already taken subject to recapture by IRS.

Cost of renting equipment is deductible, as is interest if the partnership borrows money to purchase equipment.

If the partnership sells its interest in the property after holding it for an entire year, any gains from the sale will be taxed at long-term capital gains rates. (This is true even if the company defaults and then sells after a year of holding its mining interest.)

It may be advantageous to the partnership to sublet the mineral rights to the property instead of selling them. Then the partnership can receive royalty payments, as well as annual minimum royalty payments and perhaps even a down payment from the new lessee. If the company has held its interest for more than a year, royalty income will be eligible for taxation at capital gains rates. However, only cost depletion may be used (see Chapter 17).

By subletting the rights the partnership relieves itself of the risks of the mining venture, but still receives income. Nifty, yes?

Evaluating a Coal-Mining Deal: Mining is no different from any other capital T Tax Shelter in that it has its risks and rewards, its problem areas, and its own set of pitfalls. The following suggestions may help you factor out some of the riskier programs and steer you toward the few better deals:

1. Know the general partner, the miner or coal company masterminding the deal. Read the prospectus to determine the past track record of the firm. Check the net worth of the general partner to see that it is sufficient to meet IRS requirements. Satisfy yourself that you are dealing with a reputable outfit (see Chapter 15). Does the prospectus indicate the general partner's intention of staying with the deal?

2. What is the quality, estimated quantity, type, and location of the coal? Is it steam coal, which is used as an energy source, or metallurgical coal, used in steel production? The latter brings the higher price. How "dirty" is the coal? If your coal is dirty there will be an additional expense of washing it. The lower the sulfur and ash content of the coal, the cleaner and more desirable—and easier to market—it is. How does the coal rate in BTUs (British thermal units)? High-BTU coal is of better quality and brings a better price. Will your money go into strip mining or deep mining? Are the reserves sufficient? Are they "proved" recoverable, or merely "in place"? Is the price you are paying reasonable?

The prospectus will answer some of these questions for

you. But if you are planning to invest much, the additional cost of hiring an independent metallurgical engineer to investigate the land and the coal will be money well spent. Review the results and studies of all independent engineers and geologists who have analyzed the mining site and the quality and quantity of coal.

3. Ideally, there should be good transportation facilities near the property. What does the prospectus say about roads? About nearby railroads with loading facilities? If you do not find the answer, call the general partner and ask.

4. Will equipment be leased or bought? At what price? From whom? (Watch out for conflicts of interest here.) Does the operation have a tipple (which crushes coal and loads it onto railroad cars)? If not, what plans have been made to obtain one? Are there adequate reserve funds set aside for repairs and replacement of equipment?

5. What royalty are you paying on the mining lease? Is it reasonable? (One way to check is to call around and find out what other investment groups in the area are paying.) Are the operating expenses of your program in line with those of competing coal partnerships?

6. Is there a fully detailed mining plan? The prospectus or offering circular will give details but if something appears to have been left out or if the plan appears to be oversimplified, discuss it with the general partner. You can get a backup opinion from a mining engineer.

7. What is the labor situation in the mining area? Will your mine have union or nonunion workers? What arrangements have been made for payment of royalties and debts if production is stopped by a strike? What about disaster insurance? What about conditions within the mines? Does the prospectus indicate that all federal and state regulations on mine safety will be followed to the letter? If the prospectus leaves you unsatisfied, talk to the general partner. If your questions are met with evasive answers pass on the deal.

8. Has the partnership entered a sales agreement ("end user" contract) with a utility or steel company? Are the terms of the contract satisfactory? Is the contract easily terminated by the end user? If there is no end user contract, will the spot market be adequate, or will you be left with thousands of tons of coal and no buyers?

9. Is the deal structured so you can make a profit? Your tax adviser can help you with this, and with translating any parts of the contract that you have trouble deciphering on your own.

> There's no such thing as a small taxpayer.
> —Anonymous

24

The Pure Tax Shelter:
A Cat Ranch

Every so often a "pure" tax shelter scheme emerges, and I have saved the best for the last. It was brought to my attention several years ago by an accountant friend of mine. It combines a conservative, sound investment with good tax shelter benefits.

Consider investing in a cat ranch in Mexico. The operation will start small with about a million cats. Each cat should average about 12 kittens a year, giving us 12 million cats. Skins can be sold for 20¢ for the black ones and 40¢ for the white, giving us an average price of 30¢, which times 12 million cat skins means revenues of almost $10,000 a day including Sundays and holidays.

A self-respecting Mexican cat man can skin about 50 cats per day for a wage of $3.15. It will only take 663 men to operate the ranch, so the net profit will be over $7,900 per day.

The cats will be fed on rats. Rats multiply four times as fast as cats. We will start a rat ranch right next to our cat farm. This is where the first-year tax break really comes in. Since we will be using the rats to feed the cats, we can expense the entire first batch of rats purchased during 1980.

If we can start with a million rats at a nickel each, we will have four rats per cat per day, and a whopping $50,000 1980 tax deduction.

The rats will be fed on the carcasses of the cats we skin during 1980–1981 and successive years. This will give each rat one-quarter of a cat. You can see by this that the business is a clean operation, self-supporting, and automatic throughout. The cats will eat the rats and the rats will eat the cats and we will get the skins and the tax benefits. The ecologists think it's great.

Eventually we hope to cross the cats with snakes. Snakes skin themselves twice a year. This will save the labor costs of skinning and will also give us a yield of two skins for one cat.

Compare this to tax shelter deals that skin investors as many as 365 days a year.

Appendix

CHECKLIST 1: INCOME ITEMS

Alimony and separate maintenance payments received

Annuities (to a limited extent)

Awards, except when made for some past achievement (religious, scientific, etc.)

Back pay

Bargain purchase from employer (if compensation or dividend)

Bonuses

Business profits

Cancellation of debts

Christmas bonus from employer

Clergyman, fees and contributions

Commissions

Compensation for services, whether or not paid in advance

Death benefit, in excess of $5,000, received from employer

Dividends (excess over $100)

Embezzled funds

Gains from:
Condemnation of property except if election to replace is made
Partner's sale of asset to partnership

Sales for export

Sales of government securities

Sales of patents, copyrights

Sales of property and securities

Sales of stock in foreign corporations

Gambling winnings

Group-term life-insurance coverage over $50,000 (premiums)

Interest on: Bank deposits, bonds, notes

Jury fees

Living quarters, meals (unless furnished for employer's convenience on his premises)

Notary public fees

Original issue discount on some corporate bonds

Partnership, share of income from

Patent infringement, damages

Pensions paid by employer

Prizes won at contests

Professional fees

Reimbursement for previously deducted losses or expense items

Rents, whether or not paid in advance
Retirement pay, paid by employer
Rewards
Royalties
Salaries
Soil bank payments
Tips

Unemployment benefits (limited) under:
Railroad Unemployment Insurance Act
State unemployment compensation laws
U.S. Bonds, interest
Wages

CHECKLIST 2: ITEMS WHICH ARE NOT TAXABLE

Accident insurance proceeds
Annuities (to a limited extent)
Bequests and devises
Damages, personal injuries or sickness
Death benefits, up to $5,000 for employee
Disability pay from an employer of up to $5,200 a year
Disability payments other than loss of wages
Dividends up to $100 each year received by individuals from domestic corporations
Employee death benefit, up to $5,000, from employer
Fellowship grants (to a limited extent
GI insurance dividends
Gifts
Group life insurance premiums (nonpermanent type) paid by employer
Health insurance proceeds, not deducted as medical expense

Inheritances
Life insurance paid on death
Loans (principal) repaid
Medical care payments, employer accident and health plan
Minister's dwelling, rental value or allowance
Pensions, disability (government and military personnel
Railroad passes to employees and their families
Reimbursed living expenses after casualty to dwelling
Scholarships and fellowships (with limitations)
Social Security or Railroad Retirement payments
Stock dividends not offering cash alternative
Supper money paid by employer
Tax refunds (if tax not deducted)
Veterans' benefits
Workmen's Compensation Acts, payments under

CHECKLIST 3: DEDUCTIONS FOR OUTSIDE SALESMEN AND EMPLOYEES*

Deductible *Toward* Adjusted Gross Income:

*Outside Salesmen
and
Other Employees, if Reimbursed*
Automobile maintenance and operation
Baggage costs
Convention attendance, if related to your official duties
Entertainment
Fares, transportation
Lodging—hotel, etc.
Mail costs
Meals—away from home; in case of outside salesmen, only meals purchased for customers
Porter charges
Secretarial help
Telephone, telegraph, etc.
Tips

Employee Expenses
Moving expenses
Transportation expenses shown above whether or not reimbursed

Employee Away from Home
Travel expenses above, meals and lodging whether or not reimbursed

Other
Alimony

CHECKLIST 4: DEDUCTIONS FOR BUSINESS OR PROFESSION

Accounting, engineering, and legal fees
Advertising
Attorney fees, collecting accounts, etc.
Automobile upkeep, business
Bad debts
Casualty losses (storm, fire, etc.)
Conventions, cost of attending
Depreciation—furniture, fixtures, car, etc.
Dues for organizations related to business
Education expense (travel, tuition, etc.) to maintain or improve skills required in the trade or business
Entertainment
Freight charges
Insurance—fire, plate glass, holdup, burglary, theft, public liability, storm, etc.
Interest paid to bank, etc.
Legal expenses
License fees
Light bills
Moving equipment to new location
Night watch service
Porter and janitor service
Postage
Professional journals
Rent for office
Repairs to business property
Research and experimental expenditures

* For salesmen who are independent contractors, see Checklist 4.

Safe deposit boxes
Salaries, bonuses, commissions, etc., paid
Stationery—letterheads, cards, etc.
Tax and other topical law reporters
Tax returns, cost of preparing
Taxes
Telephone
Theft losses, not compensated by insurance
Trade journals
Travel expenses
Wages paid

Discount factors for present value of $1 to be
received at various future dates and
*discounted at various interest rates**

1980

End of Year	Interest Rate			
	5%	10%	15%	20%
1	0.952	0.909	0.870	0.833
2	0.907	0.826	0.756	0.694
3	0.864	0.751	0.658	0.579
4	0.823	0.683	0.572	0.482
5	0.784	0.621	0.497	0.402
10	0.614	0.386	0.247	0.162
15	0.481	0.239	0.123	0.065
20	0.377	0.149	0.061	0.026
30	0.231	0.057	0.015	0.004

1980
Income Tax Rate Schedules
Single Individuals

Taxable income: Over—	But not over—	Tax:	Of excess over—
$ 0	$ 2,300	No tax	
2,300	3,400	14%	$ 2,300
3,400	4,400	$ 154+16%	3,400
4,400	6,500	314+18%	4,400
6,500	8,500	692+19%	6,500
8,500	10,800	1,072+21%	8,500
10,800	12,900	1,555+24%	10,800
12,900	15,000	2,059+26%	12,900
15,000	18,200	2,605+30%	15,000
18,200	23,500	3,565+34%	18,200
23,500	28,800	5,367+39%	23,500
28,800	34,100	7,434+44%	28,800
34,100	41,500	9,766+49%	34,100
41,500	55,300	13,392+55%	41,500
55,300	81,800	20,982+63%	55,300
81,800	108,300	37,677+68%	81,800
108,300		55,697+70%	108,300

IMPORTANT: If your tax table income is $20,000 or less and you claim 3 or fewer exemptions, use Tax Table A in Form 1040 or 1040A package.

1980
Joint Return

Taxable income: Over—	But not over—	Tax:	Of excess over—
$ 0	$ 3,400	No tax	
3,400	5,500	14%	$ 3,400
5,500	7,600	$ 294+16%	5,500
7,600	11,900	630+18%	7,600
11,900	16,000	1,404+21%	11,900
16,000	20,200	2,265+24%	16,000
20,200	24,600	3,273+28%	20,200
24,600	29,900	4,505+32%	24,600
29,900	35,200	6,201+37%	29,900
35,200	45,800	8,162+43%	35,200
45,800	60,000	12,720+49%	45,800
60,000	85,600	19,678+54%	60,000
85,600	109,400	33,502+59%	85,600
109,400	162,400	47,544+64%	109,400
162,400	215,400	81,464+68%	162,400
215,400		117,504+70%	215,400

IMPORTANT: If your tax table income is $40,000 or less, and you claim 9 or fewer exemptions, use Tax Table B in Form 1040 or 1040A package.

1980
Married Filing Separate Returns

Taxable income: Over—	But not over—	Tax:	Of excess over—
$ 0	$ 1,700	No tax	
1,700	2,750	14%	$ 1,700
2,750	3,800	$ 147.00+16%	2,750
3,800	5,950	315.00+18%	3,800
5,950	8,000	702.00+21%	5,950
8,000	10,100	1,132.50+24%	8,000
10,100	12,300	1,636.50+28%	10,100
12,300	14,950	2,252.50+32%	12,300
14,950	17,600	3,100.50+37%	14,950
17,600	22,900	4,081.00+43%	17,600
22,900	30,000	6,360.00+49%	22,900
30,000	42,800	9,839.00+54%	30,000
42,800	54,700	16,751.00+59%	42,800
54,700	81,200	23,772.00+64%	54,700
81,200	107,700	40,732.00+68%	81,200
107,700		58,752.00+70%	107,700

IMPORTANT: If your tax table income is $20,000 or less and you have 3 or fewer exemptions, use Tax Table C in Form 1040 or 1040A package.

1980
Heads of Household

Taxable income: Over—	But not over—	Tax:	Of excess over—
$ 0	$ 2,300	No tax	
2,300	4,400	14%	$ 2,300
4,400	6,500	$ 294+16%	4,400
6,500	8,700	630+18%	6,500
8,700	11,800	1,026+22%	8,700
11,800	15,000	1,708+24%	11,800
15,000	18,200	2,476+26%	15,000
18,200	23,500	3,308+31%	18,200
23,500	28,800	4,951+36%	23,500
28,800	34,100	6,859+42%	28,800
34,100	44,700	9,085+46%	34,100
44,700	60,600	13,961+54%	44,700
60,600	81,800	22,547+59%	60,600
81,800	108,300	35,055+63%	81,800
108,300	161,300	51,750+68%	108,300
161,300		87,790+70%	161,300

IMPORTANT: If your tax table income is $20,000 or less and you claim 8 or fewer exemptions, use Tax Table D in Form 1040 or 1040A package.

1980
Estates and Trusts

Taxable income: Over—	But not over—	Tax:	Of excess over—
$ 0	$ 1,050	14%	
1,050	2,100	$ 147.00+16%	$ 1,050
2,100	4,250	315.00+18%	2,100
4,250	6,300	702.00+21%	4,250
6,300	8,400	1,132.50+24%	6,300
8,400	10,600	1,636.50+28%	8,400
10,600	13,250	2,252.50+32%	10,600
13,250	15,900	3,100.50+37%	13,250
15,900	21,200	4,081.00+43%	15,900
21,200	28,300	6,360.00+49%	21,200
28,300	41,100	9,839.00+54%	28,300
41,100	53,000	16,751.00+59%	41,100
53,000	79,500	23,772.00+64%	53,000
79,500	106,000	40,732.00+68%	79,500
106,000		58,752.00+70%	106,000

Research and Development

New Law: Research and Development ("R and D") Incremental Credit: To encourage research and experimentation by industry, the new law provides a 25% tax credit for wages paid or incurred for services in connection with research and development after June 30, 1981 and before January 1, 1986. The credit applies only to the extent that these "qualified research expenses" are in excess of the average amount of such expenses during the immediately preceding three-year base period. During 1981 and 1982 a transitional rule provides for a shorter base period, such that for the first year for which the new credit applies, the base period is the preceding year, and for the next year, the base period is the two preceding years. Another transitional rule provides (because the credit is available only on those R and D expenditures after June 30, 1981) for a reduction of the base period amount to reflect the portion of the first year ending after June 30, 1981 for which credit is available.

In no event can the base period research expenses be less than 50% of the qualified expenses for the determined year. If little or nothing was spent on research during the base period, one half of the current expenditures would qualify for the credit.

"Qualified research expenses" eligible for the incremental credits include:

- 100% of "in-house" expenditures for wages, supplies, and certain amounts paid for use of personal property in research activities;
- 65% of "contract" research expenses, such as to a university or research firm;
- 65% of corporate grants for basic research to be performed by universities or special scientific research organizations.

The following activities do *not* qualify for the incremental credit:

- research outside the United States,
- research in the social sciences or humanities,
- research funded by others.

A three-year carryback and 15-year carryover is allowed for unused credits, and special rules provide for allocations and/or pass-throughs in the case of partnerships and Subchapter S corporations.

New Law: Contributions of Scientific Property for Research by Manufacturer: Generally the amount of a charitable deduction for a contribution of appreciated ordinary income property is limited to the taxpayer's basis in the property. But effective for contributions made after August 14, 1981, a deduction equal to basis *plus* 50% of any appreciation (but limited to twice the cost basis of the property) is allowed for contributions by the manufacturer of new scientific equipment to a college or university for research or development in physical and biological sciences.

The cost of the purchased parts cannot exceed 50% of the total cost, and the gift must be made within two years after construction.

New Law: Effect of R and D on Foreign Tax Credit: The new law provides that for the first two taxable years beginning after August 14, 1981, a taxpayer must allocate all research and experimental expenses in activities conducted in the United States to United States source income for foreign tax credit purposes. The effect of this is to increase foreign tax credit.

Index

If you found this book to be informative and stimulating and would like to be kept abreast of the latest tax laws, please write for further information to:

Stuart Ober
c/o The Dial Press
1 Dag Hammarskjold Plaza
New York, New York 10017

Stuart Ober is President of Securities Investigations, Inc., a firm specializing in tax shelter evaluations and due diligence.